# Folk Festivals
# and
# Beliefs of Radh Bengal

Understanding Through Ethnoarchaeology

# Folk Festivals and Beliefs of Radh Bengal

## Understanding Through Ethnoarchaeology

**Lopamudra Maitra Bajpai**

**Indira Gandhi Rastriya Manav Sangrahalaya,**
Bhopal-462013

**Kaveri Books**
New Delhi - 110 002

ISBN : 978-81-7479-242-6
First Published in 2022



*Published by*
**Indira Gandhi Rastriya Manav Sangrahalaya,**
Bhopal-462013
*In Association with*
**Kaveri Books**
4832/24, Ansari Road, Daryaganj,
New Delhi - 110 002 (India)
Ph. : 011-2328 8140, 4707 2321
E-mail : info@kaveribooks.com
kaveribooks@gmail.com
Website : www.kaveribooks.com

*Typesetting at* Creative Graphics, Delhi

*Cover Photographs*
Dr. Lopamudra Maitra Bajpai

PRINTED IN INDIA

# Acknowledgements

This work is an ode to those extraordinary people without whose continuous encouragement it would not have been possible to conclude the tedious journey which went into penning down this work, as their optimistic approach and outlook never felt short of supporting me throughout. I would also take the opportunity to mention about my good fortune to have the blessings of my teachers and mentors who always believed in me and inspired me enough to trust my capabilities, including the contributions of Dr. D.K. Bhattacharya and Dr. Pratibha Bhattacharya for inspiring me to begin the quest and thereby take up the study in the first place, Professor Amalendu Mukherjee for always providing me with the necessary inspiration whenever I needed it the most, Dr. Shanti Pappu for guiding me with details about formatting and editing my chapters, and last but not the least Dr. R.K. Chattopadhyay for his kind consent to guide me through the course of this work.

This work also owes to the cooperation of my many friends, companions, and acquaintances whose invaluable support at various stages of this research, helped me to gather the necessary data and also complete the chapters on times. The work was also facilitated from time to time from the significant information gathered from various museums, including the Indian Museum (Kolkata), the Ashutosh Museum (Kolkata), the Deccan College Postgraduate Research Institute Museum (Pune), the Raja Kelkar Museum (Pune), the Gurusaday Dutta Museum (Kolkata) and last but not the least, the Bangiya Sahitya Museum besides catalogue information (Bishupur, Bankura) aided the work considerably.

'The present space proves too small to pen details about varied assistance given by them and each of these individuals contributed towards formulating invaluable data, which served as the foundation of the research conducted in various districts, such as Bankura, Purulia, West Mednipur, Kolkata and Pune.'

The work also owes greatly to the Indian Council of Historical Research (ICHR), New Delhi, for granting me Junior Research Fellowship for undertaking the research and associated fieldwork.

Finally, this work would never have been completed without the constant encouragement and support of my family, though it is too small a space to speak about that, however, I would like to mention the continued encouragement of my parents- Dr. Tushar Kanti Maitra and Mrs. Manju Maitra.

# Contents

# List of Maps

# List of Figures

# Maps

**Map 1 :** Map of West Bengal, showing the districts of Radh region studied for the research1 (the three districts of Purulia, Bankura and West Mednipur are marked by semi-circles. Latitudes- 21°25’24’’N and 27°13’15’’N, Longitudes- 85°49’20’’E and 89°53’04’’E)

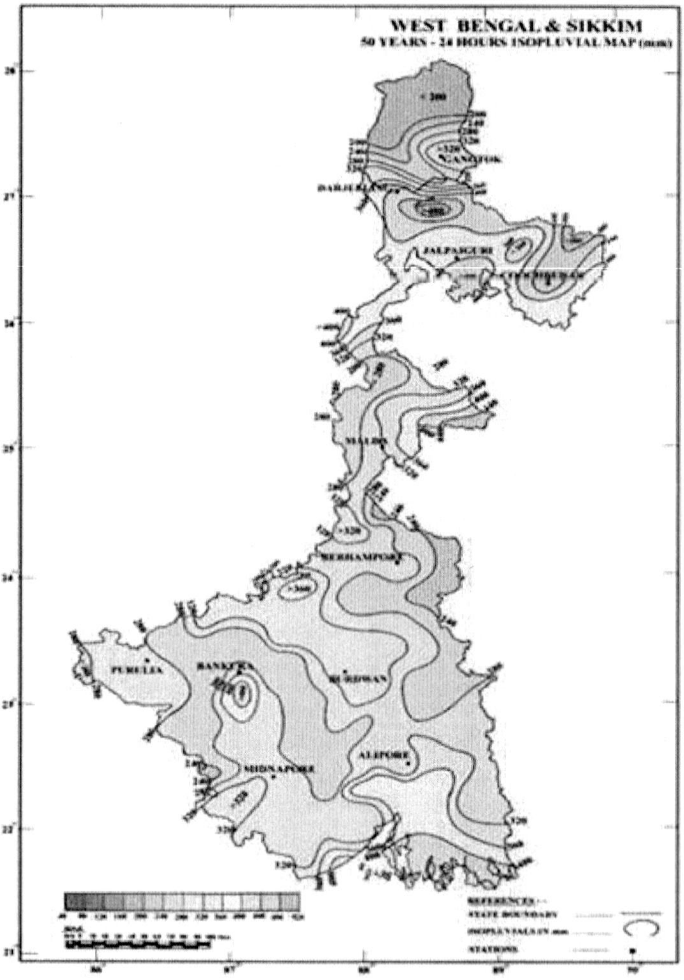


**Map 2 :** Topographic map of West Bengal, showing undulations of the Radh region

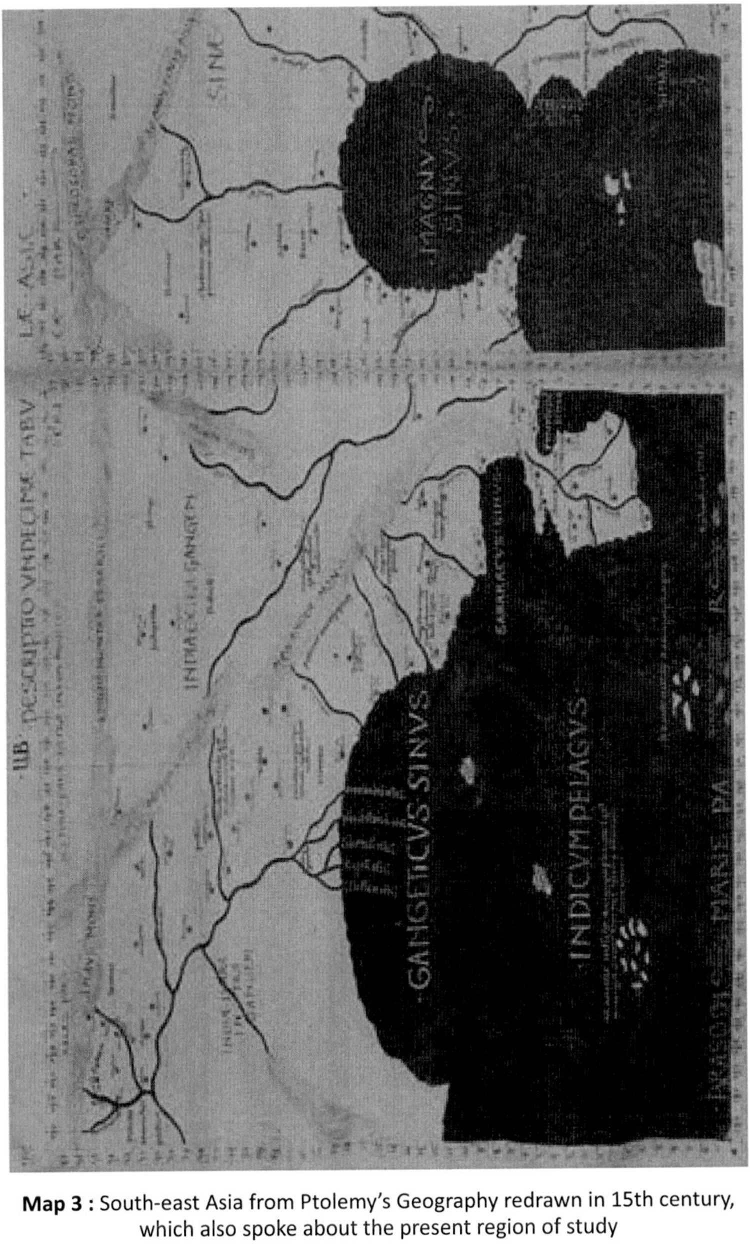


**Map 3 :** South-east Asia from Ptolemy's Geography redrawn in 15th century, which also spoke about the present region of study

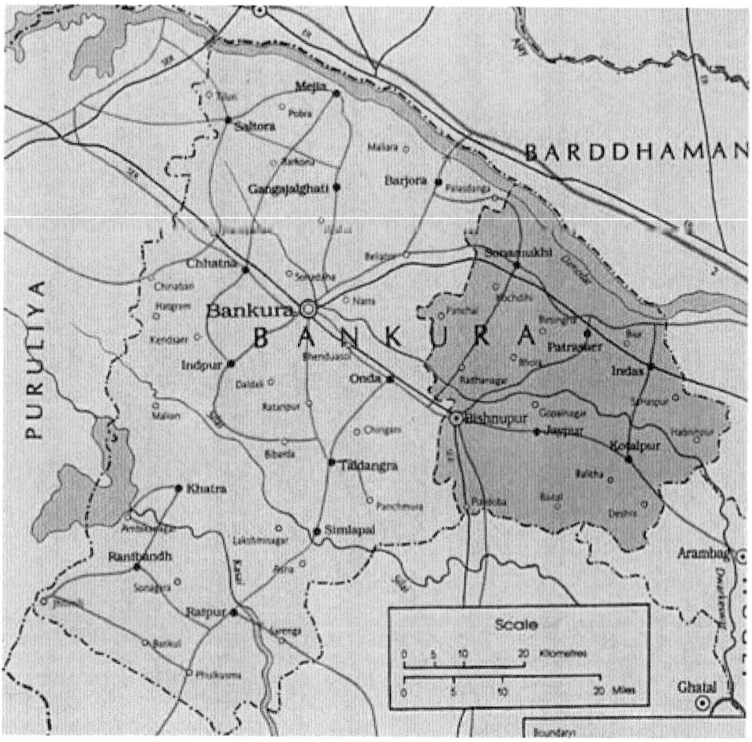


**Map 4 :** District map of Bankura showing few important villages and towns explored during the course of the work4 (Latitudes- 22°38N- 23°38 N, Longitudes- 86°36 E- 87°46 E)

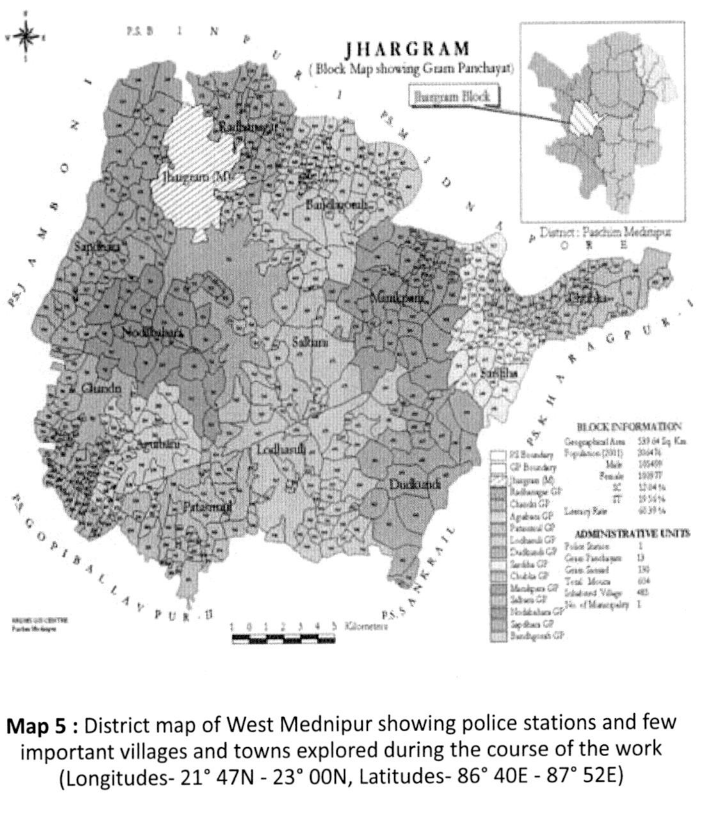


**Map 5 :** District map of West Mednipur showing police stations and few important villages and towns explored during the course of the work (Longitudes- 21° 47N - 23° 00N, Latitudes- 86° 40E - 87° 52E)

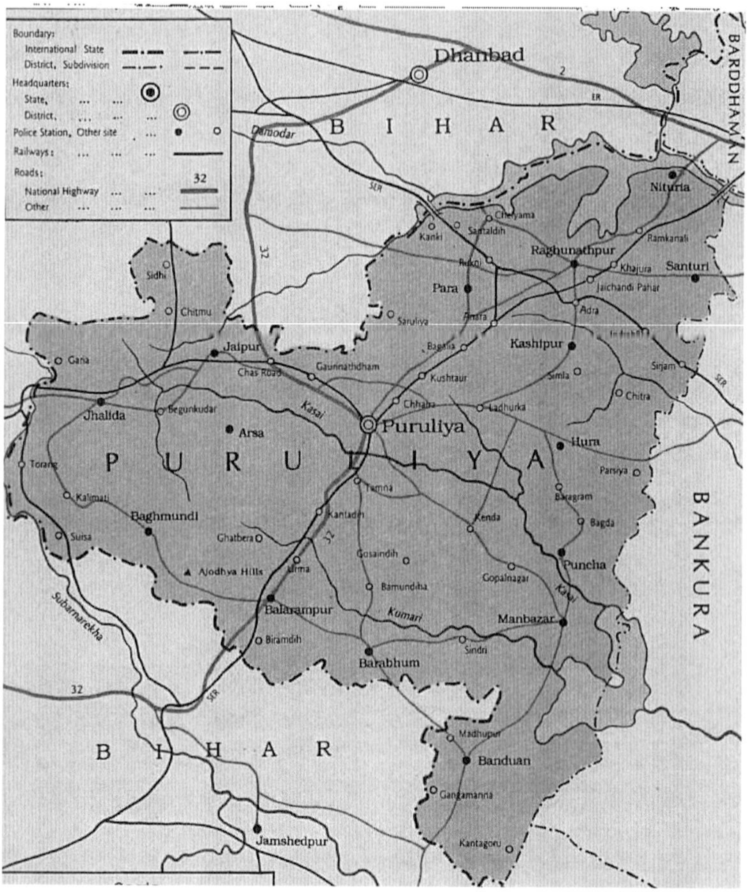


**Map 6 :** District road map of Purulia showing few important villages and towns explored during the course of the work (Total area- 6259 sq kms between 22°43N- 23°41N latitudes and between 85°49E-86°54E longitudes)

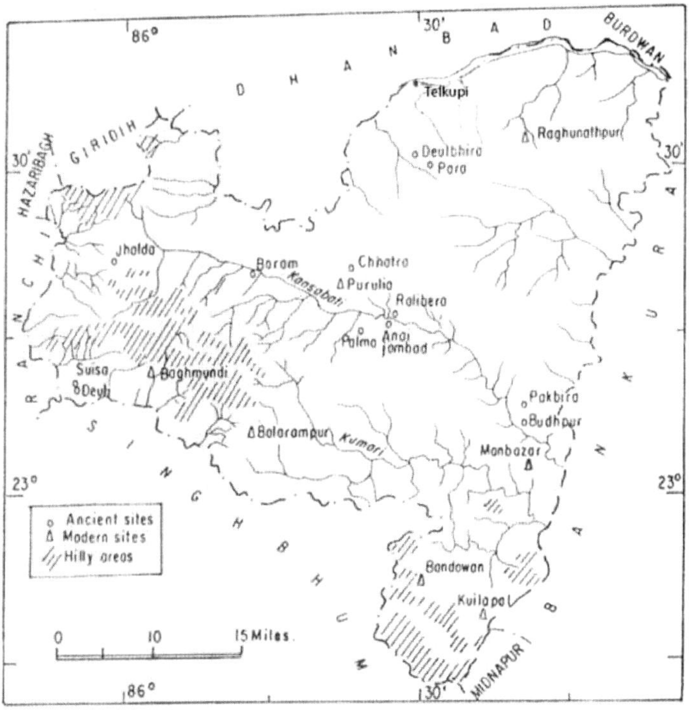


**Map 7 :** District map of Purulia showing few important villages and towns explored during the course of the work with latitude and longitude

## REFERENCES

1 http://mapsof.net/west_bengal/static-maps/jpg/west-bengal-map

2 From- http://images.google.co.in/imgres?imgurl=http://mapsof.net/uploads/static-maps/topographic_map_west_bengal.jpg&imgrefurl=http://mapsof.net/delhi/static-maps/jpg/topographic-map-westbengal&usg=__07PYR_4R8wTjASZixn9wnL6T0WU=&h=1800&w=1085&sz=156&hl=en&start=1&um=1&tbnid= HriIYZDRhhqBEM:&tbnh=150&tbnw=90&prev=/images%3Fq%3Dtopographic%2Bmap%2Bwest%2Bbengal%26hl%3Den%26sa%3DG%26um%3D1

3 From-The British Library Harley MS 7182, courtesy- http://en.wikipedia.org/wiki/File.PtomelyAsiaDetail.jpg

4 From- http://www.calcuttaweb.com/maps/bankura.shtml

5 http://paschimmedinipur.gov.in/map/jhargram.jpg

6 From- http://www.calcuttaweb.com/maps/purulia.shtml

7 After R.K. Chattopadhyay, Dept. of Archaeology, University of Calcutta.

# 1

# Introduction

The Radh region of West Bengal presents an interesting blend of thought processes and beliefs, expanding over an extensive geographic region which is an extension of the Bihar Chhotanagpur plateau and is comprised of red laterite soil. This study concentrates on three specific districts of Purulia, West Mednipur and Bankura, which celebrate various ceremonies, festivals, *melas* as well as rites and rituals that represent an interesting medley of what might be considered an orthodox Brahmanical tradition on one hand and an unorthodox folk tradition on the other. With limited historical and archaeological records, it becomes difficult to weave a continuous trend of representation of socio-cultural and religious aspects of life in the region. However, certain information from archaeology as well as history, supplemented as well as complimented by folk traditions as well as specifically observed rites and rituals, help to understand the ethos of the existence of a major part of the socio-religious life in the region. These ceremonies form an important part of the lives of the autochthones or *vratyas* who reside in the region of study. Interestingly enough, these autochthones were not originally agriculturists and are referred to as belonging to so-called lower castes and so-called upper castes of the region even in present times, with several such instances evident throughout various historical and literary records as well. The section of the population in the region— referred to as the so-called upper castes— are also mentioned in various historical and literary records to have migrated from outside the region, who gradually and over a period of time, absorbed the non-agriculturist locals as hired labours under them in their agrarian activities. The geo-physical aspect of their habitation also varies between the relatively woodlands of the tribal population with a subsistence pattern of fishing, hunting, etc. to the plain regions with agriculturists, pastorals and other *antyaja* groups. Evidences of hired labourers in agrarian fields were also prominent during the course of the field-work with many people from such classes as the Bauris, Lohars, Lodhas, Bagdis, Kayet and others working as hired labours in the fields of landed agriculturists, who evidently belonged to the so-called upper castes, including Brahmans, Kayasthas, Rajputs and others. The stories of such immigration of the so-called upper castes were also prominent through oral traditions during the course of study. It should be mentioned here that the oral traditions help to justify up to a certain extent the social association between the State of West Bengal and neighbouring states. Thus, these traditions help to highlight the significant aspect of social, cultural and religious similarities between the region of study and Odisha as well as parts of Bihar and Jharkhand. The connection between cultures is also corroborated by various historical facts, which testify the region to have been closely associated and connected to Odisha as well as Bihar, besides Jharkhand through trade routes.

Over a period of time, the so-called lower classes got gradually absorbed within the folds of the agrarian setup. In fact, no agrarian economy in Bengal can really work without taking into consideration these autonomous people who were finally absorbed as labours (labour force in the fields)—to ultimately evolve into a proper serfdom. Though various scholars debate on the existence of a proper feudal feature in West Bengal, the medieval period of the state witnessed the growth and development of various autonomous local powers as well as different vassal chiefs under them. It is also interesting to note the close association of the local aristocracy, who often had *vratya* origin and shared a close-knit relationship with the locals under them. The significant effect of this association was the assimilation of ideas and beliefs, especially of the tribals, which permeated into the agricultural group similar to a symbiotic relationship and helped to win the confidence of the people.

Several of these rites, rituals and ceremonies were influenced by economic and financial activities of the region, including the agrarian cycle. Thus, the Radh region presents an interesting blend of an array of ceremonies, festivals, *melas*, rites and rituals, all of which have a folk or Brahmanical origin or an assimilated admixture where both categories of ceremonies exist within the same socio-cultural and religious framework without a skirmish. These festivals further help us not only to understand the modern cultural scenario, but also to find traces of rites and rituals followed in the past in the region chosen for study. It is also significant to note here, the addition of the gradual process of social acceptance of certain *Mangal Kavyas* (folk epics centered on folk gods and goddesses written in Bengali), such as the *Manasamangal Kavya,* into the social setup. From 5$^{th}$-7$^{th}$ century onwards, many domestic folk festivals of the region of West Bengal were elevated to the status of mainstream agrarian tradition and culture, as they gradually got acceptance in the mainstream Puranic traditional agrarian rites and rituals. One instance is seen in *Manasamangal Kavya,* which started getting recognition by the Puranas around this time onwards. Amidst these festivals, many pertain to the sowing season, the reaping of the harvest, paying oblations to one's ancesters, fertility rites, and rituals for overall security of the village. These offerings also include various articles and artifacts from the daily life, especially the ones witnessed in rural Bengal, including the rampant use of turmeric, betel leaves, bananas, coconut, cow dung, different *alpana's*, etc. To this list, various votive offering such as terracotta horses and elephants of various sizes and shapes may be included, especially in the region of study. Over a period of time, as these traditions from the so-called lower classes of the society got accepted within the folds of the agrarian so-called upper castes, the deities also made their way into an accepted orthodox tradition gradually. Thus, the culture of the *adivasi vratyas* eventually and evidently got acceptance into the mainstream Puranic-Brahmanical fold, with some of them getting changed slightly and others maintaining their true identity. This phenomenon is quite unique to the area of Mednipur, Purulia and Bankura, as in many other regions of the country, the folk and household traditions exist as a distinct category from the mainstream Puranic traditions.

## Previous Work Pertaining to the Region

The work done so far pertaining to festivals and agriculture in India has been independent studies. There has been no attempt to sublime and amalgamate the thoughts of one discipline into the other, and expand the parameters for a more holistic study. Mostly previous works have been separate efforts to understand the systems of folk culture and traditions in the region or to understand the importance of the more popular and widely known agrarian festivals of the region, such as Durga Puja, Basantotsav, etc. The aspect of the inter-relationship of the Puranic-Brahmanic rites and rituals and the lesser known, yet widely followed, traditions was not taken into purview before to lead to an understanding of the importance of these festivals and the peculiar coexistence of different agrarian rites and rituals within the same social setup.

## Research Methodology

The method of research followed was based on extensive fieldwork in the Radh region comprising the districts of Purulia, Bankura and West Mednipur. A detailed list of the various Early Village Farming Settlements (EVF) sites of archaeology is presented in the present work under the Appendix 2 & 3, and a list of all the villages surveyed is provided under Appendix 4 & 5 as ethnographic information. The ethnogaphic data was collected based on open-ended interviews for a more qualitative research method. This exercise not only helped to understand the socio-cultural as well as religious ethos of various villages along with their original peculiarities, but it also helped to understand the various lores and oral traditions associated with different festivals as well as local history. The qualitative data obtained thus was supplemented by library work with available and published historical, literary as well as archaeological records. This information was supplemented by ethnographic accounts of the various population groups residing in the region of study.

### Scope of the Research Problem

The research work undertaken pertaining to the modern communities in the area of fringe Bengal helped me to closely observe certain ethnic agrarian community festivals in the region in modern times. Moreover, the study helped me to understand how these festivals have evolved differently over the years, which includes the assimilation of various religious thought processes, such as Jainism, Buddhism, Vaisṇavism, Śaivism, Saktaism, Tantrism and others. The essence of the study also has an intricate social perspective. Taking into purview the festivals of the region, which are widely celebrated and are ethnically of folk origin, it attempts to understand the social structure that is quite different from other regions of India. Besides, the work attempts to incorporate the understanding of various agrarian rites pertaining to women and children in the region under consideration which forms an important part of our socio-religious existence from the very ancient times. This is an important aspect, as it is closely woven into the fabric of the financial activities of the region as well as the agrarian cycle on one hand and the growth and development of various local powers on the other, which rendered a special local ethos.

The chapterisation entailed in the work is as follow:

**Chapter I— Introduction**

The chapter provides brief historiography, scope and information about the nature of the present research work along with the problems involved. The introduction also specifies the chapterisation followed for the present research work.

**Chapter II— Land and People**

It deals with specifying the region of work through a geo-physical perspective, which mentions the physical characters of the region, including rivers, forests, flora and fauna. The chapter includes mention of various population groups inhabiting the region of study. Although many of them were not encountered during the course of the intensive fieldwork. The maps incorporated within the chapter refer to the different districts covered under the present research besides depicting topographic representation of the region that deals with lateritic fringe Bengal and looks into the interpretative aspect of the work.

**Chapter III— Historical Background**

The chapter concentrates on providing a historical background of the region of study from the various literary, epigraphical as well as archaeological records currently available. It documents the growth and development of socio-cultural and religious ideas and beliefs following a chrono-cultural perspective from the available data, which attempts to incorporate various ceremonies, festivals and celebrations of the autochthones or *vratyas.* Though this information is limited in nature, yet it is supplemented by various ethnographic records which are stated in the following chapter.

**Chapter IV— Survey of Ethnoarchaeological Data**

Discussion on the content and context besides the various rituals of different villages and towns across the region of study, including the three districts of Purulia, Bankura and West Mednipur form the subject matter of this chapter. The deliberation helps to establish various cultural similarities of neighbouring states of Odisha as well as Bihar and Jharkhand and also corroborates various local lore, as mentioned in different published data and ethnographic information.

**Chapter V— Discussion**

It is the conclusion chapter which discusses important information pertaining to the assimilation of religious ideas and beliefs in the region of study and its social significance— down the path of history as well as in present times. This is important fact in the present social scenario, with several ethnic parameters weaving into the fabric of the bigger picture of a global social network. Besides, it provides vital information about folk culture acting as a significant mode of communication all along history and carries strains of various culture, beliefs and ideas which make the region of study an important entity by itself.

# 2

# Land and People

The region of lateritic Bengal under study comprising the districts of Bankura, Purulia and West Mednipur lies in the western fringe area of the state and comprises part of the extension of the Chhotanagpur plateau region. It mentioned in different geographical, historical and statistical documents as Radh region as well as the region of red or red-laterite soil. Drained by several rivers, the humid region of the Radh Plain has several *bils* and ox-bow lakes, which result from the frequent changes in the stream courses and provide water for settlements besides acting as a chief source of fish that form common diet of the people of the region. The presence of water in the region has also facilitated water-borne traffic since ancient times, and the proximity with the Bay is important for maritime fishery as well as establishing maritime connection with the outside world. Such is the geo-physical character of the region that it creates a very prominent picture of the land and the people inhabiting it, especially that of *bhumiputras* or *adivasis*[1] as well as the early settlers and autochthones of the region, who seem and to have influenced every aspect of lifestyle of the region of study from ancient times. Popularly mentioned to have an Austro-Asiatic origin, the name *Banga* is mentioned to have been formed from the Santali term meaning "holy" or "supernatural power". This facet shows the relation of the place with an old Austric-speaking group in the region. It is the essence of these original inhabitants of the region who impart an essential touch of history. Socio-culturally too, the aforementioned population groups present a distinctive picture of their own which renders a touch of ethnic ethos portraying myriad features of festivals, rites and rituals. Not only is the diversity of the cultural elements and ceremonies, important in this case but their existence within the same socio-cultural fold without a skirmish. The region also comprises of large and small towns, industrial centres, agricultural lands, vast expansive drainage systems, barren as well as fallow lands and forested areas with a wide range of flora and fauna, though endangered to a great extent.

## Topography, Natural Features and Geology

The Radh region finds special mention in the context of topography and geology of West Bengal (from 212̣5″24″″N and 271̣3″15″″N latitudes and 854̣9″20″″E and 895̣3″04″″E longitudes). The districts constituting the Radh region, such as Mednipur (both Purba or East and Paschim or West Mednipur), Bankura, Bardhaman, Birbhum and Purulia, are of low plateau in character, especially the eastern part of these districts and western part of Murshidabad, Hooghly and Howrah districts. This region has rugged terrain out of which Purulia is most rugged than the rest. The plateau region appears as peneplain due to erosion. Monadnocks are also formed in some places. The height and ruggedness of the terrain gradually decreases towards north-east and south-east.

The Radh region is an area constituting specific geo-physical traits as compared to other regions of West Bengal. K.S. Singh mentions the region to be amongst one of the seven physiographic divisions[2] of the State of West Bengal. Ashutosh Bhattacharya in his *Paschim Banger Sanskriti* mentions the area to constitute mainly the western lateritic region of hilly and forested tracts, which extend from the northern part of Subarnarekha River in Jhargram, Mednipur District towards the north, till the banks of Ganges in the north of Birbhum District. R.L.

Singh mentions (1971:295-296) the existence of the region of Lower Ganga Plain, which also constitutes the Radh region, to possess, "apparently a homogenous geographical en tity" that "exhibits significant variations in geographical phenomenon, both physical and cultural, which render feasible the delineation of somewhat more uniform lower order units depending on different attributes." The region bordering Chhotanagpur Highlands has relatively more stable configuration with vast diversity of physical resources and consequent differentiation in the cultural landscape. This region also forms an important part of the three divisions[3] of the Lower Ganga Plains (*Ibid*:296) and can further be sub-divided into:

1. Birbhum-Asansol Radh, which consists of
   - Birbhum Plain and
   - Ajay-Damodar Interfluve,
2. Bankura Radh, which consists of
   - Damodar-Dwarakeshwar Doab and
   - Dwarakeshwar-Kasai Tract and
3. Mednipur Radh, which consists of
   - Eastern part and
   - Western parts.

This lateritic region, with exposures to the Gondwana, experiences different climatic conditions from the rest of the Lower Ganga Plain. The characteristic feature of "the region comprises of semi-compact and sprinkled settlements, with occasional riverside lineations" (*Ibid*: 298).

Settlement wise, the Radh Plain exhibits a variety of natural characters. The gradual upcoming of mining areas, engineering, paper, aluminium and other ancillary industries along with iron and steel industry in the Asansol-Raniganj areas take together with the factor of close proximity with the central city of Kolkata through well connected railways, has resulted in the rapid growth and development of population in the areas. At times, however, the area faces drinking water problem, resulting from lowering of water table and depletion of soil moisture, especially in the villages, and it is difficult for people to revert to agriculture, their traditional occupation (*Ibid*:275-277). It is important to note the lower population density with a predominant agrarian economy, except in the Ajay-Damodar interfluve.

The analysis of the drainage system of the region chronologically is no less important as it is necessary to correlate the evolution of landforms in such an area of shifting river courses. The topograph of the region hardly speaks of any well-defined stage of the evolution of drainage. The monotonous surface is dissected frequently by the channels of the tributaries or distributaries of the main streams Ganga and the Brahmaputra, the two distinct river systems.

The Ganga system with Hooghly as its main stream joins the Bay near the Sagar Island and the Brahmaputra system, skirting the Meghalaya plateau, joins the Bay a little north of Chittagong. General slope of the Lower Ganga Plain, as revealed by the drainage system, is towards the south-east, which is natural in a hinge zone and tends north-east to south-west. Important rivers flowing through the region include Mayurakshi, Damodar, Kasai, Subarnarekha, Kopai, Bansloi, Dwarakeshwar, Shilabati and Kangsabati, which finally drain the south-western part of the state and discharge into the Bay of Bengal (*Ibid*: 258).

Of the rainfall and natural vegetation cover of the region, mention may be made of the significant *sal* forests and the average annual rainfall which varies between 1200 to 1500 mm/year, thereby making it a comparatively dry one as compared to other regions of West Bengal. This region often faces drought, and heat in the month of May becomes severe. The soils in the western part are generally lateritic with deficiency in humous content, and red loam soils of medium fertility are found towards east (*Ibid*:265-266). These soils are associated with the deciduous and scrub vegetation that cover greater part of the western region (299,000 hectares, as mentioned by R. L. Singh:1971) comprising Mednipur (both East or Purba and West or Paschim), Bankura, Burdwan and Birbhum.

Irrigation becomes a necessity in the region with little help from the though fairly average, yet irregular monsoon showers. This phenomenon is coupled with dry winters. Moreover, water balance is adverse in the Lower Ganga Plains at various intensities. The completion of DVC and Mayurakshi projects has provided the locals with lots of employment opportunities.[4]

Rice is the most important crop of the region, which constitutes more than 85% of the total cropped land and 75% of the total sown area. The main types of crops in the region include *Aman* (dominant throughout the region), *Aus* (grown mainly is Malda, Cooch Behar, Nadia, Murshidabad and Bankura) and *Boro* (significant in only 1% of the total cropped area and confined to the marshy tracts of Howrah, Hooghly and 24 Parganas). Jute stands next in importance in agriculture (with 4.3% of total cropped area), followed by *Til* in the western margins, Tobacco in Cooch Behar and vegetables in suburban zones. Crop rotation is an important phenomenon in the region comprising two main types that are as follows:

1. *Aman* fallow—*Aman* system in the low-lying fields with little evidences of crop rotation in the *Aman* rice fields and
2. *Aus*—Jute-rabi pulses or vegetables systems in the upland fields where irrigation might provide several crop rotation systems, especially where maize,

potatoes, vegetables, jute and rabi pulses are grown. In the Radh, three crop associations have developed.

The importance of waterbodies in the region has led to the development of fisheries. Riverine fisheries are important in 24 Parganas, Murshidabad and Mednipur, which account for more than 90% of the riverine catch. With a coastline of 65 kms, though there is ample opportunity for seafishing, yet improper facilities hamper the process which limit the facilities to only 32 kms between Junput and Digha.

**Society and People**

Just as the region itself, the inhabitants there also bear specific importance. West Bengal is divided into three cultural zones, of which the Radh region has a special place of its own in forming a "geo-historic area" (Singh, 2008:11-13). A plateau area of lateritic soils, which is also the seat of tradition and culture, the area is often divided into Uttar Radh and Dakhin Radh. Certain communities with an identity in terms of sub-division of the area, like Kayastha and Mahishya, are divided into Dakhin and Uttar Radhi, as well as the communities of Kumbhar and Napit. This division becomes important during marriage alliances since more often than not, their establisment across these two sub-divisions is generally not permissible. The region consists of population groups of various classes, which are both so-called higher and lower in status. Thus, the region includes so-called higher castes, such as Brahmans, Kayastha, Baidyas and Sadgops along with other communities out of which many belong to the scheduled tribes, scheduled castes, and other backward classes. This region has the largest number of people belonging to Mundari speaking group, namely, Munda, Santals, Kora, Mahali, Bhumij and Birhor. There are some communities which are specific to this region and that too in the plateau area, including

Birhor of the scheduled tribe community and Khaira of the scheduled caste community. Other communities like Kharia, Lodha, Sabar and Pahariya, as well as Sarak (who once professed Jainism), Baishyas, Let and Bhalla are also found only in this region. However, in recent times, they have spilled over from original region or habitat. Other communities like Kanui and Bauri, though have spilled over to other places, are still mainly concentrated here. A few tribes like Santals, Oraons, Mundas, Lepchas and Bhumijes are distributed all over Bengal and do not have a distinct concentration, like the Lepchas and Bhutias who scarcely occur outside Darjeeling, as against Rabhas and Meches who are mainly confined to Jalpaiguri. The Santals, the earliest inhabitants of Chhotanagpur as well as Bankura, occur in large numbers in the western tracts of Bankura, Burdwan and Mednipur districts Thus, the tribal population is not uniformly distributed throughout the region, and, roughly it can be mentioned that the Mongoloid population like the Lepchas, Bhutias, Rabhas and Garos are mostly concentrated in a certain part in West Bengal, while the Proto-Australoid population groups consisting of such tribes like Santals, Bhumijes, Oraons, Mundas and others are dispersed throughout the state (Das *et al.*: 1966:ix).

Culturally speaking, this region has a specific character that has evolved over centuries through association with people of various castes and creeds as well as religious ideas. The region has come under the influence of Buddhism and Jainism, as well as Vaishnavism, and in later years, Islam and still later, Christianity. Even today, the importance of Vaishnavism, Tantric Buddhism and Jainism is witnessed through several pujas of the region, especially those performed by the so-called lower communities; for instance, the puja of Dharmaraj that is performed during full moon day of Buddha Ajanta or the day preceeding it. Of all the seven regions of West Bengal, Radh has the maximum number of pilgrim centres, and some centres grew up in places where it is believed that parts of the body of *Sati* fell. The region also has specific folk festivals that render a distinct touch to it when compared to other regions of West Bengal. To name a few, Tusu, Bhadu, Sharul, Karam, Bandna or Soharai and Chhata *parab* are all important and well-known regional cultural occasions of this region. Chhou is a very well known folk dance of the region, especially associated with the district of Purulia.

**Population Groups**

According to the 2011 census reports of the Government of India, the population of West Bengal is 9.13 crores, an increase from figure of 8.02 crores, as seen in the 2001 census. Total population of West Bengal as per 2011 census is 91,276,115 of which male and female are 46,809,027 and 44,467,088 respectively. In 2001, total population was 80,176,197 in which males were 41,465,985 while females were 38,710,212. The total population growth in this decade was 13.84 percent while in previous decade it was 17.84 percent. The population of West Bengal formed 7.54 percent of India in 2011. in 2001, the figure was 7.79 percent. Out of this, 27.5% belonged to scheduled caste communities (with 78.7% males and 62.5% females) and 7.8% belonged to scheduled tribe community (with 74.4% males and 57.7% females) (Rural Development statistics-Source: Ministry of Health and Family Welfare, Health Statistics 2011). In fact, there are several scheduled castes and scheduled tribes inhabiting the state. According to the 1961 figures, there were 41 scheduled tribe communities (with a total population of 20,54,081) and 63 scheduled caste communities (with a total population of 68,90,314) (Das *etal.* 1966). As per the 2001 census, the Radh region alone consists of the maximum number and percentage of scheduled castes and tribes inhabitants. Baske (Baske,1987:29) speaks of the 1976 Scheduled castes and Scheduled Tribes Orders (Amendment) Act" wherein 38 population groups of West Bengal are mentioned, of which 27 inhabit region of study.[5] A similar picture is available from the writings of Bhowmick (Bhowmik, 1994:6-7) according to whom, as per the census of 1981, a total of 476 tribal communities existed in India comprising a total population of 51,626,638 out of which 74 belonged to PTG or Primitive Tribal Groups. (*Ibid*: vi-viii). Furthermore, in the accounts of Russel and Hiralal as well as in the four volumes of *The Tribes and Castes of the Central Provinces of India*, one can come across the data pertaining to the population groups inhabiting the region of study, especially those belonging to the so-called lower classes of the social order. However, the most updated information is provided in the *People of India series Vol XXXXIII* of 2008 (Singh, K.S. ed.) in the two volumes for the State of West Bengal, which mentions 49 communities belonging to Scheduled Castes (24.14%), 28 belonging to Scheduled Tribes and the rest as other communities. This list also encompasses the population groups mentioned by Baske, following the Scheduled Castes and Scheduled Tribes Orders (amendment) Act of 1976. According to the updated information from Singh (2008), the tribes inhabiting the region of study, in alphabetical order, are as follows: Aghori, Aguri, Angarok, Bagdi, Bagti, Baida, Baidya, Bairagi, Baishya, Bajkar, Bathudi, Bauri, Bedia, Bhumij, Birhor, Brahman, Gareri, Gahasi, Ghunnya, Gour, Ho, Jalia-Kaibarta, Jola, Jugi, Kahar, Kakmara, Kalal, Kalu, Kamar, Kandra, Karan, Karanga, Kayastha, Kela, Khaira, Khalifa, Khandait, Kharia, Khatik, Koeri, Kora, Kudmi, Kumhar, Lalbegi, Lodha, Lohar, Mahar, Mahishya, Mahli, Malhar, Mali, Marwari, Mayara, Mete, Mirshikar, Muchi, Munda, Musahar, Napit, Oraon, Oriya, Pahariya, Pan, Patni, Pod, Portugese, Rajput, Rajput Solanki, Raju, Rajwar, Rautia, Sabar, Sadgop, Sahis, Sankhakara, Santals, Sarak, Siyalgir, Sunri, Sutradhar, Swarnakar, Tamboli,

Tanti, and Tili. Appendix 1 mentions an updated list of the various population groups, based on the reports of Singh (2008) along with a brief preview of the rites, rituals and ceremonies of the various groups who were prominent during the course of the fieldwork. Of these groups, several features which are similar in character, but are repetitive, have been omitted obviously to avoid monotony of facts. All the groups have rice as their staple diet cereal, with some of them consuming *rotis* also. The women of all the tribes and castes, barring a few, are seen to have a social status lower than men and do not generally inherit father's property, are engaged in household chores, providing financially for the family. Almost all the including population groups are educationally backward and have very low literacy rate, especially the ones who fall under the category of tribes and castes. It is also important to note that almost all the population groups, including the various scheduled castes and other backward classes, with few exceptions, worship similar deities like, Durga, Kali, Siva, Lakshmi, Saraswati, Basanti and Narayan or Satyanarayan. For these people, the important socio-religious festivals are also similar, for instance, Durga, Kali, Saraswati and Lakshmi pujas, Siva Gajan and Charak, Dol Yatra and Ratha Yatra, amidst others. Prevalence of animism also exists, especially among the population groups listed under PTG. Of the many deities, several have a tribal origin, but are widely worshipped, including Manasa and Sitala, who are important regional deities of the area under study. These deities are worshipped with equal pomp and splendour and regularity like the mainstream Puranic goddesses, such as Durga or Kali. Almost all the population groups speak and write Hindi as well as Bengali, and some of them are adept in the Oriya and Roman script as well besides Jharkhandi-Bangla and Manbhumiya-Bangla. Such admixture of languages is witnessed in the population groups inhabiting border areas of Odisha or Bihar and Jharkhand. The Brahman is the presiding priest for performing rites and rituals of almost all the population groups, excepting a few who appoint priests from their own communities. Since almost all the population groups profess a majority religious belief, the sacred centres of pilgrimage for them are also similar, which include places like Nabadwip, Tarakeshwar, Dakshineshwara, Moutor, Rameshwar, Kalighat, Belurmath and Mayapur within West Bengal, Haradwar, Puri, Vrindavan, Mathura, Gaya, Kasi, Gourinathdham, Kalyaneshwari, Beneras, Kamakhya and other parts of India. Most of the population groups cremate the dead, and after observing a mourning or profanity period of certain duration which varies from group-to-group as three to thirty days, they perform a *sradh*, primarily with the help of a Brahman priest and at times, with the help of a priest from their own communities. In order to understand the various ceremonies, festivals, rites and rituals of the locals, it is important to identify with them through a historical perspective which is connected to the economic and socio-cultural activities of the inhabitants. This activity is attempted in the following chapter.

## ENDNOTES

1. These *vratyas* formed significant population groups of the region of study and are prominent till today. They form a majority of the population groups and are also often referred to as primitive, which is a term indicated towards *adivasis* or early settlers in a region. Many times, they are referred to as *Vanyajati, Girijan* or *Upajati* (Bhowmick, P.K.:1980:1). Though, after coming and living in close contact with other groups, several traits may have diluted over a period of time, including linguistic oneness—as in the case of Lodhas of Mednipur or Oraons of Sundarbans who speak Bengali, instead of their own mother tongues—yet, they maintain several intrinsic properties of their own. However, till this day, several of these autochthones continue to worship their own tribal deities, but the tribes have entered the Brahmanical polity in various positions. Some of their leaders who were dominant in the early period were admitted to the Kshatriya or Rajput caste, and the origin of few Rajput clans can be

traced to the Bhar and other tribes. Again, several communities of the aristocratic or land-holding class were permitted to rank with the Brahmanical cultivating castes. At times, some of the castes retained their original possession of land in the centre of the Brahmanical population, like the Andhs, Halbas and Manas. On the other hand, those tribes who were subjugated and permitted to live with a servile status in the Brahmanical village have developed into the existing menial castes of weavers, tanners and others constituting the lowest social group. Some tribes lived apart from the villages, in their own existence in the forest tracts and kept possession of lands. Thus, they rank somewhat so-called higher than the ones residing within the villages and are considered as low castes and untouchables (Russell and Hiralal:64-65). The autochthones, therefore traversed a long path of history with various socio-cultural and religious changes and came in close touch with other cultural groups over a period of time. This phenomenon finally resulted in the transformation of their own culture "'to a considerable extent that blended according to the demands of the situation or circumstantial exigencies. Thus, it can be said that the tribes are not permanent crystalline structures belonging to one 'stage' of historical or social development. However, it is important to notice the conversion of tribes into Puranic religion, and several of them profess Brahmanical religion in recent times. It is also important to notice the existence of the 'impure castes', the touch of whom exudes profanity. "The debased and servile position of the impure castes corresponds to that which, as already seen, is attached to the Sudras of the classical period" The class of sudras was usually regarded as untouchables and it included the tanners, bamboo-workers, sweepers, hunters, fowlers, gypsies, vagrants, village musicians and village weavers (Russell and Hiralal:73). The surnames of the communities are also important, which bear testimony to a lot of factors, including their original habitat, traditional occupation and stories of migration, and they indicate features of adaptation, alteration and adjustment. A number of communities also take in synonyms to sanskritise their names or link with traditional occupations to raise their status in regional social hierarchy by adopting synonyms with or without formation of myth. Speaking about associations of castes, occupation of the castes needs special mention, which is an "important phenomenon in determining the division and social precedence of castes in India" (*ibid*). An enormous majority of castes are occupation-based, and their social position depends on their caste calling. There are also agrarian classes whose origin can be traced to different sources, but who, on obtaining land have acquired the cultivating status and retain their separate caste organisation and name. There are also classes formed from military services, as well as those who were formed from a religious sect or order. However, amidst all, occupation remains to be the dominant factor for determining a caste. This phenomenon also speaks about the various countries of the origin of different castes and classes. However, in recent years, this system of untouchability, though not completely eradicated, has changed, thereby resulting in the transformation of occupation-based social hierarchy. Changing socio-cultural scenario and insecurities associated with lack of job has often resulted in the transformation of the traditional and primary occupations, which are fast being replaced by other secondary occupations like agriculture or share-cropping or daily-wage working in construction sites of agricultural lands, rickshaw-pulling, etc. In this context, it is also important to look at the various festivals, rites and rituals as a channel of the expression of the various sentiments, including fear, anxiety, happiness, joy, and sorrow, amidst others, of the people concerned. A major part of these ceremonies is occupied by agrarian activities and the concept of production. Finally, the ritual concept in agriculture is also important. Apart from the association of rituals with the productive activities that legitimises the entire mechanism of production, it is also important to note how rituals help to activate religious idioms in the actual context and how cultivators rationalise their religious behaviour in the face of technological changes (Chakrabarti:1986:5-6).

2. The seven physiographic divisions of West Bengal according to K.S. Singh are as follows: 1)Darjeeling Himalayas, 2)Terai Region, 3) Northern Plains, 4)Delta Region, 5)Low Plateau and Radh Region, 6) The Sundarbans, and 7)Coastal Region'.
3. The three divisions of the Lower Ganga Plain are: 1) The North Bengal Plains, 2) The Delta Proper and 3) The Radh Plain or the Western margins of the Delta. Furthermore, there are 8 second order and 21 third order regions (*Ibid*:296).
4. The highest percentage of irrigated area (60%) by government canals lie in Burdwan, followed by Birbhum, Bankura (30%), Hooghly (29%) and Murshidabad (14%). Irrigation from local ponds and *bils* is most popular in areas like Murshidabad, Mednipur (both East or Purba and West or Paschim Mednipur), Howrah (40%), followed by Birbhum, Bankura and West Dinajpur (32%). Well irrigation is not so popular, except in Nadia, Malda and Cooch Behar with 20% of irrigated area falling under well irrigation, and double cropping is only seen in the *Duars* and the delta region of Nadia and Malda (30% each), Hooghly (17%), Murshidabad (15%) and 24 Parganas (11%).

5. Baske (Baske, 1987:29) speaks of the 1976 'Scheduled Castes and Scheduled Tribes Order (Amendment) Act' wherein there is mention of 38 population groups of West Bengal, of which the ones inhabiting the region of study include (*Ibid*: 30-32) (in alphabetical order) the following: 1. Bedia (Purulia), 2. Bhumij (Purulia, Bankura, West Mednipur), 3. Birhor (Purulia), 4. Chero (West Mednipur), 5. Garet (Purulia, West Mednipur), 6. Garo (West Mednipur), 7. Ghond (West Mednipur), 8. Ho (West Mednipur), 9. Karmali (Purulia), 10. Kisan (Purulia), 11. Koroa (Purulia), 12. Koda (Purulia, Bankura, West Mednipur), 13. Lepcha (Purulia, West Mednipur), 14. Lodha, Khariya (Purulia, West Mednipur), 15. Lohar (Purulia, Bankura), 16. Mahali (Purulia, Bankura, West Mednipur), 17. Maholi (Purulia), 18. Mal Pahadiya (Purulia, West Mednipur), 19. Mech (West Mednipur), 20. Mog (West Mednipur), 21. Mru (Bankura, West Mednipur), 22. Munda (Bankura, Purulia, West Mednipur), 23. Oraon (Bankura, Purulia, West Mednipur), 24. Rabha (Bankura, West Mednipur), 25. Santals (Bankura, Purulia, West Mednipur), 26. Shabar (Purulia), and 27. Shaoriya Pahadiya (Purulia).

# 3

# Historical Background

Bengal has an important historical background, encompassing socio-cultural, religious and economic history of yore that went into rendering this specific part of the subcontinent a very intrinsic ethos and identity. Forming a significantly distinct part of Bengal is the region of study Radha Bengal. With its variety of physiographic units, diversity of tribal life and the richness of its forest products and mineral distribution, the historical background of the area has much to offer to understand the modern mode of folk life, religion, festivals and ceremonies, and in the process, it connects history with present times. A major part of these stories are retold through archaeological excavations and also surviving epigraphical, numismatic and literary records of erstwhile times, with its most part constituting the history of the original inhabitants or *vratyas* of a land. This history, often unwritten, finds little or no mention in the literary records of court historians and yet travels through generations in the form of oral traditions, including various ceremonies, festivities, rites and rituals. The present study and this specific chapter is an attempt to look into this region, dating from the time of the earliest records available. Nevertheless, the task is a difficult one due to the lack of continuous historical data. The various beliefs, practices, religious thoughts and ceremonies of the masses, often supplement the historical and archaeological data pertaining to the lifestyle and subsistence pattern of the inhabitants. At several times, such religious beliefs and practices were patronised by royalty and were often adopted as state religion as well; but throughout time, there remained a dominant belief of the original inhabitants or the *vratyas*, which was not replaced by the patronised religious ideas. The following pages represent a brief data pertaining to the pre, proto and historic records of the region of study as available from archaeological and historical data, which attempts to reflect such religious ideas, including ceremonies and festivals. The supplementing and complimenting ethnographic data is represented in the following chapter.

## From Earliest Times till the Gupta Period

Archaeological research, in much parts of the region of study and adjoining areas, goes back to 19th century and covers a time span from the very earliest prehistoric times till very recent time of the Muslim period of Bengal. There are important sites that have yielded significant information regarding the cultural continuity of the same, especially pertaining to distribution of different types of sites and the reconstruction of their stratigraphy and basic cultural details. Though few recent researches have attempted to understand the composite cultural history and "interrelationships between the different geographical segments of this region" (Chakrabarti, 1993:186), yet the analysis of folk religion, ceremonies and their representation, and understanding in proper cultural contexts is very less, with most of the data reflecting associations of royalty, their land grants and evidences of territorial expansion. Nevertheless, some information helps to surmise the socio-cultural life of the ancient inhabitants. Historical records correspond with archaeological assemblages from only a period of Early Historic or Chalcolithic and Iron Age period onwards.

## Prehistory

The reconstruction of prehistory of the region of study is entirely through archaeological assemblages. The evidences from Purulia, Bankura and West Mednipur of West Bengal is further supplemented with the data from other sites in Chhotanagpur Plateau, including districts like Palamau, Hazaribagh and Giridih, Ranchi, Singhbhum, Santal Parganas in Jharkhand, and Burdwan as well as, Birbhum in West Bengal. All these sites have yielded enough materials to suggest a closely forested tract and stone tools of Lower, Middle and Upper Palaeolithic affiliations and thereby, a possible suggestive hypothesis arises, about "the hunting groups wandering in the forests and losing some of their tools as well as artifacts in the course of a working day" (*Ibid*:187-188). Since the above reference also includes the region of study, it can be surmised that the beginning of the prehistoric era in the area was the same.

Speaking about Palaeolithic occurrences, mention may be made of the foot of the Netharhat Plateau that yielded evidence of Upper Palaeolithic occurrences, but these need to be studied further for a complete picture. Chakrabarti (*Ibid*:188) mentions such artifacts as chopping tools, handaxes, scrappers and others from sites like Chainpur-Bishnupur areas as well as Ranchi[1], which provide information in relation to original inhabitants and the Neolithic stages.

The Lower Palaeolithic stage in the region of study also points to the significant existence of a forest cover in the western part of West Bengal,[2] where the upland stretches are distinctive in relation to the surrounding plains. Although heavy plantation has been carried out by the Forest Department, but judging by the forest tracts in these areas, it can be suggested that all these areas of lateritic gravelly uplands of West Bengal were once under natural forest cover.

The Palaeolithic assemblage of the region of study have also been studied earlier by several, including, D. Sen, A.K. Ghosh and Meera Chatterjee (1963)—especially in the contexts of the areas near Bankura town and Kumari-Kangsabati confluence[3] and Upper Palaeolithic evidences from Dhaba in Purulia and also in Burdwan, Bankura and Mednipur.

The prehistoric stage in West Bengal also includes the mention of a range of rich fossil finds from Susunia in Bankura district. Though scholars[4] have pointed out that the tool collection in the site lacks proper records and thus, the geological stratigraphy of the area as well as archaeological stratigraphy of the different localities still remain unrelated, but the fossil finds in good numbers indicate a rich natural setting amidst which contemporary people used to reside. The earlier fossils include such items like *Bubalus palaeindicus, Bos namadicus, Bos sp., Palaeoloxodon namadicus, Equus namadicus, etc.*, which were assigned to an upper Pleistocene Age. Later investigations revealed such extinct items like *Bos cf namadicus, Bubalus bubalis var. palaeindicus, Boselaphus namadicus, Palaeoloxodon sp., Crocuta sp.*, and *Hystrix crassidens.*[5] Amongst the living forms are *Antelope cervicapra, Cervus duvauceli, Cervus unicolor, Axis axis, Muntiacus muntijac, Sus cristatus, Equus onager khur, Panthera cf. leo, Gavialis gangeticus* and *Batagur baska.* The assemblage suggested a late Pleistocene to early Holocene bracket and helps to ascertain upto a certain extent the rich fauna that early man in the region was exposed to.

The prehistoric period also includes the microlith-users. In this scenario, it is important to note the rich availability of microliths in the region in "easy abundance in the forests (of the Ayodhya hill area of Purulia), along the river banks (of the Tarafeni and Bhairavbanki valleys, the Sanjai river banks, etc.) and on the hill slopes (northern Palamau, the hills near Jhalda). They also occur profusely around the outcrops of raw materials, mostly quartz" (*Ibid*:199).

From the region of study, there have been no published data pertaining to living activities of the microlith-using prehistoric population, but adjoining areas have reported some, which can also be extended to the region of study, like Egara Mile area of Burdwan or Paruldanga of Shantiniketan.

Chakrabarti (*Ibid*:200) considers it as possible explanation to the fact that microlithic hunter-gatherers were living in a condition of increasing aridity when strong aeolian actions were depositing a mantle of yellowish sands (e.g., in Birbhanpur and other places), and they were unlikely to have been rooted to a single place for long. This condition also meant that they could have been using makeshift huts of leaves and branches of trees. Even in modern times, similar arrangements are noticed, and this situation was also seen during the period of fieldwork. Thus, perishable cultural debris could not be located, and the non-perishable ones in the form of stone tools could only be found in archaeological assemblages. This can further be analysed by locating a proper early Mesolithic occupation level in the region, which will provide data on the way people lived.

The Neolithic horizon of the present region of study is not clear from the work carried out so far. The discovery of many stone tools in terms of neoliths have been reported from various regions, including Mayurbhanj (Odisha)[6], Belpahari, Susunia and certain other regions of Mednipur and Bankura. Similarly, stone tools in association with BRW are found from most of the sites of the districts of Bankura, Burdwan and Birbhum. Published data regarding this period does not furnish any information about the available standard of life of the original inhabitants or their religious beliefs and practices. A coordinated search might prove helpful to give insight into the Neolithic stages in Bengal, including the region of present study and assist in answering specific questions on certain issues. The early beginning of food production in the context of Chhotanagpur Plateau and data about assemblages of iron slag, black-and-red ware along with microliths and large number of Neolithic Celts could be connected to such sites of the region whese copper-mining activities occurred. However, it was not till the early historic times and the period of Chalcolithic and Iron Ages that one comes across references of literature to corroborate the existence of the original inhabitants or their religious life.

## Chalcolithic and Iron Ages and the Early Historic Period

Corresponding to the archaeological period of Early Historic times, the mention of *Banga* is found in literary references that can be traced as early as 5$^{th}$ century BCE. in some ancient Indian Sanskrit texts that refer the region to be geographically meaning as a riverine, low-lying, flood-prone terrain. These references can also suggest the region of study to mean that it was swept by rivers, as is also found in the assemblages during the prehistoric times within alluvium levels. However, the references can only point to the direction of the existence of the original inhabitants in the region and not about their mode of living, their religious beliefs and practices. Nevertheless, these are important to point out the fact that the region could have already witnessed outside population gradually coming in to settle, because of which the original inhabitants were made to clear the forested lands with stone tools and move further inside towards the interior of the lands. This evidence is more prominent from the time of the use of microliths onwards.

The beginning of the Chalcolithic and Iron Ages associate this period with iron and black-and-red (B&R) ware evidences, with various radiocarbon dating assessments estimating a long chronological span of 1500 BCE. to 400

BCE. But, scholars also argue otherwise, as it has been suggested that Iron Age began in the region around the end of the second or the beginning of the first millennium BCE., with around 500 years of iron-free existence. However, the debate still continues on the beginning of use of iron in the region, but none of the evidences so far have yielded any reference regarding the lifestyle and pattern of religious activities of the region, for which, one has to refer to the historical evidences. The beginning of Early Village Farming (EVF) settlements and their association with B&R ware is well represented by several numbers of sites distributed across the districts of Mednipur, Bankura, Burdwan and Birbhum. The most represented sites include Mangalkot, Pandu Rajar Dhibi and Bharatpur (Burdwan District), Bahiri, Manisadal and Haraipur (Birbhum District), Dihar and Pakhanna (Bankura District), besides Moghalmari and Tamluk from Mednipur District.

The individual cultural traits of the Chalcolithic and Iron Age period in the region provide information of uniformity regarding the range of potteries, wattle and daub huts with mud-plastered floors and courtyards, beads of semi-precious stones, cultivation of rice, wide availability of cattle and buffalo, limited use of copper and a large use of small stone tools, with "no doubt detailed functional associations," etc. (*Ibid*: 203-205). Another important aspect to relate to the period is the abundant availability of deer and antlers in the excavated sites. These also suggest the countryside to have been more wooded, grassy and open, a fact that can lead to surmise that there was a marked change in the increase in rainfall in the region, as against the arid condition of the Mesolithic Age. Towards the end of this phase, iron smelting seemed to have been an important activity, as is prominent from Birbhum, Burdwan and other areas. The remains from Tamluk also suggest that during the $2^{nd}$ and $1^{st}$ millennia BCE., farmers were "courageous enough to have moved till the proper delta" (*Ibid*:205).

On the other hand, these stages of Chalcolithic and Iron Ages and the Early Historic periods correspond with certain classical historical records in the form of epigraphical and literary evidences, dating as far back as $1^{st}$-$2^{nd}$ century BCE., These have the earliest mention of the region of Radha as well. Mention may be made of Jain and Buddhist texts as well as rock edicts. The latter speaks of the region and neighbouring areas and helps to understand considerably the socio-cultural and religious lives of the inhabitants under the influence of royalty. The earliest reference regarding this fact can be made of the Mahasthan rock edict ($3^{rd}$ century CE)[7], which though could not be located exactly within the region of study, nevertheless, was included within its territory, revelation due to the geographical proximity of the same (Sen,1991:17-19)[8]. This plausibly is also important as the region is often considered as the easternmost limit of the contemporary Magadhan empire under Asoka. Another important piece of document, corresponding to about the same time, is the Asokan rock edicts of Dhauli[9] near Bhubaneshwar and another in present Jaugad[10] under Ganjam District in Southern Kalinga region and both speak about local life. These findings impart a sense of geographical assertion, that upto a certain extent, helps to visualise the region of former Bengal under the influence of Magadhan empire, especially under King Asoka in $3^{rd}$ century BCE. (*Ibid*:16-17). There are also similar inscriptions in the area, close to the vicinity of the present region of work, which also speak about patronisation of Buddhism by Asoka.[11] The Dhauli and Jaugad inscriptions also point to the fact that agrarian festivals existed in contemporary times, which correspond with the modern day festival of *Tusu* (*Ibid*)[12].

There are also literary evidences that correspond to archaeological time span of Early Historical period that helps to throw light on the original inhabitants and their socio-religious life. Jain text *Acharanga Sutra* is one such source of historical work. Though the composition of the work can be ascribed to a later date in $6^{th}$ century CE., yet, these literary evidences speak of a time that goes back to around $6^{th}$ century BCE. Originally composed in Prakrit, the work has the earliest mention of the region of Radh and is significant not only from the historical point of view, but also due to the fact that it speaks about the spread of Jain thoughts and beliefs in the region under the auspices of Mahavir at an early stage. The travels of Mahavir are mentioned through *Subha* or *Sumhabhumi* and *Vajja* or *Vajrabhumi*[13] in the country of the *Ladhas* or *Radhas*, of which the present region of study including Purulia, West Mednipur and Bankura form an important part. There is also a mention of the inhabitants of the region who came in touch with Mahavir and incidentally, resulted in a hostile reaction on part of the autochthones who let loose their dogs after him (which is mentioned in the text). Apart from Jain texts, ancient Buddhist texts (like *Arya Manjusri Mula Kalpa* and *Anguttarayanikaya),* too mention the original inhabitants of the regiona whose composition, under the auspices of Asoka, can be ascribed to an earlier date, as compared to the Jain texts. *Arya Manjusri Mula Kalpa* mentions the people of Bengal to belong to the "*Asura* community and that the *Asura* language was the language of the *Bengalis*." (Roy,1981:10)[14]. *Anguttarayanikaya* mentions the region of Bengal to have been under the Magadha rule and that it was once under the influence of Buddhism. These documents also argue against statements by many scholars in recent years regarding the advent of Buddha in-self in Bengal as having no concrete historical records (*Ibid*). Still, of a later date, corresponding to the archaeological time span covering Early to Later Historical period exist literary evidence of the writings of various Chinese pilgrims who visited the region of study and mention variously about local religion of the people as well as the patronised religion of the royalties. This fact has been explained in the following pages, under the chronological section of Early Historical period.

Within the time period of around 600 years after the Mahasthan rock inscription, there is almost no availability of any written data or epigraphical work pertaining to Bengal, till the finding of the Susunia rock inscription, dating to $4^{th}$ century CE. that speak of the existence of King Chandravarman. Though, it is a piece of evidence related to ascertaining the historical expanse under royal influences, and there is no mention of the masses, yet, it is significant as it is the first component of historical evidence of the appearance of names of kings in an acceptable manner in any written evidence in Bengal. Haraprasad Sashtri has attempted to identify Chandravarman with the brother of Naravarman of the Varman dynasty of Malwa, which is also seen from the Meherauli Iron Pillar inscription. There is a dichotomy between scholars behind the true identity of Chandravarman, stating that "the Malwas never extended their region beyond the eastern limits of Rajasthan" (Majumdar, 1943:30), and some identify them with the Chandra Varma of Meharauli inscription (near Qutub Minar) in Delhi, while others identify them as non-resident rulers who could be possibly from the region of Pushkarna in Rajasthan. However, from what is deciphered in the inscription, Sen mentions, "The king of Pushkarn (or Pushkarna), Sri Singha Varma's son Sri Chandra Varma created the inscription." (Sen,1991:33-34). The Early Historic evidence of Susunia in Bankura is an important turning point in historical records of the region of study. Though the information is meager, yet it helps to throw light on Chandravarman of Pushkarna, a worshipper of Visṇu, and local influence on Pakhanna explains an assumption regarding settlement of a capital city of Chandravarman located 25 kms from Susunia.

The archaeological and historical significance of these epigraphical records also help to ascertain few important details about contemporary society, including the territorial limits of the Gupta Empire or the *janapadas,* which also incorporated the region of study[15] and the existence of local administrators, which acted more like vassals under the main royal powers in the region[16]. Majumdar (*Ibid*:2-5) pointed out four main divisions, which refer to the available copper grants of the Gupta Period, besides suggestion that the geographical divisions of the region of Bengal was under the influence of Samudragupta of the Gupta Dynasty at one stage (approximately between 330-375 CE). The entire region was divided into *bhuktis* that Majumdar mentioned as 'allotment', which used to denote the biggest administrative unit within a kingdom or an empire. These *bhuktis* were subdivided into a number of *vishaya, mandala* or *vithi.*[17] These sub-divisions included such places like *Vangas, Pundras, Suhmas, Radhas, Gaudas* and *Gaudiyas*. The aforesaid partitions were mainly on the basis of geographic landscapes that also corresponded to the territorial divisions of ancient times of the various communities who inhabited the region. Of these, the main ones were *Bango* (now Bangladesh), *Radh,* i.e., western part and *Barendra* or northern part of modern West Bengal; however, their boundaries constantly shifted from time-to-time (Singh, K.S. pp. xiii-xiv)[18]. Specifically, there is a mention of three *bhuktis* in the area of the present Bengal, which include Pudravardhana, Vardhamana and another one that consisted of Suvarna-vithi and Navyavakasika.[19] The regions of Uttara Radh and Dakshin Radh also appeared for the first time during the Gupta Age and were further mentioned at the time of Lakshmansena of the Sena Dynasty many centuries later. These two regions of Uttar and Dakshin Radh formed sub-divisions of the Vardhaman-*bhukti,* which is known from the inscriptions of the Pala-Sena Period, along with others like Danda-Bhukti-Mandala, Paschima-Khatika.[20]

Though, as mentioned earlier, the boundaries of these territorial divisions kept shifting, but amidst this change, certain regions emerged important in later years. *Puṇdravardhana bhukti's Varendri* was one such district. A well-known district, it lay north of the main branch of the Ganges, later known as Padma and stood on the west of Brahmaputra, embracing Rajshahi Division and the State of Cooch Bihar. Of the Burdwan Division or *Vardhamāna-bhukti*, an important and considerable part constituted the region of *Rādhā*. The central part of Bengal lay embracing the majority part of the Presidency Division and a considerable part of Decca Division between the Bhagirathi, the Padma, the lower reaches of Brahmaputra and the estuary of the Meghna.[21] And, finally, there was the Chittagong Division that stretched beyond the Meghna and included the remains of the royal seat of Samatat.

Socially, the period under the Gupta Age did not witness any division between the Brahmans and the non-Brahmans. Caste rigidity that was seen in succeeding times, was also not perceived. From the time of 5$^{th}$ to 6$^{th}$ century CE., the Gupta kings advocated the spread of the official language of Sanskrit in the region and all official records were written in Sanskrit. Important Brahmans, who have been variously mentioned by scholars to have been brought from the west and were well-versed in the Vedic knowledge, helped to further the cause of the Sanskrit documents and official records. In the social sphere, there was much importance accorded to local chiefs. This fact is known from the land grant unearthed from the Village Mallasarul in Burdwan, which provides information about the growing importance of local chiefs even during the declining period of the Guptas. This land grant dates back to during $6^{th}$ century CE. with the mention of local king Vijaysena found on it, possibly under the rule of King Gopchandra (Sen,1991:37)[22].

Historical and archaeological records also suggest significant expansion of local influence through economic activities. This position is also verified by the fact that the coins made of gold and silver of the Gupta Age continued till later times, even years after the decline of the Guptas (*Ibid*:45-46) in Bengal. Few such *dinars* of Gupta rulers have been unearthed, like that of Narsimhagupta III, Chandragupta, Vishnugupta and Jaygupta. The Gupta king who first introduced his gold *dinars* in the region is Bainagupta around-188 Gupta era or 507 CE., as known from the Ghunaighar copper inscription (of Vainya Gupta)[23] of Tripura in modern Bangladesh (*Ibid*). Moreover, mention should be made of the Early Historic finds from archaeological excavations of the sites of Pokharna, Dihar, Tamluk, Tildah, along with several others[24] from adjoining districts, as well as from Bangladesh consisting of the sites of Mahasthangarh (which is not far from Bangarh in Bengal) and Wari-Bateshwar in the Meghna Delta. All the above sites have yielded significant information about the growing economic network in the region, thereby making the Ganga Delta a very important zone. However, it should also be mentioned that, considering "not a single, specifically early historical site in the plateau portions of the districts within the region of study—Bankura, West Mednipur and the whole of Purulia, need not lead us to believe that these regions were not within the economic network of the Early Historic West Bengal" (Chakrabarti,1993:209).

The importance of some sites in political, economic and social setup is also corroborated through ancient literary evidences. The site of Bangarh, which is highly mentioned in ancient literature, is identified with the ancient city of 'Kotivarsa'. Bangarh is mentioned to have been at the centre of administrative division, which was a part of the still larger administrative division and had its capital at Mahasthangarh. Tamluk has been identified with ancient Tamralipta, and amongst the sites of Kotasur, Mangalkot and Chandraketugarh, the last one is identified with the capital city of Gangaridae. This mention has been made in the writings of classical Greece, from which it is known that Bengal formed the dominions of the king of the Prasii, i.e., Magadha, as early as the time of Agrammes, i.e., the last Nanda king (Raychaudhuri, 1953:309-10). Though displaced geographically to a lower region and need further verification, yet the mud fortifications at the site of Chandraketugarh, which are not earlier than 2$^{nd}$ century BCE., also speak about occupation from the Mauryan phase onwards, till the time of the Palas. It is well known that the Bengal Delta, especially the Bhagirathi Delta, played an important role in Early History in maintaining India' s relation with South-East Asia and elsewhere, and the overall Early Historic situation in Bengal suggests such a picture. The distribution of Early Historic sites in Bankura, Birbhum and Burdwan suggests the emerged route to have been associated with major politico-administrative units of ancient Bengal. Trade routes were important. From Burdwan, one can enter Bankura via Dihar and go to south. Pokharna is across Damodar in the Panagarh section of Burdwan and is suggested to lie., in the important trader outes besides connecting Bankura and beyond. This position is also inferred from the fact that if Susunia was within the administrative units of King Chandravarman, it can be assumed that his kingdom extended further into the lateritic and Sal forest areas of the plateau region. In such a scenario, it can be also logical to infer that the resources of the plateau were being more securely integrated into the economic system of the region, than what is known. A thriving economic activity in the region is also suggested by the evidence of a gradual development of a local system of currency that also incorporated Kushana devices and different weight systems[25]. (Chakrabarti, *Op.cit*: 209). The region of Radha also saw the evolution of Kushana coinage, which is known as Kushano-Vanga or Kushano-Radha coinage. Radha was an important trade centre at the time of Kanishka, i.e., around 78-100 CE., when Kushana coins were introduced in the region. A large number of coins, representing the Kushana coins were also unearthed, especially from such places like, 24 Parganas (South), Burdwan, Mednipur, Bankura and Purulia, of which the finds from the plateau region of Bankura and Purulia are the maximum. These coins seem to have been in circulation from 2$^{nd}$ century CE. onwards till about 4$^{th}$ or early 5$^{th}$ century CE, when the early Gupta Age was continuing. This fact can also help to infer that the plateau portions of the districts of Bankura, Mednipur and Purulia along with Burdwan could have witnessed a distinct geographical and political unit, with their base at Pokharna in the Bankura stretch of the Damodar Valley. The region is also said to have experienced trade from traders coming from the northwest who used Kharosti Script and dealt in food grains and horses (Mukherjee, 1991). This transaction also connected the region with the southeast. Though the region witnessed serious development of economic activities, yet it is important to note, as also pointed out by Chakrabarti (*Ibid*:208), that the western parts of the districts mentioned above and the district of Purulia "do not have any reported early historic settlement. The implication is that these regions could go on housing their hunter-gatherers."

All the archaeological evidences from the time of black-and-red ware phase onwards suggest the ancient settlements in West Bengal to have formed a locational nucleus, which is still used by modern settlements of the area. Thus, both the historical and archaeological evidences mentioned above point towards the fact of a growing socio-economic importance of the region of Radha (or Uttar Radha), as well as Suhma (associated with coastal Mednipur and the area to the north) and indicate towards both to have come up as important geographical and administrative unit by this time. Though none of this yielded information about the religious beliefs and practices of the original inhabitants, yet, it can be surmised that the growing and developing socio-economic activities, new settlements in the region, and fresh contacts with relatively new regions did not completely leave the original inhabitants free from influence.

**Late Historical Period and the Medieval Period Post Gupta Age**

The Later Gupta Period and the Post-Gupta Age also saw the region of Bengal expanding considerably in territorial limits, as finally by the time of 6$^{th}$ century CE. during the reign of Sasanka[26] (595-621 CE.) and the early 7$^{th}$ century when Gauda ruled Western Bengal that extended upto Odisha or Utkal, as the latter was formally known. It is also important to note that this period could be the time of the foundation of the Kingdom of Panchkot in Purulia in the northern section of the district. The importance of the political stability offered by the Kingdom of Panchkot is also mentioned by Chakrabarti (1993:211), as he adds, "It is doubtful if without the political stability offered by the state of Panchkot, Purulia would have had so many later historical remains."[27] Archaeological evidences also point to the fact that from the time of 7$^{th}$ - 8$^{th}$ centuries, the region witnessed organised political territories/kingdoms, and it also was possibly constituted within the political territories of Magadha from the Post-Gupta Period onwards. Available ruins of a spurt in temple and image-making between $8^{th}$-$10^{th}$ century CE. also possibly point towards the process of secondary state formations, which includes the Kingdom of Panchkot, and there could have been several smaller states within the forested and hilly tracts of the West Bengal-Bihar-Odisha borders. Culturally, the Odisha Style of temple building exercised the most profound influence and can also include the parts of the region of study, which could have been included within different kingdoms of contemporary Odisha. This fact, however, needs to be further verified as historical evidences are very few.

Archaeological information about the Gupta, Post-Gupta, and Pala and Sena Periods is aplenty, as obtained from excavations in various regions, including Chandraketugarh, Mahanad, Mangalkot, Ballal Dhibi, Rajbaridanga or ancient 'Karnasuvarna', etc. This period also coincides with the Post-Gupta Period of the Pala and Sena rulers. The process of unification of tribal formations of Bengal continued under Pala and Sena kings (between 8-13 century CE.), and gradually Bengal emerged as an 'ethnic territory'. Between $8^{th}$-$9^{th}$ centuries, the Bengal region emerged as a geographic entity, as the Pala administration established itself as, single authority commanding the land on the left of the Ganges was established as *Varendra Bhumi* or *Varendri*, meaning *"srehstha sarasbhumi or utkrishta Indrapuri"* (or ideal establishment of the God Indra) (Sen:1991:12). "At the same time, the land on the right came to be recognised as *Radh Bhumi* or *Radha"* (*Ibid*).[28] The Pala and Sena ruins are much distributed in Malda and West Dinajpur districts of Bengal in the form of stone images and temple ruins, large tanks and single-occupational burnt brick sites. The Terai region of Bengal also provides enough evidence to support that this period saw the reign of Pala and Sena kings and it possibly could have offered routes to the Tibetan Plateau across the northern sector.

Socially, the time witnessed a significant part of the spread of Buddhist ideas and beliefs amongst the masses, and Buddhism—which was the royal religion—received further impetus for social acceptance under the Pala rulers (from approximately $8^{th}$ century to $10^{th}$ century CE.). In this context, it is also important to mention the large-scale penetration of Jainism in the area, which could have failed to survive in historical records due to lack of royal patronage. However, its widespread reach in the plateau region is corroborated by the availability of several Jain images, dating to $8^{th}$-$10^{th}$ century CE. onwards. The maximum number of such Jain ruins in the form of images of *Tirthankaras*, alongside Brahmanical images is also found in such areas like Singhbhum, Purulia, and Bankura. Though Singhbhum is not included within the region of study, but it helps to ascertain the extent of the penetration of Jain and Brahmanical religious principles, nevertheless. In the district of Bankura in the Bankura-Bishnupur sector, the temples of Bahulara, Saileswar, Sanreswar, and Ekteswar probably marked the easternmost stretch of this development and spread related ideas and beliefs. On the other hand, the ruins found at Harmasra in the western and southwestern parts of Bankura District could have signaled a close link and continuity with the Purulia area. It is also noteworthy to mention here that similar activities were also witnessed in the district of Burdwan at the temples at Barakar, Sat Deuliya, and the northern boundary of the district on the bank of Ajay (Ichhai Ghosher Deul).

Several of the available images are dated and provide an information pertaining to the period $7^{th}$- Early $9^{th}$ century CE, like the images from Pakbira in Purulia (debated to have been between 7th-8th century CE. or at most, middle of 9th century CE). Several sites are also mentioned to have been contemporary with Pakbira, along the Kangsabati, including, Budhpur, Ralibera, Anai Jambad, Palma, Boram, etc. Similarly, in the northern part of the district, one finds sites of similar period, which include Para, Toisama, etc. Most of these sites could have been connected through trade too as seen in case of Puncha, near Pakbira, which is considered as an important trading capital of the district in the 19th century. The old Benares road from Calcutta passed through the Raghunathpur area in the northern part of the district. Another major route could have been through the Kangsabati River. Most of these ruins were even visible during the time of field work. Thus, the remains and the sites could have been connected to the old trading routes of the area. All these ruins taken together, help to infer the presence of organised political power on the local level in the plateau portion of the region of study.

The period saw assimilation between Brahmanical religion and Buddhism under the Palas,[29] who introduced themselves as secular and reigned till almost the end of 12th century CE. in succession by 18 kings of the same dynasty.[30] Under Dharmapala, the reign extended till Varanasi. He conquered Kanyakubja for which he was awarded the title of *Uttarapath's Raajchakravartin.* Though with time, the extensive expanse of the reign reduced, yet Magadh was within the Pala suzerainty till the end, and the last of the Pala rulers Madanpala was only limited to Magadh. In between, during the time of Mahipala, the region of Barendri slipped from the Pala rulers to a local Kaivartya chief—Divyok or Dibo. During the time of the rule of Bhima—the son of Dibo, the region again passed into the Pala administrative power. The Pala rule also witnessed the escalation of the importance of Buddhism in the region.

This change is reflected through the initial Buddhist *slokas* at the beginning of the administrative declaration of every Pala king, starting from Dharmapala till the last ruler of the dynasty as well as the construction of several Buddhist monasteries, as mentioned in the texts of Lama Taranath (7th century CE) that speaks about Buddhist history in India and describes the Vikramsila vihara, which was an area of Mahayana Buddhist learning. He also mentions the *'tarka sabhas'* or philosophical debate and argument meetings at the Vikramsila vihara between Brahman pundits and the Buddhist monks. Amongst other monasteries, the one at Tamralipti was very popular. Several Chinese scholars visited the region, like Fa Hien, who spoke about the presence of a stupa that was erected by King Asoka, as well as other Chinese pilgrims Tao-ling, Ta-Cheng-Teng as well as I-tsing (671-695 CE)[31], who are mentioned to have studied Buddhism at Tamralipti. I-tsing has also spoken about several Buddhist monks, both male and female, at the royal court of King Rajbhatta.[32] Several Buddhist scholars also helped to spread Buddhist preaching like, Shilabhadra and Atish Dipankar, who taught at the Buddhist centres of learning at Nalanda and Vikramsila and also earned fame and respect by traveling to Tibet.

Socio-culturally too, the period was important, as it witnessed the origin of the modern Bengali Language. Alongside, the time also saw an escalation of the importance of the use of Sanskrit. Various texts were also composed in Sanskrit, like Asvaghos' s *Buddhacharita* and *Saundarananda*. "Sanskrit was a popular language amidst the Buddhist in Bengal and not Pali or Buddhist-Sanskrit" (Sen, *Op.cit*:79). Since, under the Pala kings, Brahmanism also received equal incentive, land grants were made to various Brahmans and help was provided to establish temples and worships of various Puranic deities. The Pala *mahamantri* or chief minister was also from a line of a family of Brahmans.[33] A considerable area of the region of study was also under the Pala administration. This information is known from the time of Nayapala (II), the son and successor of Mahipala (approx 1038-1055 CE). At this time, Karna, son of Gangeyadeva of Kalchuri Dynasty, had attacked Nayapala (II), causing much damage and devastation. Karna attacked once again during the time of Vigrahapala III (1055-1070 CE), the son and successor of Nayapala (II), "and mostly probably, occupied a big part of the region of Uttar Radh". However, Vigrahapa III defeated Karna and married his daughter—Yovanashri (Sen:81). This piece of information is significant to note, not only because of the idea of the extension of the Pala power in the region of study, but also helps to understand that from the time of Vigrahapala III, the Pala power was facing onslaughts from various sides.

As Buddhism and Brahmanism thrived side-by-side, it was only a natural consequence that Buddhism tried to imbibe Puranic religion during the Pala Period (Roy, 1981:2-3). The influence of Buddhism on the religion of the inhabitants is also evident from the rise of Tantric Buddhism, which saw the assimilation of Brahmanical and Buddhist ideas and also witnessed the rise of Sakti worship, as has also been mentioned by Roy (Roy:1981:2-3) due to influence by Brahmanical religion. Moreover the religion of Buddhism, in turn, is seen to have received an extra feature that "transformed it into a kind of Tantric Buddhism." This situation further led to a gradual change in the importance ascribed to womenfolk in the society against the prevailing Brahmanical order.

In the middle of 12$^{th}$ century CE, when the Pala power was at its decline, the Senas established their supremacy in Bengal. However, before the Sena power was established, Bengal also saw the rise of the Varma at the time of the middle of 11th century at the hands of the Jaatvarma, who had their capital Vikrampur and the regions of Samatat-Harikel was under their influence. As a dynasty, they were related to the Palas, being distant blood relations. However, the fact that they favoured Brahmanical religion and encouraged the Brahmans in their activities is known from the fact that they had the Vishnu-*cakra* as their seal and symbol on currencies.

The Senas came to power routing out the Varmas and the Palas.[34] During the time of Lakshmansena (1201 CE) and later three generations of the Sena rule, an important change took place in the region, which also affected the rest of Bengal equally and resulted in important socio-cultural and religious changes in the future for centuries that were to follow: These changes occured due to the invasion of Bengal by Ikhtiar-uddin Muhammad-Bin-Bakhtiyar Khalji, which has also been variously labeled as the '*Turki akraman* or invasion' or the 'invasion of Islam.' A large section of the western part of present Bengal was under present region of Odisha and was mainly under local Brahmanical feudatories, tribal chiefs, etc. In 1306, there was the intrusion into South-West Bengal, as mentioned in the *Sirat-i-Firuz Shahi* that Sultan Firuz Shah Tughluq came into Sikharbhum and Manbhum. The same text also mentions the prevalence of 36 vassal chiefs in the region and after the defeat, the Sultan reached Jajnagar (Odisha).[35] The Senas have been referred to come from Karnat and were present in an important section of the Radh, Damodar and Ajay basin areas (Sen, *Op.cit*:88). The fact that the Senas were patrons of Siva is evident from the copper plate inscription of Lakshmansena (1179 to 1205 CE), had an inscribed Siva image at its top besides a *sloka* written in praise of Lord Siva. Moreover, Vijaysena and Ballalsena were Saivaites, which is evident from the fact that both are referred to by the title *Parammaheshwar.* Patronising the contemporary Brahmanic society, the rule of Ballasena is credited with socially dividing the Brahmans into the ones who migrated from the West and the ones who already inhabited Bengal. Socially and culturally too, the region made progress to enrich the history of years to come by prose and poetry written in Sanskrit in these times. Here, mention may be made of Umapatidhar—the minister of Ballalsena and Lakshmansena, whose Sanskrit compositions were famous in contemporary times (*Ibid*:90-92).

The Later Historic Period also saw proper delineation of geographic territories, especially in the region of study—the Radh region. This fact has been corroborated through various literary evidences of contemporary period. From 9th to 10th century, there is a mention of the region of Radh into two divisions, Dakshin and Uttar Radh, mostly evident from the time of Lakshmansena onwards.[36] Though variously the territorial borders and geographical limitations of Uttar and Dakshin Radh have been attempted to be delineated by historians down the ages[37], yet there remains a sense of ambiguity regarding determining the exact position of the regions[38]. However, a gradually expanding geographic boundary connected through trade and commerce with other parts of India as well as important parts of the world[39] is seen to exist. A similar work that connected the trade activities in the region with local festivals was also provided by Bhattacharya and Chattopadhyay, which pertains to the offering of terracotta horses as votive offerings to Goddess Sini, particularly in the district of Bankura[40]. This information brings to mind the mention of the port-city of Tamralipti, whose mention in Ptolemy's *Geography* is the 'earliest dated reference' (Majumdar, *Op.cit*:29) alongside its fame as an important site in Early historical period.[41] This state continued into the Later Historical Age, though with reduced importance and finally replaced by Saptagram around 8th century CE, by which time with decreasing economic activities, new trade contacts emerged when the region of Bengal saw the introduction of the Muslim rule. Before 15th century began, during the time of the Islam in Bengal, the period witnessed the emergence of small, independent autonomous kingdoms. Some of them are famous as the *Baro Bhuinyas,* who had become considerably significant and important.[42]

This period also witnessed the development and distribution of population groups according to social classes and occupations. Trade was once again encouraged during the Mughal Age, which further helped to delineate social divisions. After the creation of the Bengal *Subah* under Akbar, Raja Man Singh was appointed as the governor and he brought traders, businessmen and artisans from Rajasthan and carried back an image of goddess Kali from Jessore to Jaipur and established a colony of Bengal Brahman priests in Jaipur.[43] Still, in later times, in 18th century, the plundering of the Bargees also left behind a socially important impact in Bengal, with several soldiers getting mixed with the local population and thus, giving rise to such Maratha communities, like the Baishya or Bassi, who are little known agricultural communities of Purulia. Some Maratha Brahmans settled in Burdwan and bear the name of Layek. Other local communities bear surnames, such as Deshmukh, Senapati, Tendulkar, Bassi, Adhikari, Sarvadhikari and other names, with a suffix of 'kar' used as Bengali surname. Mention is also found of a second generation of Maharashtrian scholar, Sakharam Ganesh Deshkar (1869-1910), who produced Bengali work *Desher Katha* in 1904, which is the story of the freedom struggle of Bengal (Singh, 1992:xvii). Thus, the origin of certain present day tribes can be historically traced to the Late Historic Period.

The process of territorial expansion further continued in Bengal throughout the tenure of the British rule and even afterwards. This phenomenon helped to chalk out new parameters for socio-cultural and religious contacts under the English East India Company between 1757 and 1790 and throughout this time, the British gained complete control over the administration of the area. Under the British, the region of Bengal was considered as an important area for trade and commerce and economy. Socially, there was a definite rise in pluralism during the colonial times in Bengal. Christianity, brought and introduced by the English, spread and distributed rapidly amidst the tribal population groups of the region and lower Brahmanical castes. The changing socio-religious significance of the society was mentioned in the trading accounts of several English traders as well[44]. At this time, Kolkata rose as an important centre for industrial belt along the Hooghly and the region of Durgapur-Asansol rose as important centre of mining. This development entailed influx of population from different parts of India associated with occupations like artisans, traders, professionals, etc. New rules and regulations introduced in the society, which pertained to education and social changes, like widow remarriage and introduction of English education, were met with various tepid and sore responses across Bengal. This influx of population continued even after independence and by 1950 and the later years, a range of population belonging to various occupations crossed over from the region of former East Pakistan to various places across Bengal and settled down, like Namasudra caste of sharecroppers or agricultural labourers, Chhutor or carpenters, Kamar or blacksmiths, Kumbhar/Kumor or potters, Keot or Kaivartya or fishermen, etc., as well as a number of landed aristocracy, including Brahmans, Kayasthas, Vaidyas, etc. These groups constituted both the lowest rung as well as the so-called upper castes of the Bangladesh society. In the socio-cultural as well as religious sphere too, new entrants helped to further delineate novel beliefs and thereby, encouraged new religious activities of the original inhabitants.

## ENDNOTES

1. Chakrabarti (1993:187-188) speaks about the finds of Lower Palaeolithic chopping tools, handaxes, scrappers, flakes, levallois cores, cleavers in the lowermost level of a gravel conglomerate in Chainpur-Bishnupur areas and around Ranchi by Vidula Jayaswal and others and several Neolithic celts from Ranchi from Later Asura sites (but without any contextual data). He also mentions the Lower Palaeolithic finds of A.K. Ghosh, including such artifacts as choppers, handaxes and scrapers in the lateritic gravel overlain by a thick silt deposit, and Ghosh mentions the find of microlithic tools in the upper reddish soil, which possibly meant, "in this case surface soil."
2. This has been stated by Chakrabarti (*Ibid*:190) through a study of the locality of Egara Mile (and was traced at Parihati, Mohanpur-Satbanki, Nakbindi, Patina, Jagannathpur and Ganganir Math) where all the tools occur at lateritic gravelly uplands of this region.
3. Chakrabarti (*Ibid*:192) quotes from Ghosh and Das (1967) about the West Bengal palaeolithic sites in the context of Bankura and Mednipur as "1)bedrock, mainly Archaean, 2) deposits of secondary or detrital laterite, and 3) alluvium" (from Ghosh, A.K. and Das, Ranjana. 1967. Palaeolithic Industries of West Bengal. In *Bulletin of the Cultural Research Institute* 7:112-23).
4. *Ibid*:198
5. "The fossil identification studies were made principally by M.V.A. Sastry, D.C. Dassharma and S. Biswas (1967) and D.C. Dassharma, S. Biswas and A. Nandi (1982) and also Sahu, 1988" (after *Ibid*).
6. The Neolithic Period is also variously suggested to be the beginning of food-production in the context of early microlith-using communities in this part of India and also the beginning of the wide use of Neolithic Celts which had specific functional utilities (*Ibid*:202). The site of Kuchai in Mayurbhanj showed a stratified Neolithic stage. Within West Bengal, the only metal-free Neolithic stage in West Bengal is at Pandu Rajar Dhibi (Period I, *IAR, 1984-85:97*), and it is also "unlikely that this level is confined to Pandu Rajar Dhibi alone" (*Ibid*).

7. This circular shaped rock inscription in Mahasthan, Bagura District of Bengal, gives scattered and varied information about contemporary life. The site was probably the headquarters of the local administrator (of the eastern section of the empire), its name during that period having been *Pundranagara,* as is mentioned in the inscription. The *mahamatta* of *Pundranagara* is described as in-charge of measures for famine relief. So far, excavations at the site have revealed terracotta of the Sunga Period.
8. Sen mentions (1991:17-19) the scholars who contributed considerably to the deciphering of the Mahasthan rock inscription Ramkrishna Bhandarkar, Benimadhab Barua and Dineshchandra Sarkar. He referred to the deciphered documents of Sarkar and mentioned parts of details which speak to a certain extent about the life and society of erstwhile times. He mentions the existence of granaries and the importance of purchasing in a group such items like houses and grains. He also mentions that the word *'gando'* in the inscription could point to the name of contemporary currency or a system of barter and exchange in the form of *kori.*
9. DHAULI (Major Rock Edicts)—The Dhauli inscription has been cut high on a rock in a group of hills which rise abruptly from the surrounding plain. The site has been identified with Tosali, which is mentioned by Ptolemy as a metropolis. It was situated near the sacred pool of Kosala-Ganga and thus developed into a religious centre as well. The identification of Dhauli with Tosali is most convincing and is borne out by the text of the 1$^{st}$ Separate Edict which is addressed to the *mahamattas* of Tosali. It seems reasonable that the edicts would be as near the city as possible if not actually within it.
10. JAUGADA (Major Rock Edicts, similar to the Dhauli version).The inclusion of the two separate edicts among the Jaugada series would point to its presence within Kalinga. It is now a ruined fort in the Behrampur *taluka* of the Ganjam District in Odisha. It is situated on the northern bank of the Rishikulya River. The two separate edicts are addressed to the *mahamattas* of Samapa, which was probably the name of the town in the Mauryan Period. The area covered by the ruins would suggest that the town must have been a fairly large one, and the presence of the fort might point to its being a military centre. Its proximity to the sea may have given the town an added advantage in trade and maritime activities.
11. Another rock inscription of Asoka is in modern Barabar Hills (referred to as Khalatik in ancient times), located near Gaya Asoka, and the grandson of Asoka, Dashrat, had carved few viharas for a residence of Ajavika monks during the four months of monsoon in the region.

From the inscribed illustration at the entrance of one of the caves, one can ascertain the framework of the village huts constructed in ancient times in Bengal. "These illustrations of Barabar Hills are the oldest illustrations explaining the feature of habitation in India. From this position, one gets to know that in eastern India, the huts used to be constructed of mud and clay with a framework of bamboos and a roof of straws." (Sen, 1991:17).

12. This celebration used to be held regularly, though it might have differed in practice and ceremony from what they are perceived in present times. These rock edicts speak about listening to them on specific period of the *Tishya Nakshatra* or constellation, which corresponds with the period of *Tishya* even in present times. The other name for *Tishya* is *Pushya* (Sen,1953:65). In Dhauli and Jaugada *Shilanushashans* (Rock Edicts) Asoka speaks about two specific folk harvest festivals concerning the month of *Paus*. The Dhauli Rock Edict (located in Puri District, near Bhubaneshwar and referred to as Number 1 Separate Kalinga Rock Edict) records, "This edict should be heard at the time of *Tishya Nakshatra* (Tishya Constellation). Outside the period of *Tishya*, it can be heard individually as well, from time to time"(Sen,1953:93). Sen explains it as "Every *Tishya* period, probably, a gathering was held for listening to this edict." The Jaugada Rock Edict (located in Ganjam District in Odisha and referred to as Number 2 Separate Kalinga Rock Edict) records, "This Rock Edict will be heard for a period of four months during the time of *Tishya Nakshatra* (Tishya Constellation). Outside the period of Tishya, at other times as well, this edict can be heard. If need be, it can be heard individually as well" (Sen,1953:93). Though no specific date of these rock edicts are ascertained, however, based on the formation period of the Rock Edicts, it can be postulated that they were composed more than two thousand years ago. Sen also elucidates, "Numbers 5 to 14 Rock Edicts were put up during the $13^{th}$ and $14^{th}$ years of his reign, including the 1 and 2 Separate Rock Edicts."

    With this approximate date, these ancient Rock Edicts help to portray ancient winter harvest festivals. The other name for *Tishya* is *Pushya*. The month of winter witnessed the reaping of the *aman* harvest. This position denotes that the festival existed without any royal patronage (Maitra, 2008:215-216).

13. Though there are various debates amidst scholars about the exact locations of these regions, as several ascribe the region of Vajjabhum to be Birbhum, others identify Vajjabhum with Singhbhum and Manbhum and still others with Mayurbhanj. However, the region mostly corresponds with the present regions of parts of Birbhum,

Burdwan and Hooghly Districts and parts of the region of present study. It is also said to correspond with the modern forests area of Jharkhand and comprises of the erstwhile regions of Simbhum, Manbhum, Mallabhum, Samantabhum and Varahabhum.

14. In Vedic and post-Vedic literature, the *Asuras* were known to be anti-gods, i.e., they were opposed to the Vedic gods. The word *Asura* is mentioned in the oldest section of the Vedas, and Vedic literature indicate that they were highly civilized. "*Asuras* were versed in magic, which indicates they belonged to the tradition of *Atharva Veda*. Their proficiency in architecture is also evident from the stories of Mahabharata, where *Asura Maydanab* built a castle." (Roy, 1981:10).
15. District-wise, these include Birbhum-Kotasur, Bahiri, Burdwan-Mangalkot, the upper levels of Pandu Rajar Dhibi showing Kushan-type terracottas, 24-Parganas or the Bhagirathi mouth-Chandraketugarh and a few miscellaneous and not very dependably documented sites, Maldah and Dinajpur-Bangarh and Kushan terracottas from Kandaran. (from Chakrabarti, 1993:206). In Bangladesh, these archaeologically significant sites include Mahasthangarh (which is not far from Bangarh in Bengal) and Wari-Bateshwar in the Meghna delta (*Ibid*).
16. Sen(*1991*:37-38) mentions that besides Samatat and Kamrup, the fact that the rest of Bengal was under the influence of the Guptas during the time of Samudragupta is evident from the availability of 15 copper plate inscriptions between the time period of mid-5$^{th}$ century CE. to mid-6$^{th}$ century CE. All these documents pertained to the purchase and sale of land or land grants. These included one in Burdwan District, five in Dinajpur District and the rest in Bangladesh, including three in Rajshahi District, three in Faridpur and one in Tripura District and another one in Bagura District. It is from these documents that the divisions of *bhuktis* of the time of the Guptas are known, that mainly included the Pundravardhana bhukti and the Burdwan bhukti.
17. "*Vishaya* and *mandala* are, however, at times, used as synonyms. At the time of the Guptas, the term *vithi* is not clear. In later times, it appears as a sub-division of the *bhukti* as well as *mandala*. Other sub-divisions of *mandala* in epigraphs are *khandala*, *avritti* and apparently *bhaga*. The *avritti* was further sub-divided into *chaturakas* and the latter into *patakasî* The *pataka* seems to have been the lowest administrative unit" (Majumdar,1971, pp. 23).
18. *Ibid.*
19. Of these, seven *bhuktis, namely,* Pundravardhana, Vardhamana, Tira, Srinagara, Kankagrama, Danda and Pragjyotisha are known from

the records of the Pala and Sena to have formed a part of the Gauda Empire. Furthermore, Tira *bhukti* (Tirhut in North Bihar), Srinagara *bhukti* or Magadha *bhukti* (in South Bihar) and Pragjyotisha *bhukti* (in Assam) lay beyond the limits of Bengal proper (*Ibid*:pp. 23-24).

20. This information is obtained from the Mallasarul Plate of the 6th century CE, the Irda Grant of the 10th century and the Naihati and Govindapur Grants of the 12th century. This region included the geographic areas of the valley of Damodar River and is known to have included the Uttar Radh and Dandabhukti *mandalas*. At times, it stretched from the river Mor in the north to the Suvarnarekha in the south, but it is a matter of doubt whether it covered such an extensive area as early as 6th century CE. In the east, it extended as far as the western branch of the Ganga, now known as the Hooghly. In the 10th century, the southern boundary was till the lower reaches of the Suvarnarekha. About mid-12th century , the northern boundary extended beyond the river Ajay to include the village of Vallahitta in the Uttar Radh *mandala*. In the last quarter of 12th century, at the time of Lakshmansena, Uttar Radh formed a part of the Kankagrama *bhukti* (*Ibid*:26kl-27).
21. The mention of these areas have also found a place in the writings of ancient Greek historians Ptolemy and Pliny, who refer the region as the territory of *Gangaridai* (a name originally given to the people living in the valley of the estuarine Ganga) and also in the writings of poet Kalidasa as the land of the *Vangas* who were specially noted for their skill in handling boats.
22. Sen also mentions (*Op. cit;* 45-46) the finding of another copper plate inscription that could not be discovered in India as it was carried off to England. The inscription is from Karnasuvarna and speaks about the northern part of the present district of Burdwan and southern part of the district of Murshidabad that were under the administration of Samanta Narayanbhadra, "who seems to have been an important local chief compared to the king as he himself made the land grant."
23. The prevalent times witnessed an incentive for Buddhists as well, which can be seen from the Ghunaighar Inscription (of Vainya Gupta), dated between c. 5th to 7th century CE., it speaks about the purchase and donation of wastelands and also water-logged areas related to cultivation. It also mentions a gift of five plots of land to a Buddhist monastery as *Sunya-pratikara-hajjika-khila-bhumi* (water-logged and waste-lands paying no taxes) (Maity and Mukherjee. pp. 67,70, Vol VI, pp. 56, 59, 60). There are also clear references to deforestation on which the Tippera Copper plate supplies valuable information. It speaks about the settlement of a community of Brahmans in a forest

area which was the resort of deer, buffaloes, boars, tigers, serpents, etc. (EL Vol XV, pp. 307, 311). Such humongous task could not have been possible without the help of iron; but in the region of Bengal, there is no clear evidence so far to ascertain the date of introduction of iron.

24. District-wise, these sites include Birbhum-Kotasur, Bahiri, Burdwan-Mangalkot, the upper levels of Pandu Rajar Dhibi showing Kushan-type terracotta, 24-Parganas or the Bhagirathi mouth-Chandraketugarh and a few miscellaneous and not very dependably documented sites, Maldah and Dinajpur-Bangarh, including kandaran with terracottas from the Kushana Period (from Chakrabarti, *Op.cit*:206).
25. Chakrabarti (*Ibid*:209) quotes from B.N. Mukherjee (1991. Trade, Traders and Media of Exchange in Pre-Gupta Vanga. In Jha, A. ed. *Coinage, Trade and Economy*, pp. 46-51) regarding the information about the development of a local system of currency. He mentions that "Though Kushana coins began to be imitated in the lower regions of West Bengal in the days of Kanishka I or shortly after him, the territory soon developed a currency system of its own incorporating Kushana devices and a different weight system."
26. Sasanka was mentioned as an arch rival of Harshavardhana, and he was regarded as a Śaivaite, whereas Harshavardhana was a Buddhist. In this scenario, Banabhatta's accounts should be viewed with caution. It is not expected that Banabhatta, as well as Hiuen Tsang, both of whom ware patronised by Harshavardhana, are not expected to present a positive image of Sasanka. However, it is also mentioned by Hiuen Tsang that Karnasuvarna, the capital of Sasanka, had several Buddhist viharas where several Buddhist monks resided and practiced Buddhism. This position could not have been possible if Hiuen Tsang is to be believed about the atrocities of Sasanka against the Buddhist monks, especially the fact that he caused the exodus of several monks from the monastery at Kusinara.
27. Purulia remains have been closely studied by several scholars, including K. Bhattacharya, P.K. Mitra and A.C. Bhowmick,1986; Bhowmick 1984; Dasgupta 1971, 1973; De, 1970; Mitra, 1983, 1984; Mukhopadhyay, 1977 (*Ibid*:211).
28. As Sukumar Sen (*Op.cit.*:12-13) mentions, if according to Jain text *Acharanga Sutra*, Mahavir had travelled through the region of Radh, then it is older compared to its counterpart Varendri. According to the Sanskrit dictionary, the meaning of the word Radh is beautiful or *Baibhav*.
29. From a *sashon-patter upakramanika shloka* or introductory *shloka* or an administrative document of 9$^{th}$ century CE, it is known that the

region of Bengal underwent several small divisions of kingdom after the death of Sasanka, from the time of the end of $8^{th}$ century. Several kingdoms were busy in conflicts and fights within themselves throughout the time period, which was finally put to rest by the election of a king called Gopala whose son Dharmapala extended the importance of Bengal in the political map of the nation in years to come. The Pala Dynasty ruled for nearly 400 years henceforth. Regarding the years of reign of Gopala, there is a dichotomy between historians, as according to Vincent Smith, he reigned between 730 (or 740) till 800 CE, however, Rakhaldas Bannerjee mentions the same as being 785 (or 790) CE to 790 (or 795) CE. There also exists a confusion regarding his coronation as a king and accepting the royal religion of Buddhism. In this respect, it is also important to note a feature highlighted by Sukumar Sen about the choice of Gopala as the ruler of Bengal. Sen mentions (*Ibid*: 69) that, as popularly believed, Gopala's unanimous election to the position of chief and placement on the throne is hardly unlikely given the politically unstable situation of the contemporary times. It could well correspond to what is mentioned in the land grant of his son Dharmapala which states that a heirless king married Gopala to his daughter and placed him on the throne. The religion of Gopala was unlikely to be Buddhism, as his father is mentioned to have the name Bappavisnu and grandfather was Dayitavisnu. He himself was called Gopala. So it is likely that he was a follower of Vaishnavism, but his wife, named Dedda Devi was a possible Buddhist and he accepted the religion of the state of which he was appointed a ruler. Thus, the Pala Dynasty took up Buddhism.

30. The Pala Dynasty had the following rulers: Gopala, his son Dharmapala, his eldest son Devapala, his eldest son Surpala, his brother's son Vigrahapala, his son Narayanapala, his son Rajyapala, his son Gopala II, his son Vigrahapala II, his son Mahipala I, his son Naypala, his son Vigrahapala III, his eldest son Mahipala II, the second son of Mahipala III- Surpala II, the youngest son of Mahipala III, Rampala, his eldest son Kumarapala, his son Gopala III, and Rampala's youngest son Madanpala. This information is provided by the copper plate inscription of Surpala I (Ibid:70).
31. He visited the regions of Tamralipta and Magadha to closely study *Vinaysastra* and collect manuscripts. He reached Tamralipta in 673 CE. and after residing there for a few months, he reached Magadha and resided for ten years before returning to his homeland. At Tamralipti, he met Hiuen Tsang's disciple Ta-Cheng-Teng, who was residing there for thirteen years and trained I-tsing in Sanskrit. Ta-Cheng-Teng also brought him to Nalanda. I-tsing's records were compiled in his book that he wrote in Sumatra, from where it was send over

to his homeland in China. His book *Nan-hai-chi-kuei-nai-fa-ch'uan*, speaks about his travels and encounters in Magadh and Tamralipti. This book it was later translated into English by J.Takakusu in 1896 who named it *A Record of the Buddhist Religion as Practiced in India and Malay Archipelago* (Sen., *Op. cit*:61).

32. The metal votive stupa at Asrafpur and the two copper inscriptions of Raja Devkharga verify this. I-tsing fact mentions the two kings, as Khargodyam and Rajbhat. (Datta, 1980.119).
33. Sen (*Op.cit*:71) mentions, that *mahamantri* of Dharmapala was Birdeva's son Garg that who was from a *Shandilya bangsha* or lineage and belonged to Panchal *gotra.* Under Dharmapala's son Devapala, the minister was Gargadeva's son Darbhapani and his son Someshwar, including grand Kedarmishra. Devapala was succeeded by his brother's son- Vigrahapala, who had Kedarmishra as well as Kedarmishra's son Gurabamishra as his ministers.

    After this period, the names of ministers are non-available. In later times, it is, however, known that even under the later Palas, the Brahman ministers continued to occupy special place in administrative setup as it is mentioned that under Mahipala, the *mahamantri* was Bhatta Baman. Vigrahapala III had Jogdeva as his minister, whose son Bodhideva was the minister of Rampala. Kumarpala succeeded Rampala, whose minister was Vaidyadeva.

34. *Sekhsubhodaya* speaks of a story concerning the origin of the reign of the Senas. The founder of the Sena Dynasty, Vijaysena, was a poor woodcutter who would gather wood daily to sell in the market to run his house and worship Śiva. On a certain day, without any wood to sell, Vijayasena had to part with his only axe to fetch enough money to give his wife as well as worship Śiva. On another ill-fated rainy day, without finding any wood to sell in the market, Vijayasena spent the whole night in the rains in the forest, scared to return home to his wife empty handed. On the same night, Śiva appeared in his dream and blessed him, as he understood that inspite of being a fool, Vijaysena was his true-hearted worshipper. Śiva also appeared in the dream of Sahadeva Ghosa, a minister of the Pala Dynasty, and instructed him to get Vijaysena replace Rampala. This exactly is event what happened in later times. Though this story needs to be verified for its authenticity, yet it points to two important facts that the Senas were not rich by birth and origin and that an internal minister of the administration of the Palas rendered help in removing them from power and replace by the Senas (Sen., *Op.cit*:87).

35. Mukherjee (2003:21-22) had quoted from an old Persian manuscript preserved and available in the Bankipur Library No. 547, Vol VII of the Bankipur catalogue.
36. This region of Dakshin Radha was identified as *"sadachari Brahmanbhuyistha"*, as mentioned by Sen (*Op. cit*:12).
37. There is also a mention of Radha region in Vrindaban Das's *Chaitanya Bhagavat*, where the region has been referred to as *Radh Desh*. The main city of Uttar Radh was Karnasuvarna. Dakshin Radh was within the earlier *sukhho* or region, whose principal city was Bhurisreshthi and port was Tamralipta (*Ibid*:12-13). These facts have also been highlighted by Majumdar, as he mentions "This far-famed territory was like *Vanga*, divided into two parts *viz.*, *Dakshina* or South Radh and *Uttara* or North Radh. This mode of division which can be traced back to the 9th century CE, apparently replaces the older segmentation of the area into Vajjabhumi and Subbhabhumi" (Majumdar, *Op.cit*:21-22). The significance of these two divisions of Uttar and Dakshin Radh can also be traced to various historical records. About Dakshin Radha, mention may be significantly made of the Gaonri Plates of Vakpati Munja (981 CE,). Once again, ten years later, it featured in historic literature, *Nyayakandali* of Sridharacharya and figures in the Chola records of 1023-25 as Takkanaladam. There are also other references amongst which significant is the Amaresvara Temple Inscription of Mandhata (Nimar District in the Central Province) composed by Halayudha, the *Prabodha-chandrodaya* of Krishna Misra and the *Candi* of Kavikankana Mukundarama. All these records help to throw light on geographic limitations and boundaries about Dakshin Radh. According to these records, Dakshina Radha included Bhurisrishti or Bhurisreshthika (modern Bhursut) and Navagrama in the Howrah and Hooghly Districts as well as Damunya (to the west of the Damodar) in the Burdwan District. Thus, the territory embraced a major part between the two rivers Ajay and Damodar of which the southern boundary may have reached the Rupnarayan and the western boundary may have extended far beyond the Damodar, into the Arambagh sub-division. However, according to the Radh region mentioned in the *Digvijaya-Prakasa*, it is only limited to the territory lying north of the Damodar.

    On the other hand, the northern part was recognised as Uttara-Radh (i.e., the *Uttiraladam* of Chola Inscription), as early as the time of Ganga king Devendravarman. This information is known from the Plates in the Indian Museum of the Ganga year 308 that possibly falls in the 9th century CE. This district is also known from the Belava and Naihati Grants. According to the recorded document, it was within the Vardhamana *bhukti*, but at the time of Lakshmansena, it was part of the Kankagrama *bhukti*. Majumdar also mentions specific places mentioned in the Plates which were situated in Uttara Radh. These included Siddhalagrama, which has been identified with modern Siddhangram in the Birbhum District and Vallahitta with Balutiya on the northern borders of the Burdwan District. The Saktipur Grant of Lakshmansena suggests that the *mandala* of Uttara Radh also included villages in the Kandi sub-division of Murshidabad (*Ibid*: 21-22).

38. The sense of ambiguity pertaining to geographical assertion of Bengal, including Radh, is also expressed by Majumdar (Ibid:22), when he states, that at most times, the River Ajay was taken to have constituted the dividing line between the two Radh regions, but the inclusion of the Katwa sub-division within Uttar Radh may also imply that, at times, the Khari, rather than the Ajay, was taken as the dividing line. Regarding the northern limits of the Uttar Radh, it is mentioned that the Jain text Prajnapana knows Kotivarsha or Bangarh in the Dinajpur District as a city in Radh. The Chandraprabha of Bharat Mallika refers to a part of Radh that lay north of the Ganges (Uttara-Gangaradham). "It is, however, clear from contemporary inscriptions and the Tabaqat-i-Nasiri that in the 12th and 13th centuries, the Ganga formed the boundary between Ral and the city of Lakhan-or" on the one hand and "Barind and the city of Diw-kot on the other." Thus, it can be surmised that the difficulty in ascertaining geographical limits was due to the continuous shift in the borders of the two Radh regions.

39. It is also interesting to note and mention the attempts of Samaren Roy here as he tried to associate the worship of the Goddess Bhāduli with sea voyages and thereby, with the relation of the original inhabitants of the region with Crete through trade and commerce. This worship seems to have originated at the time of the height of maritime activities in Bengal: "between 3rd century CE. to 10th century CE. and subsequently prohibited by Ballal Sen's dictate." (Roy, *op.cit*:22). The worship of Bhāduli is full of symbolic features, like, the time was August when the worship used to take place during which the rivers were full and the monsoon was high. In the torrid rains and the seas, the people were anxious for the welfare of their dear ones. Though particulars about the Goddess Bhāduli are not known and in one of the hymns she is called as the mother-in-law of Indra similar to reference of the Laul (who too is an obscure god worshipped by Bengali women, but there is no trace about his present form or origin) and in another passage it seems these are later attempts to connect them to the Vedic pantheon. According to Dr. D.C. Sen, the

clay figurines made in connection with this celebration had a strong similarity with the clay figures discovered by Evans in Crete of the Third Millennium BCE, and some of the finds of Pandu Rajar Dhibi suggest an affinity between the two (*Ibid*:21-23). There needs to be more evidence to prove the relation of trade with cultures outside India and its impact on the original inhabitants from where the worship of Bhāduli might have originated.

40. It is significant here to mention a recent study pertaining to the local religious beliefs pertaining to folk Goddess Sini of Bankura, carried out by D.K. Bhattacharya and R.K. Chattopadhyay. The study refers to the votive offerings of terracotta horses and elephants at various sacred places, often and mostly located at the outskirts of villages, referred to as Sini *sthans*. Though such votive offerings are not only limited to the Goddess Sini alone in the region but most other local gods and goddess as well, however, Sini forms an important part of concept—representation of a deity in folk tradition of the region under study. This feature was also evident in the case of several other folk deities, like, Dharmaraj, Burha-Burhi, Baram and others during the course of fieldwork. These deities are mostly portrayed through conceptual representation only, though few evidences of anthropomorphic representation were also witnessed in recent times throughout Bankura, Purulia and West Mednipur. However, in all the representations, irrespective of the presence of an idol or otherwise, the deities are seen to have been offered votive offerings in the form of various sizes of terracotta horses, which have reins and also terracotta elephants and often variously bear the gallant decorations that befit a rider who might sit astride on an elephant's back. According to Bhattacharya and Chattopadhyay (Trends in Social Science and Research, Vol 4, No. 1, June 1997— Special Issue Culture Studies— Selected Papers from the 6th Congress of the National Academy of Psychology [NAOP], India), these terracotta votive offerings are cognitive representations of the importance associated with the pilgrims and traders who used the routes as a passage to travel between the regions of Odisha and Jharkhand. Mostly frequented by traders on horse and elephant backs, these animals were regarded, over a period of time, as symbols of prosperity. Thus, in later times, as the route was less frequented by traders, as well as pilgrims, these symbols still remaining prominent in the cognitive recollection, were regarded through the terracotta horses and elephants, which were offered to the village deities for general well-being of the village and its inhabitants.

41. Majumdar (*Ibid*) mentioned that the area was already known in the Mahabharat, as in case of the *Digvijaya* section of the *Sabhaparvan*

where it is distinguished from territories known to have been situated in the northern, eastern and central Bengal, and also from Suhma. In later times, it was a part of Vanga at the time of Jaina *Prajnapana* and that of Suhma at the time of Dandin, who was the author of *Dasakumaracharita*. The core of the territory was in modern Mednipur District, and the region has been identified with the Tamalites of Ptolemy, i.e., the modern Tamluk. During the visit of Hiuen Tsang, it lay over 900 *li*, which is about 150 miles from Samatat and was approx. 1400 *li* (similar to miles) in circuit. "The land was low and moist," forming a bay where land and water communication met. Mention of Tamralipti is also found in the writings of Fa-Hien and I-tsing who were Chinese pilgrims and visited the region of Tamralipti, both before and after Hiuen Tsang, respectively. Tamralipti is also mentioned in *Dasakumaracharita* of Dandin. All the references point to the fact that Tamralipti was connected to the "regions of Ceylon, Java and China in the east and the land of the Yavanas in the west." *Kathasaritasagara* also records people embarking on ships at Tamralipti and sailing off for Katina, possibly in the Malay Peninsula.

42. They were also mentioned in various poems in the *Dharmamangal Kavya*, e.g., *Baro Bhuinya bossy cache bake diva dhal* (*Baro Bhuinya* is sitting armed with a shield), which goes to explain the importance of the support these kingdoms got from the royalty. Interestingly, it can be mentioned that the Samanta administrative head that was instituted by Rampala in 11$^{th}$ century, to stand against the Kaivartya rebels, was definitely a predecessor of these *Baro Bhuinya*.

43. Several scholars are also of the opinion that the word 'Bengal' was not known before Muslim conquest and emerged only during the medieval period. The English name 'Bengal' and Portugese counterpart *Bengala*, were derived from *Vangala* and not from *Vanga*, which is the name adopted by the Muslim rulers for the province in 12$^{th}$ century. According to Baul-i-Fazl, the name *Ban galah* was originally *Bangla*, and the name is to have come from the *al* or embankments, which its former rulers had laid throughout the province—10 yards in length and 20 yards in breadth, and this was the suffix of the name *Ban galah*. According to modern writers, the name *Vangala* has come from *Vangala*, i.e., *Vangala* or home of the *Vanga*, which "seems probable." The name *Vangala* might have derived from the word *Vanga*, as *Pavana* was to denote a separate unit of *Vanga*. "The word *Vangala* never disappears and figures in Nethar Plates (805 CE.) of Rashtrakuta Govinda III that speaks of Dharma and Dharmapala as king of *Vangala*. A later Tirumalai Inscription (1025 CE.) of Rajendra Chola speaks of Govindchandra as lord of *Vangala-desh*. From Vanga

to Vangala to Bengal in the Anglicised form—a natural course of development of nomenclature."

44. The Palas also called themselves Lord of Gauda that had a three-fold connotation: The term Gauda denoted the name of the capital city, name of Bengal or North Bengal and name of the whole of India.

45. The East Indian Company merchant, Thomas Bowrey, resided in the region between 1669 to 1679, and from his personal accounts (that mainly concentrated on the geographical understanding of the region), a glimpse of the erstwhile society is also available. Written in a typical manner with spellings and grammatical syntaxes that befit the Victorian Age, Bowrey's accounts speak about the importance of the worship of Siva, including the Charak and Gajan festivals with the process of *banphor* (piercing various parts of the body with sharp objects as a mode of repentance, self torture for cleansing and worshipping) being an important aspect of the worship. The significance in the observation is the prevalence of the ceremony more than four centuries ago that had acceptance of the Brahmanical order of the day (Temple, *op. cit.* pp. 197-200).

# 4

# Survey of Ethnoarchaeological Data

## Brief Review of Socio-Cultural Evidences from Archaeology

Literary, epigraphical as well as archaeological records furnish information about the erstwhile mode of living of the contemporary society in ancient Bengal. This chapter especially deals with information from specific archaeological evidences including prehistoric and historic remains of culture in ancient Bengal, with special reference to sites that correspond to the Early Village Farming sites of Bengal (Appendix 2 & 3) as well as ethnographic and archaeological data gathered during field work from the region of study (Appendix 4 & 5). At the very onset, it should be mentioned that both data are intensive but not exhaustive and they bear direct significance to the work and its area of research as far as the survival of folk festivals, rites and rituals and religious tradition in fringe Bengal is concerned.

The prehistoric remains of Bengal[1] are also important from the point of view of understanding a trend of continuity till modern times. The Chalcolithic settlements emerged on the fringe of the pre-historic settlements, by utilising the natural resources of the zone opened up by its Stone Age dwellers, who were essentially a community of hunters and gatherers. Speaking about the region of study, several artifacts pertaining to prehistoric times have been cited, much part of which is also available in published data formats. This fact has been referred to in the earlier chapter about the history of the region. It is also significant to mention that the distribution of Palaeolithic artifacts (Chattopadhyay 1989, Datta *et al.* 1992), which have been so far reported and published, explain only scattered occurrences. With this reference, significant examples which can be cited include the area of Sonamukhi-Kusadwip, thereby suggesting a late arrival in comparison to the Susunia region, though their strategraphic positions remains unknown. The above information is revealed through important excavations from such sites as localities falling under the Police Station area of Sonamukhi, Patrasayer and Bishnupur, areas in and around Kusadwip, Pandua, Bhadkul, etc. as has been reported by Datta *et. al.* (Datta *et al.* 1992, Chakraborti and Bhattacharya 2001, Bhattacharya 2006-07). Besides, all important references from Susunia and Purulia confirm the existence of a Palaeolithic stage. Though a detailed chronological study for the periodisation of events is needed for further postulation of facts, yet none of published papers so far, points towards the existence of rites, rituals and festivities of the locals in prehistoric times. In fact, this evidence is only available from late-historic/ early medieval period onwards. The ethnoarchaeological data supplements as well as compliments the information with a possible trend of continuity in existence of cultural traditions and economy and also points to the existing festivities in modern times. It is also important to consider that, as mentioned by Chattopadhyay *et.al.* (2009:83), the reconstruction of behaviourial history of the region has a bearing on the archaeological assemblages reported so far. The recorded assemblages suggest a possible continuation of the Palaeolithic tool-making tradition in various parts, like the woodland areas of Sonamukhi, Kusadwip, Gamidhya and Jaipur, amongst others. Moreover, it is important to consider the possible presence of a late Palaeolithic hunter-gatherer in the same ecological set-up adjoining to Bishnupur.

For the Mesolithic period, the spread of population could also be ascertained from archaeological sites along rivers. The distribution of microlithic occurrences can be found adjoining to rivers like Dwarakeshwar and Damodar. In the region adjoining to Bishnupur, for example such confirmation of the spread of Mesolithic hunter-gatherer and their survivors can be geographically located along the rivers Dwarakeshwar and Damodar and their tributaries. In a similar manner, the Sonamukhi Forest and the undulating tract of Kakardanga-Kusadwip are also important, as well as other sites of Bankura like Gamidhya, Dharapat, Kakardanga, Hatkrishnanagar, etc. The distribution of scattered microlithic assemblages in sites which are in close proximity to each other also speaks of transhumance cycle of the residing communities (*Ibid* 1989, *et al.* 2007 & 2009:83-84).[2]

A study of the areas corresponding to the Early Village Farming/BRW phase, often also referred to as the Neolithic stage, based on agro-pastoral economy of the Protohistoric period (roughly datable to the middle of the second and the first millennia BCE), has also yielded various microlithic tools[3] (see Appendix 2 & 3). Mention may be made of such places like, the valleys of Ajay, Damodar, Kansai, Rupnarayan, Suvarnarekha and Burhavalang, all of which originate from the Chhotanagpur Highlands.[4] These sites also show example of movement and existence of population in and around the rivers. Mention may be made of Dihar (Figs. 76-79) in the Dwarakeswar Valley and Pakhanna in the Damodar Valley, besides other newly explored and excavated sites along the tributaries of Sali and Kana Nadi. The ancestors of these early prehistoric population can be traced to the hunting-gathering zone of the Sonamukhi-Kusadwip area, little away from the alluvial plain, who later shifted to the above said plain and led a sedentary way of life instead of a nomadic one (*Ibid*:86-87). However, in the absence of any stratified digging to determine with certainty the chronological and cultural sequences of the Neolithic as well as its preceding times[5], the work becomes difficult,[6] but several parts of the region, especially Bankura, has shown remarkable evidences of ground and polished stone tools in association with the BRW (*Ibid* 1989, *Ibid et al.* 2007) cultural phase besides stray occurrences. Though speculations still differ, some scholars have also suggested an association of the Late Stone Age culture with the Neolithic culture. Such tools were needed for the Neolithic culture, which began the process of cultivation, harvesting, carpentry, fishing, etc and is suggested to have continued from the Late Stone Age culture (Banerjee, 1997, pp. 51).[7]

The following Chalcolithic stage corresponded with the use of metal (copper or bronze) which was corroborated by the evidence of food grains for the first time, and various excavations ascertain the fact through Carbon 14 dating. Certain archaeological sites produce good examples to ascertain a long protohistoric epoch, such as the site of Tamluk, which is the port city Tamralipta of yesteryears. The 1955 excavations of the Archaeological Survey of India sufficiently proved the existence of a Neolithic cultural phase, before the emergence of a kind of pottery affiliated with Northern Black Polished (NBP) Ware. The Painted Black-and-Red Ware, like the excavated examples from Pandu Rajar Dhibi, highlights a protohistoric phase in this connection. The protohistoric evidences from Tamluk reveal important information regarding flourishing connections through maritime trade with the Greco-Roman world. The influence is also found reflecting through various figurines, especially of *apsaras* and *yaksinis* of Sunga-Kushana Period, all of which reflect a divine grace and are lyrical in appeal, and one good example is the *Oxford Figurine* in Sunga

Style, which represents a graceful style of female divinity.[8] With important foreign influence through maritime trade and commerce, the region of Tamluk is also important to have yielded a vast range that even portrayed local culture, including classical themes and folk-mythology of the past, like a bull-headed being on terracotta could have occurred from legends, while winged horses on terracotta could depict fairy tales (Dasgupta, pp. 7-8).

Of the early and later historical archaeological remains, it should be mentioned that a major part constitutes land grants and inscriptions, variously from Gupta, Pala and Sena Periods that speak of the pattern of the arrangement of lifestyle in contemporary times, as well as the popular religious beliefs of the people upto a certain extent. It is from these arrangement of habitation, as is seen through the epigraphic as well as literary evidences, one gets to have an idea about the developing socio-cultural modes of living in an organised manner, of which mention may be made of Puranic temples as well as Buddhist and Jain viharas within each village.[9] Another instance is Baigram Copper Plate Inscription, which speaks of the temple of Visṇu (Govindasvamina). Similarly, Khalimpur Copper Plate records the temple of Sarasvati (Kadamvaridevakulika) in the village Krauñcha śvabhra and Govindapur Copper Plate of Lakshmansena referred to the Mandapa of Lengadeva in the village of Viddarasasana (Lengadevamandapi) (Chattopadhyay, 2002, pp. 85). It is also important to mention that during the Post-Gupta Period, consolidation of power took place in the region under the auspices of Vijayasena whose administration was in the realm of the reign of Gopachandra belonging to 6$^{th}$ century C.E. This is suggested from the proximity existing between Mallasarul (on northern bank of river Damodar and the Antra, Hadalnarayanpur) and other sites of the same region on the southern bank. The Mallasarul Copper Plate of Vijayasena bears further evidence to the above stated fact with abandoned structural ruins, including debris of extant temples, and stone images of Puranic and Jain divinities, along with other artifacts that serve as stray references (*Ibid*, 2009:88).[10]

Though a majority of these inscriptional evidences, forming important parts of archaeological records of erstwhile times, do not exactly correspond to the region of study, nevertheless, they help to come to an understanding about the important and mainstream religious beliefs of the region. Thus, it can be said that very similar to modern times, even in ancient times, there used to be a special place for socio-religious gathering of the masses to perform various rites and ceremonies. The kings, as well, never pursued any policy of religious intolerance but patronised, irrespective of their personal religious beliefs, all important religious principles, ideas, rites and practices. This position is evident from the presence of Brahmanical temples along with Buddhist as well as Jaina monasteries within the same village. Regarding this, it is important to mention a source, as cited by Chattopadhyay (*Ibid*:86)—the Dhulla Copper Plate of Srichandra, which mentions Buddhist king Srichandra taking active part in Brahmanical observances like *Adbhutaśnti*, during the *Hōmachatushṭaya* or the Four Homas,[11] implying that the villagers of ancient Bengal resided in perfect religious harmony, quite like the present times.

An important aspect evident throughout the present fieldwork is also the scattered presence of various stones, mostly laterites, in different areas, referred to as herostones. Mostly horizontal in structure, several of these stones were also seen ornate with carvings. At several instances, these evidences were seen clearly visible on the earth's surface and at many other instances, they were seen only partly visible above it. Though the exact reason for the original utility of these stones through historical times is yet to be ascertained by scholars, but the fieldwork throughout the region of study, suggests several of these herostones to have been possible parts of old temples—including Puranic, Jain and Buddhist, or marking the limits of these temples, as well as sacrosanct lands or even graves at few instances. The herostones of Purulia were seen to be standing erect from the ground with a cylindrical base and a rectangular top. Many of these could be considered as belonging to parts of Jain temples, especially structures in front of a temple, which supported the façade. Typical examples are particularly prominent, especially in the form of structures at Deulghata (in front of the first temple on the right) and several similar structures found in front of the entrance of the temple at Banda (60 km approx from Purulia Town, Thana-Raghunathpur, Panchayat-Mangalda-Moutor). An important aspect of acculturation is reflected through the present worship of several of these stones as various folk gods/goddesses all over the region of study. Cases in point are many, of which mention may be made of the herostones of Chhatna[12] (Bankura) (Fig. 1), Pakbira (Purulia). There are also several herostones worshipped as village deities, which are specially located within open spaces, ploughing fields and at the outskirts of villages. Such examples can be seen in the herostones within a ploughing field about 1 km from Chharra (Purulia) (Fig. 2) as well as several scattered examples of herostones in an open field, on the left bank of Kangsabati (2 km from Ralibera, Purulia) (Fig. 3) and another one, worshipped as Siva is located 2 ½ km from Puncha (towards Budhpur, in an open field on Manbazaar main road) (Fig. 4).

Another important and significant information pertaining to the region of study, which is corroborated through archaeological as well as historical references and was also evident throughout the ethnographic fieldwork in the region, is the emergence of large, regionally-based ruling powers in Bengal by the middle of $18^{th}$ century. This information speaks about early formation of medieval society in Bengal. Religion also was important, as many believed in revival of concepts of Puranic religion, or patronised Buddhism or Jainism. This also brings to notice another significant information to the fore- the procedure of integration within the frameworks of the state formation through legitimisation of power and the affiliation of temple reconstruction. (*Ibid et al.* 2009:88). The ruins of temples and palaces of several of these local royalty, survives till date, like, the Mallabhum royal family or the Panchkot royal family. These also provide important archeological examples of the religion patronised by respective ruling authorities. (brief information about location and measurements of herostones and other historical artifacts is provided in Appendix 4).

## Reviewing Data from Ethnographic Fieldwork

It is the innate nature of depiction, arising out of the conglomeration of various thought processes, as well as the belief of the locals and autochthones that renders the socio-cultural and religious representation a distinct value of its own. Thus, the assortment of patterns from channels of Jainism, Buddhism, Śaivism and Vaisṇavism, along with belief manifested in the innate worship of the Mother Goddess and thereby the influence of the Sakti Cult portrays an interesting blend of beliefs and practices in the region of study. Adding to this, is the prevalence of the already existing bonds of beliefs and ideas towards life, including the observance of *brata* rites and the worship of elements of nature, like the worship of *ghata* (clay pot), trees, hills, sun, the moon, the *lingam*, or the worship of local deities like, Sasti, Sitala, Manasa, Bhairab, Dharmaraj, Sini, Candi and others. It is also important to see the Śaiva influence appear most prominently and noticeably suggesting an important patronage of temples possibly from the local rulers of Śaiva faith. A similar trend is also seen about the Vaisṇava faith, especially in and around the region of Bishnupur, scattered evidences in West Mednipur and also parts of Purulia, which received patronages from different royal families, like Vaisṇava royal family of Bishnupur or the Mallabhum royal family, the Panchkot royal family or the different vassals of these families as well as the royalty of Odisha. Though the evidence of Saktaism is meager, but local traditions and their association with Śaivism might also possibly suggest the importance of Sakta faith in the region. Other forms of ethnoarchaeological information in the region correspond to the data bearing testimony for the worship and appearance of cult-spots and the sites of *grāmadevatās* or village deities. Regarding this, it is important to notice the prevalence of Bhairab, Dharmaraj/Dharmathakur, Sini, Manasa, Sitala and Candi in various forms denoted by various names in the present area of study. Often related to a theriomorphic existence, at several instances, the anthropomorphic details also provided information to supplement the ethnoarchaeology data. All these point towards the existence of animism, nature worship and worship of mother goddess as an important part of folk religion. The survival of folk religion is also perceived through the birth of such medieval Bengali texts, like the Mangal Kavyas: *Dharmamangal*, *Manasamangal* and *Candimangal* in the recent past, which provide sufficient information about the prevalence of specific religious traditions in the region. The local temples and deities, including *grāmadevatās*, village deities, etc. also were influenced by proximity with other cultures. A close examination in the arena of art history suggests absorption of styles derived from Odisha (Chattopadhyay,1999-2000:20-21), with specific reference to the Varaha and Varahi from Salda belonging to the Bishnupur/Vishnupur Sub-division (*Ibid et al.*, 2009:89). The Odishan influence was also evident during the course of the ethnographic fieldwork, particularly the presence of Utkala Brahmin, especially in Western Mednipur as well as Western and Central Bankura (*Ibid*, 1999-2000: 20-21). Similarly, the importance of the religion of Islam was also evident in certain places, like, architecture as well as presence of Muslim population in various villages, especially in Bankura and West Mednipur.

Several significant features became evident during the course of fieldwork, including the modern spread and mass popularity of Vaisṇavism in the region of study. In all the three districts of study, Vaisṇavism was seen to enjoy a growing status of importance, especially amidst the so-called lower classes who till date are considered inferior by the so-called higher classes in the villages, like the Brahmans, Kayasthas, Rajputs and others. This state could be the result of finding solace through a deliberate method for social acceptance, away from the rigid forms of Brahmanism. However, inferences cannot be completely deduced without further ethnographic studies, but the growing number of *naamsankirtan atchalas* (cemented podiums for gathering and worship with a roof, supported by encircling pillars) in almost every village for the performance of bi-annual, annual or monthly *Chabbish Prahar Naansankirtan* (*Naamsankirtan* conducted for continuous twenty-four hours) points towards this fact. Finally, it is important to mention, as was noticed throughout the course of fieldwork, the region, till date, maintains an important stance towards various forms of folk and Sakta religion, which was always a predominant force in the region even before the spread of Vaisṇavism. Deities such as Manasa, Kali, Bhairab and Baram continue to enjoy primary status amongst people inspite of the widespread patronage extended towards Vaisṇavism. The folk deities continue to maintain their independent status amidst the spread of Vaisṇavism, and the feature is maintained till date, as evident from the observance of *Dolyatra* and *Raaslila*, along with the worship of Baram and Bhairab within Bishnupur till date (Ghosh, *Op cit*: 340-341).

Another important aspect of modern living in the area of study, which was also prominent throughout the course of fieldwork, is the maintenance of several *pujas* by local *Gram Sholoanna Committees.* Patronised by local royalty in the recent past, several of the *pujas* survive in present times with the help of the cumulative efforts of modern benefactors. This characteristic has become more prominent in the recent years with the dwindling socio-economic status of the modern successors of the various local royal/ zamindar families. These ceremonies include modern as well as old religious practices related to Visnu, Śiva as well as various forms of female deities like, Durga, Kali, Annapurna, etc. The *Gram Sholoanna Committees* look after every detail of worship including the daily worship or the *nitya puja*, as well as ascertainment of the officiating priest of the temple or even arrangement for monthly or yearly fairs and festivals associated with respective deities.

## Sects of Puranic Religion

The Purāṇic religion is basically characterised by the growth and development of a number of sects, with each of them showing devotion towards a specific God. The two most important sects in the region of study are Vaisṇavism and Śaivism, though Śāktas too hold significance.

### Vaisṇavism

Several epigraphical as well as archaeological records testify the popularity of Vaisṇavism in the region of Bengal, with the religion often described to have an early beginning of about $4^{th}$ century CE. and spreading especially under the influence of royal patronage. However, in course of fieldwork, the significance of Vaisṇavism associated with royal patronage could only be traced to a time in the recent past that dates back to Early Medieval/Medieval Period. An important instance, verifying such data is the spread of Vaisṇavism, especially in Bishnupur and adjoining areas, which were under the influence of the erstwhile Mallabhum royal family. In a similar manner, the spread of the religion in various parts of West Mednipur under the different vassals/ zamindars subordinate to the royalty of Odisha was also important.[13] In present times, the association of the spread of Vaisṇavism and its popularity under royal patronage is also evident from the various architectural details of the region of study. These details include resplendent *Rasmanchas* of Bishnupur town, Hadalnarayanpur, Ayodhya, etc., as well as magnificent huge *Raths*, which mark the participation of the entire village during the time of *Rathyatra* every year.

The association of local royalty to the spread of Vaisṇavism could be gathered from many evidences during fieldwork, and one such important instance was seen in the village of Bālsi (Bankura), pertaining to the reign of king Gopalchandra of the Mallabhum royal family. The royal patronage assigned the responsibility of the temple of Lakkhinarayan Jiu (Fig. 8) to a certain local Choudhury family. The researcher was fortunate enough to have a glimpse of the original documents and manuscripts of the royal order (Fig. 5, 6 & 7). A similar example of royal patronage was seen at the temple of Sri Sri Radhakanta Jiu in Muninagar (Bankura) (Fig. 9). The temple is ascribed to have been established by Bir Singha, according to a plaque at the entrance of the temple.

Apart from the direct influence of royalty, Vaisṇavism also spread under the influence of the vassal, the local chiefs and zamindars of the region. Such instances are also many, like, the Madanmohan Jiu Temple that was established by the local zamindar family at Asada (West Mednipur), the temple of Radhadamodar Jiu of Khirpai (West Mednipur) (Fig. 10), the local royal family of Hadalnarayanpur (Bankura) (Fig. 11), or the temple of Krishnachandra of the Chunchor royal family under the Malla kings in Hatkrishnanagar (Bankura). Thus, during the course of fieldwork, the spread of Vaisṇavism in and around Bishnupur, could be traced to the last few hundred years under the patronage of the Mallabhum royal family and their various vassals and chiefs in various parts and regions. Even places which were far off from the direct influence of the seat of Malla royalty, were seen to be related to the patronage of the royal family. Mention may be made of the Lakkhinarayan Jiu temple of Metla (Bankura) (Fig.12), or the ruins of the Visṇu temple of Dumurkoh (Purulia). The temple of Metla, which is located several kilometers away from the seat of the Bishnupur royal family, was constructed under the patronage of one of the vassals of the Mallabhum royalty by the title/ surname of Singha Deo Rao. The locals still speak about the vassal chiefs in their village lore, and the approximate date of the construction of the temple under the local vassal chief is about 1718 CE, as mentioned by the people in the region. The temple of Dumurkoh is also mentioned in the local lore in association with the Panchkot royal family. In a similar manner, several temples, dedicated to Visṇu also find mention in the region of West Mednipur, with possible patronage of the local royalty, which were under the king of Odisha. Mention may be made of the Rahghunathji Temple (West Mednipur) of Garbeta, which is ascribed to have been made by Malla king Raghunath, or the spread of the religion at Naipur (West Mednipur) under the auspices of the local *zamindar* family, that is, Kanungo. Similar occasions are evident in almost all the villages under various police stations in West Mednipur, including Mednipur, Shalboni, Danton, Garbeta, Kharagpur, Narayangarh, Pataspur, Bhagabanpur, Jhargram, Sankrail and others. The spread of Vaisṇavism is also associated with the popularity of the worship of Jagannath and the prominent lore around Chaitanya, who is believed to have travelled through the region to reach the temple of Jagannath in Puri.

Though the patronage of royalty expanded the horizon considerably in the past regarding the spread and penetration of the religion in the society, however, its recent spread could be ascribed to a certain extent, to the attempts of the respective *Gram Sholoanna Committees.* This aspect is not only true for the religion of Vaisṇavism, but other religions as well. Pertaining to Vaisṇavism, the instances are several and mention may be made of Dwarika, Uliara, Pandua or Penera, amidst several others (Bankura). The process of modern spread of Vaisṇavism also aids in understanding attempts of accepting the royal religion, with possible efforts of social elevation in the status of the local population. This facet was most evident in regions which have significant population belonging to so-called lower classes. In this regard, mention may be made of interior places in Purulia, such as Palpal, Sirkabad, Balarampur, Gobindopur and Bagmundi, Kalimati or Palma, or in interior Bankura like, Penchashimul (spelled Pecha-shimul), Biskodor, Paharbedia or Jugunthol, bordering Susunia hill region. Similar instance of the recent spread of Vaisṇavism in West Mednipur can be seen in places like Parulia. The current popularity of Vaisṇavism is also associated with extensive building of *atchala* for the performance of *Chabbis Prahar Harinaam Sankirtan.* It is important to mention here the cognitive association towards the Malla royal family of Bishnupur. Even in remote and interior parts of Bankura, such as Koro, Dhumkoro, Gangajalghati,

Chayanpur, Banasuria, Deuli, Susunia, including others in northern part and Indpur or Bheduasole in central part of the district—which are far from the seat of the Malla royalty—every attempt of the recent spread of Vaisṇavism is always associated with the Vaisṇava Malla kings of yesteryears. This position is also apparent from the words of the locals and can be seen as attempts of social change through the emancipation of social status in the modern world. The association of royalty renders a universal edge, as if cutting across all social barriers of caste.

## Śaivism

The spread of Śaivism in its fully developed form in Bengal comprising the cults of Rudra, Śiva and the phallus (including the ordinary and the more developed *mukhaliṇga* form), and the Purāṇic mythology about them, probably evolved during the Gupta Period. The early Sena rulers were followers of Śaivism—a tradition which continued even amidst the later Sena rulers, who continued to have the image of Sadāśiva engraved on their royal seal despite Vaisnavism assuming the place of royal religion (Majumdar, 1971: 516-517). However, during the course of the fieldwork, evidences could only be gathered of a later period that dates back to late historical or early medieval periods.

Popular belief and reflections in local lore speak of Śaiva religion in the region of Bankura, Purulia and West Mednipur as older than Vaisṇavism. Mostly presided over by Brahman *purohits*, the *nitya puja*, as well as the annual festivals and Gajan *melas* are attended by people across all religions, caste and creed—a practice that was also inspired by the royalty of yesteryears. Several temples also received local patronage of zamindars/vassal chiefs due to which these structures have ornate architectures, for instance, the temples of Budhpur (Purulia) or Khargeswar Temple of Kharagpur or Parbatinath temple of Khirpai (both in West

Mednipur) (Fig.13). It is also interesting to note that, though Vaisṇavism flourished under royal patronage, especially in and around the regions of Mallabhum of Bankura or the various parts of West Mednipur, yet an undercurrent of Śaivism survived, which helped to keep the ancient belief alive. A typical example is seen in case of Village Tiliboni Basantapur (Bankura), where local lores associate it with the frequeut visits of the Malla King Bir Hambir. The temple of Bhuteswar Śiva (Fig. 14) in the southern part of the village within the Brahman para is also said to have been inspired by the royalty. Similar examples of royal patronage of Śaivism can also be seen in the twin temples of Saileswar and Sanreswar in Dihar (Bankura) (Fig.15, 16 & 17), both of which enjoyed royal patronage in $14^{th}$ century and are even described in local lore of the region till date. Archaeologically rich, the region of Dihar has yielded important information that not only associates it with a flourishing site under the royal patronage, but also with a trade centre known for its rich financial activities. Both sites contributed for the gradual affluence of the region.

Various other sites also yield information about royal patronage of Śaivism, which is verified by local lore such as the temple of Kameswarnath Jiu of Nera Deul (West Mednipur). The temple, though could not be localed durig the field work, is popularly known to have been constructed by King Umapati Bhatta, and it attributes its name to the fact that the top of the temple could not be finished. Another similar instance is Khargeswar Śiva of Kharagpur (West Mednipur), which is stated to be constructed either by the King Kharga Singha of Dherenda or King Kharga Malla of Bishnupur Malla royal family. Several of the present ruins of temples speak about royal patronage like, the temple of Deuleswar in Kusadwip Village (Bankura) (Fig. 18). The broken down laterite temple only houses the *linga*, without sidewalls and a roof, but the pattern of remaining architecture attributes its construction period to correspond to the later period of Malla royal family. To this day, *nitya puja* is held in the temple along with annual Gajan festival and *mela*. A similar character is associated with the Buddeswara Śiva Temple of Budhpur (Fig. 19) or Uma-Maheswara Temple of Deulghata (Fig. 20), both in Purulia District. The ruins of all these temples speak about the grandeur of sculptural details and the patronage received from the local chiefs. Their popularity is ascertained from the *nitya puja* that still takes place on the ruins and is indicative of trend of continuity throughout.

Similar to the revival of several other *pujas, melas* and festivals in modern times, Śaivism too has received an impetus under the patronage of various *Gram Sholoanna Committees* in different villages presently. With accumulated finances, the concerned villages perform the festivals, Gajan and *pujas* along with distribution of *prasads* across all castes and creeds throughout the village. Typical examples cited during the course of the fieldwork are many, such as, Bhara, Prakashghat and its adjoining village called Chchilimpur, the Śiva of Deulghata (Purulia), Dugdheswar Śiva Temple of Gamidhya (Fig. 21), or the Deuleswara Śiva Temple of Pataspur (Bankura) with its annual special *puja* on *Caitra Sankranti*: All these religious structeres are located in Bankura District. Though smaller in extent, yet similar examples can also be seen in Sirkabad, Palpal, Deulbhita, Mangalda, Gobrandha, Moutorh, Gobindopur, Bagmundi and Burda and other places in Purulia District. Various initiatives of the *Sholoanna Committees* are also seen in form of sponsor of several weeks or even month-long *melas* associated with the annual Gajan festival, as was seen in reference to Baruneswar *mandir* of Talajuri (Purulia) (Fig. 22) which holds a three-day long *Caitra* Gajan *mela*, starting from 27$^{th}$

of the month. Examples of other initiatives are by village Uliara (Bankura), which organizes a month-long Gajan *mela* that starts from *Phalgun Sankranti* and continues uptill 1$^{st}$ *Baisakh*, or by the village Chumashna (Bankura), where the same *mela* is held between 16$^{th}$ *Phalgun* to 2$^{nd}$ *Chaitra*. Here, mention should also be made of the very popular festival of *Palas Parban* of Deulghata (Purulia), which is annually held for three days and is attended by people from far off places like Kolkata.

**Female Deities**

Significant to note is the association of the worship of female deities, patronised by royalty. Mostly corresponding to mainstream Brahmanical deities, evidences are many, such as the Mallabhum royal family, as well as other smaller areas under various chiefs and vassal chiefs, like Jamkuri royal family, Panchkot royal family, or Kashipur royal family deities. With reference to such worships, mention may be made of the Sarbamangala Goddess of the royal family of Bagra in Garbeta (West Mednipur). In the Mallabhum royal family and within the town of Bishnupur, such instances of the worship of various female divinities are many like, the Mrinmayee *mandir*, which is referred to as the oldest temple in Bishnupur based on the date popularly noted in 997 CE. by King Jagatmalla, who was supposedly instructed by the goddess in his sleep. Sarbamangala *mandir*, which does not bear the exact date of construction, though local lore assumes it to be a recently built piece of architecture; Radhalaljiu *mandir* that was established in 1658 by King Bir Singha; and the Chhinnamasta *mandir* (a com*para*tively recent construction of 1973, though the idol dates to earlier times and was a part of the Bishnupur royal family treasure)[14] are some other instances of the worship of female divinities. Another important example is the deity Radharajrani of Jamkuri (Bankura) (Fig.23). It is an important deity in the region and has its *nitya puja* supervised by the descendants of the local royal family—the Singha Deb family. Another significant example is the Raj Rajeswari Temple of the royal family of Kashipur (Purulia) (Fig. 24), which was established under the auspices of the local royalty—Maharaja Jyotiprasad Singha Dutta Bahadur in 1331 *bangabda* (1924).Though recently established, yet the popularity of the deity has a mass appeal throughout the region as a royal deity of considerable significance. She is also associated with various local lores, which further signifies her importance in the royal family. The noteworthy worship of goddesses at the Hadalnarayanpur (Bankura) royal family also deserves special mention, which is reflected in the annual Durga *puja* and also the regular worship of the Radha-Damodar *mandir* of the *Bara Taraf* of the family. Similarly important is the *kuldevata* Radha-Krisṇa of the vassal/zamindar family of Gangajalghati. Here, mention should also be made of the worship of Ma Brahmani, which is seen to be popularised in Hadalnarayanpur as well as Kasba Narayangarh (West Mednipur). In both instances, the patronage of the royal families is most significant. In Hadalnarayanpur (Fig. 25), the *Bara Taraf* of the royal family sponsors a major part of the *puja* even today. The deity at Kasba Narayangarh, who is worshipped for a day in the month of *Aswin*, was established by King Gandharba of Narayangarh.

## Jainism

Ancient Jain religious texts, dating to an early historic period often has references of Radh region, which has been mentioned in the earlier chapter. Supplementing as well as complementing the data, archaeological accounts have also proved the nature of widespread extension of Jainism in the region. Regarding the widespread prominence of the religion, Niharranjan Roy (2003: 493) can be referred to, as he explains the influence of Jainism between 4th to 3rd century BCE in Pundravardhana and Northern Bengal. However, the archaeological examples of possible Tirthankaras and deities which are found all across the region of study, can only be dated to a historic period of Late Guptas to the time of the Palas/Senas in Bengal. The architectural grandeur of these remaining idols speaks volume about the penetration and spread of religion in the region as well as the architectural dexterity of the craftsmen of yesteryears. Several of these Jain idols, which are a part of the ruins of former temples, are worshipped under transformed features. Thus, the continuity of religious tradition exists in a metamorphosed manner in recent times. This facet was extensively witnessed throughout the course of the fieldwork, especially in some parts of Bankura and West Mednipur and the majority of Purulia. In most of the places, the local people are aware about the Jain or Buddhist origin of various idols due to the benevolent method of preaching of various educationists and historians of the area, including their fieldworks in recent times. The various idols of possible Jain Tirthankaras and deities that were seen to be worshipped during the course of fieldwork are Manasa, Śiva and Dharmathakur/Dharmaraj besides others. Citing some of the examples observed during the course of the fieldwork, mention may be made of the worship of Yamraj idol in *Para* village (Purulia) (Fig.26) of the Bauri *para*, or the several remains of possible Jain idols housed in a Dharmaraj *mandir* in the Dom *para* of Charra (Purulia) (Fig. 27-30). In the village of Bhara (Bankura), a similar example of theriomorphic representation is seen to be worshipped as Lord Hanuman in present times. Mention should also be made of Suissa (Purulia) (Fig. 31, 32), where the recovered remains of several Jain idols are housed within an enclosed area that also bears the protective board of West Bengal State Archaeology Department. Nevertheless, several of these idols are locally worshipped as local/folk gods and goddesses with red vermillion smeared on them. Another such important example of a Jain idol is in Pakbira (Purulia) (Fig. 33, 34). The deity is worshipped as Bhairabnath—an incarnation of Śiva, with regular *puja* on Mondays and the officiating priest belongs to the Ray *para*. other important places are Anai and Jambad (Bankura) (Fig. 35), with both villages situated within a short distance of 1½ km from each other. Anai has a Paresnath Mahadev Bera Ananda Ashram on its southern side, which comprises at least 12 idols of Jain origin out of which two are worshipped as Paresnath, two as Adinath and other two as Chandraprabhu. Located within the ashram temple, under trees or in open air, these deities were also seen to be referred to as the *grāmadevatās*. Significantly, mention may also be made of the Visṇu idol at Dharapat (Bankura) (Fig. 36), which in present times, is worshipped as Nangta Shyamchand Thakur, especially by married women who seek blessings for a child.

An important aspect to this transformed feature is the association of male idols with the female power of regeneration. The fieldwork revealed several idols of possible Jain origin, which are worshipped as female gods, mostly worshipped by married women or couples to get blessings for a progeny. One particular reason which the researcher cosidered as a possible reason for this practice is the architectural particulars of the idols in nude standing positions and the associated sculptural details of snakes, lotuses or trees and other types of flowers that are often connected with symbols of fertility. Across the road from the place where idol of Visṇu at Dharapat is located, is housed a seven-hooded idol of Parsvanath (Fig. 37) within a modern construction, which is worshipped as Manasa. A similar example of a possible Parsvanath idol which is worshipped as a female deity is Khandarani Goddess of the village of

Bheduasole (Bankura) (Fig. 38). Though no *nitya puja* takes place at the temple, yet the deity is revered as an angry village goddess whose wrath befalls on people who, in the words of villagers, 'do not listen to her'. The ignored temple lies in the southern end of the village amidst a cultivating field and shrouded in a small gathering of *chor kanta* (*Chrysopogon aciculatus*) and babul plants (*Acacia arabica*). Other such examples include the deity of Chhinnamasta or Basulimata of Muninagar (Bankura) (Fig. 39), the Kali and Mahavira images of Penara (Bankura), several relics and remains of idols of Palma (Purulia) (Figs. 40-43) within personal properties and houses of people. Another significant example of association of a possible Jain deity is the Pashan Kali of Dwarika (Bankura) (Fig. 44). Though the deity is worshipped as Kali, yet its strong association with folk goddess Manasa, which is worshipped on the days of Manasa *puja* in the month of *Sravan* and every Tuesday and Saturday of the year, makes its association with folk culture significantly prominent. This deity is famous for fulfillment of desires or *manasik* of all people across all castes and creeds, which is very important, especially since the village of Dwarika has a large Muslim population.

Thus, throughout the course of fieldwork in the region of study, it was noticed that inspite of the Jain origin, it is the folk influences that have led to these deities, idols and ruins survive hundreds of years in a transformed form within the parameters of the folk culture.

**Buddhism**

Though several ancient Indian literary texts verify the travels of both Buddha and Mahavir in the Radha region, yet, during the course of field work, it was the influence of Jainism which was perceived to be surviving the maximum. It was only at one instance where a proper influence of Buddhism could be identified, as evident from the architectural details of the idol worshipped as well as the lore associated with it. This occurrence is at the village Radhamohanpur (Fig. 45, 46) in Bankura. Inspite of the presence of the *mandir* of Gobindochand or Gobinchand, which is a *samadhi mandir* of a local preacher, it is the significance of a *mandir* of Buddhadev which dominates the religious activities of the village. Located within the Mondol *para* of the village (on the north of Sonamukhi block and towards the south of Damodar), the regular worship of the deity is mostly limited to the so-called lower classes of the village. However, participation in the festivals of Buddhadev includes people across all castes and creeds, especially in the six-day long *mela*, beginning on the day of *Maghi purnima*.

### Folk Tradition: Gramādevatās and Various Village Deities

The various *grāmadevatās* within a village are often identified within a specific village, towards whom, the villagers have unambiguous fondness and respect. Broadly, all the types of village deities who were evident during the course of the fieldwork can be divided mainly into three categories, based on the extent of their areas of worship. Firstly, there are several deities who are considered sacrosanct, especially within a particular village. Throughout the course of the fieldwork, several such examples could be seen, such as Bisahari of Bisra (Fig. 47) or Kaliburi of Gamidhya (Fig. 48) (both in Bankura) and others. Secondly, there are other village deities who are considered important in a comparatively larger region, including several villages taken together. Such examples are many, with significant ones being various forms of Sini, Dharmaraj as well as that of Śiva bearing the title of *grāmadevatā.* In this respect, the worship of Siva is important, as the recognition of the status of a *grāmadevatā* renders a different feature to the worship. Finally, it should be mentioned that a category of village deities include the gods and goddesses, who are famous not only within few villages but also in a couple of neighbouring districts in a manner similar to the deity Māriyamman in South India. An avid example is the worship of Goddess Manasa in the present region of study, whose popularity is not only seen throughout the region of study, but also in other parts of northern India. Other similar examples are that of the deities Bhairab and Dharmaraj.

## Mainstream Gods and Goddesses Worshipped as Grāmadevatās

An important aspect witnessed during the course of fieldwork is the devotion shown towards *grāmadevatās* in a similar manner as is often shown towards deities from mainstream Puranic religion in some of the villages. This gradual change in perspective is in reference to the offerings and *prasad*, observation of certain rites and rituals, adornments of the deities as well as several local lore associated with the deity. The practice is a recent phenomenon and has grown over the last few years, especially in villages which did not adhere to any particular *grāmadevatā* tradition. Amongst all the deities worshipped thus, the female forces were seen maximum. A typical example is seen at the Jagatgouri *mandir* of Rautkhanda (Bankura) (Fig. 49, the idol was not allowed to be photographed), who appears to be the central point of worship of the village. Inspite of the folk association of the deity, she is worshipped as Manasa and Durga every day during the *nitya puja*. The popularity of the deity for special *pujas* every Tuesdays and Saturdays were evident during the course of the fieldwork as the researcher visited the site on a Tuesday. The temple is thronged by people from all across Bankura who come there for *manasik* and wish fulfillment. The offerings, temple decoration and embellishments as well as the rites and rituals of the *nitya puja*, all reflect attempts of the association of a *grāmadevatā* to the status of a mainstream goddess.

On the other hand, at several places, certain mainstream goddesses were seen to be worshipped as *grāmadevatās* by the autochthones, for instance, in the village of Penara (Bankura) (Fig. 50). The village entrance has the ruins of a brick temple, which houses three female deities : Bipadtarini, Singhabashini Durga and Sankattarini (respectively from the left in Fig. 50). The ruins of the temple still stand to mark the extent length of the original temple, which possibly flourished under the patronage of Malla royalty. Though there are no specific idols, the deities are worshipped through votive offerings of terracotta elephants, which are placed on an elevated mud platform to accommodate the figurines. In this context, it is also important to mention the Raksha Kali *puja* of the village of Gharaigera (West Mednipur) in the month of *Caitra*, followed by a month-long *mela*, which is locally believed to be at least a hundred years old. The Kali, of Antra (Bankura), though recent in origin, is also considered to be the central deity of the village within the Bagdi *para* of the village. The roughly built brick temple with four walls and a tin shed for a roof, only has an *abayab* for worship in the form of a *ghat*. Similar in importance is the Kali Goddess of the village of Moutorh (Purulia), which is famous for the *puja* of the deity and goat sacrifices in all neighbouring villages. A similar example of importance associated with a mainstream deity is in the village of Kusadwip (Bankura), within the Tili *para* in the *mandir* of Mahamaya. The temple receives *nitya puja*, twice daily, officiated by a Brahman from the Brahman *para* of the village.

## Candi

The important and powerful forces of Candi could be seen to be worshipped through folk culture in various forms. Mention may be made of Kekai Candi inside Chhilimpur Village (Bankura) (Fig.51), 100 mts from the centre of Prakashghat village, towards the western outskirts. This *sthan* is formed of a heavily eroded laterite stone which is placed loosely on a niche in a broken wall of a house along the main road. However, the aspect of *nitya puja* every Tuesday of *Caitra* and *Bhadra* and its association with Devi is evident from the *alpana* of the symbol resembling Goddess Laxmi's feet, which are seen drawn near the feet of the eroded structure. The Candi is referred here along with Goddess Laxmi to bring good luck and fortune.

Often associated with malevolent forces, the deity is also worshipped for blessings against natural calamities, illness and sickness. Such a typical instance was noticed in the village of Jagmohanpur (Bankura), where special Candi *puja* takes place during the outbreak of small pox in the months of *Phalgun* and *Caitra* to ward off the evils of pox and cure the patients. Located on the eastern limits of the village and managed by the *Gram Sholoanna Commmittee,* offerings made of conch shell bangles and saree[15] are made by married women to get blessings for a progeny. At several other instances, Candi was revered for overall goodness of the village as in the case of Candi of the villages of Penchashimul and Biskodor (both in Bankura), as well as the of Lohardanga (Bankura), where the deity was seen to be worshipped in the month of *Magh,* corresponding with the day of Saraswati *puja* and accompanied by *khichuri bhog* and *kirtan* singing. Similar instance is the Candi of Asada (West Mednipur), which resembles a possible male deity of Narsingha. The headless deity is locally worshipped as Candi and is popularly believed to have been caused by the plunders of Kalapahar. With an increasing popularity, many deities are also recognised far from their villages, a typical example being the Basanta Candi Mandir of Patrasayer (Bankura) (Fig.66), which accompanies the Kenduli *mela* from 9th *Magh* every year till the following six days. The officiating priest is a Nayak from a non-Brahman local family. Interesting to note is the theriomorphic representation through an idol of a laterite stone, who is referred as Candi.

**Manasa**

Geo-physical reasons often lead to harsh weather conditions in the region of study, which range from severe summers to very cold winters with the monsoon season in between that sees tremendous floods. Water-logged lakes, ponds and other water bodies indicate an approaching harvesting season. It is also the time for various snakes to frequent the marshy areas, in a manner similar to which they take refuge outside heated surfaces in the summer time and appear in open ground, causing trouble for the farmers/field labourers and fishermen. Thus, the popularity of the deity of Manasa is not uncommon in the region. Almost every village has a Manasa *sthan,* and it is not surprising that she occupies the eminent position of a *grāmadevatā.* Instances are several, such as, the Manasa deity of Talajuri (Purulia), which occupies the seat of a *grāmadevatā* and receives a special *puja* on 1st *Magh,* along with goat sacrifices.

Apart from the *nitya puja,* the deity receives special *puja* on Saturdays and Tuesdays, and an annual *puja,* festivals and fairs are held in the months of *Jaisthya, Asad, Sravana* or *Bhadra* in various villages, which are decided in recent times, mostly by the *Gram Sholoanna Committees.* However, the date decided by the *Committees* varies, for instance, Hadalnarayanpur (Fig.52) holds special annual Manasa *puja* on *Sravan Sankranti,* quite like the Manasa deity of Chuamashna (Bankura), who receives it on 5th of *Jaishthya* and on *Sravan Sankranti*. But the Manasa deity of Bhatra (Bankura) receives it on some predetermined date in *Bhadra*, as determined by the *Gram Sholoanna Committee* unlike the Manasa *puja* of Dhumkoro (Fig. 53), which receives its annual *puja* on *Bhadra Sankranti* every year. Though mostly located, as was observed, within the *paras* of the so-called lower classes of the village, like the Bagdi, Bauri, Keor, Dhibor *paras*, several instances show her to be residing in more than one *para*, including those of the so-called upper classes of a village as was seen in the village of Metla (Bankura District).

Manasa *sthans* with votive offerings were also seen in adjoining places in the temple complexes of various mainstream deities, for instance, Śiva as well as Visṇu temples in the region. This character also verifies the importance associated with the goddess throughout the three districts of work. A similar example was witnessed in the Manasa deity of the village of Dwarika (Bankura). There are two temples in the village out of which one stands next to a Durga Temple in the Kayastha *para* and another one in the Teli *para* close to the Janardan Temple, which receives *puja* every Tuesday. Interestingly enough, the deity of the second temple is worshipped in the form of Kali. Quite resembling in feature is another example from the region, namely, the Manasa *sthan* in the village of Uliara (Bankura). Located next to a Kali Temple, both the temples are worshipped through only an *abayab* to mark their sanctity.

In sharp contrast to the attempts of the association of the goddess to mainstream Brahmanical religion is her endowment with the status of village goddess or *grāmadevatā*. An example is Gamidhya, where Manasa is referred to as Kaliburi and stands across the main road, adjoining the Śiva Temple of Dugdeswar of the village. This deity is also called

Dasohara and receives a special *puja,* apart from *nitya puja,* for two days on the *pancami* after Dasohara *puja.*[16]

An important feature of the goddess, which was also witnessed throughout the course of the fieldwork, was the worshipping of the deity in an anthropomorphic form, reflecting the transformation from a concept to an idol. The deity, which was originally worshipped through the branch of a *sij* tree and an earthen pot of water, was seen variously worshipped as clay idols of female goddess, which is equal in grandeur to an idol of Laxmi or Saraswati as far as adornment and embellishments are concerned. Such examples are many such as the Manasa Temple in the Mondol *para* of the village of Kapistha (Bankura) (Fig. 54), the Manasa Temple within the Bauri *para* of the village of Chhatna (Bankura) (Fig. 55), the Manasa Temple of the Bauri *para* in Palpal (Purulia) (Fig. 56) and the Manasa Temple within the Dhibor *para* of Gangajalghati (Bankura) (Fig.57). Thus, though the deity is worshipped in her anthropomorphic form, the officiating priests were noticed to be mostly from the so-called lower classes of the village, with exceptions of a Brahman priest at few places. Several such instances can be cited, such as the Bauri priest of the Manasa Temple within the Bauri such as *para* in the village of Chhatna, the Keor priest of the Manasa Temple within the Keor *para* of Gangajalghati village or the Majhi and Lohar priests of the Manasa Temples within the respective *paras* of Durlovpur.

Being an important folk deity of the region, it is also important to mention certain definite characters associated with specific Manasa deities in certain villages, such as the worship of Manasa as Bisahari in the villages of Prakashghat and its adjoining village of Chchilimpur (Bankura). This aspect is significant since in all other examples of Manasa in neighbouring villages, she is considered an independent entity who is different from Bisahari. Thus, deity of Bisahari of the village of Bisra (Bankura) is considered different from Manasa and is worshipped on the day of Dasohara. Considered as a significant *grāmadevatā*, the village is named after the deity.[17] However, this deity too is associated with Śiva, as corroborated by the location of a Śivalinga[18] on the left of Bisahari—a feature which is usually witnessed within any Manasa temple/*sthans*. Importantly, mention may also be made of the Manasa deity of Radhanagar (Bankura), located within the Lohar *para*, which is referred to as a Manasa *mandir* by the Lohars, but the people from the so-called upper classes of the village refer to it as Ratan Muni. The officiating priest is one Mohan Lohar, and a special *puja* takes place every Tuesday and Saturday. Significant to also mention is the special *khichuri bhog - Pausalya* associated with the annual *puja* of the Manasa deity of Jaykrisnapur (Bankura), which is held on the Saturday and Tuesday after the 20$^{th}$ of the month of *Paus* every year, as determined by the *Gram Sholoanna Committee.*

## Sini

The region under study has several Sini goddesses worshipped under various names. Mostly located at the peripheries of the villages, these are generally marked by votive offerings of several terracotta horses and elephants of various shapes and sizes, especially in the district of Bankura. Mostly, the deity does not have a regular officiating priest nor any *nitya puja* takes place, but at several instances an annual *puja* is seen to occur. It is also interesting to note that the presence of the deity is the maximum in the district of Bankura as compared to Purulia or West Mednipur. Of the few Sini deities of Purulia witnessed during the course of fieldwork, mention may be made of Juar Sini of the Kalimati Village (Purulia) (according to the locals, the site is not allowed to be visited by women. Hence, the researcher too was not allowed to visit the site) and Hatiya Sini Pansi Mura of Harup (Purulia) (Fig. 58). The deity is associated with the annual *mela,* also referred to as Harup *mela,* which is held on *Jaisthya Sankranti.* Another important example is the Rupa Sini of Rupar Ghagra (West Mednipur), which is marked by votive offerings of terracotta horses and elephants of various sizes and occurrence of a day-long *mela* on the 4$^{th}$ of the month of *Magh,* with goat sacrifices. Important also is the Sini of Nachanjam (West Mednipur) whose *puja* takes place in *Magh* (*Makar Sankranti*), along with a *mela* for two days. Once again, terracotta horses mark the deities' sacrosanct place. Closeby, at Kharikasuli is the deity Machaisini, whose worship is considered important for the village. The worship takes place on 1$^{st}$ *Magh* and witnesses goat sacrifices as well.

In the village of Chuamasna (Bankura), on the eastern side, within the *goyala para* (cowherd area), is the *sthan* of Chuasini, locally referred to as Candi, under a banyan tree. Votive offerings in the form of small terracotta horses are enshrined within the niche of the banyan tree roots. Besides the *nitya puja,* a special *puja* is held on 28$^{th}$ *Caitra,* followed by Gajan, and its close association with Śiva is prominent.[19] Another significant Sini *sthan* lies under a tamarind tree, about 300 m from the centre of the village of Indpur (Bankura) (Fig. 59) and is known as Chukai Sini. With the help of collective efforts of the Bauris of the village, the worship is performed by one Ajit Bauri (as was seen at the time of fieldwork), a day after *Makar Sankranti.* Important also is the Bandh Sini (Fig. 60), which is located across an unmetalled road, next to Baner Bandh Pukur under Indpur Police Station (Bankura) at the rear end of the village of Halukmari. The Makra Sini (about 14 km from Bheduasole, Heerbandh Police Station, Bankura)[20] is important for blessings against calamities, sickness and illness and a four-day long *mela* at the time of *Paus Sankranti* is held to celebrate the deity. The worship of Sini is also for the general well-being of the village and villagers, which was prominent in every aspect.

### Sitala

She is the deity associated with the well-being of children, and her worship is often seen to be held especially during the months of *Caitra* and *Baisakh*—a period that is traditionally associated with the outbreak and spread of small pox (though there are no cases reported anymore for several decades now), chicken pox and measles which are seen to often affect children with low levels of immunity. Though her presence was seen at various scattered places in Bankura as well as Purulia, the maximum presence was noticed in West Mednipur. No special mention is required for any idol and thus, mention may be made of such villages like Sankrui, Belya Maharajpur, Anandapur, Nutanbazar and others, which portray her worship in an anthropomorphic form and the deity is revered by one and all to obtain blessings for the well-being of children, as well as their families.

## Discussing Grāmadevatās

### Bhairab

Considerable Bhairab *sthans* were witnessed during the course of the fieldwork at various corners of villages. Initially, some of these places were used to mark the extant periphery of a village, as in the village of Koro (Bankura) (Fig. 61) (located approximately ½ km from the village settlement area and close to National Highway No. 60 it conducts *puja* every *Makar Sankranti*), but because of population expansion, many were seen to occupy a central place within the villages. In most instances, especially in the district of Bankura, votive offerings in the form of various sizes of terracotta elephants and horses were seen to be offered at the place of worship.

More often than not, it was noticed that these *sthans* were located next to the *paras* of the so-called lower classes of the villages.

Interestingly, it was observed during the course of the fieldwork that the deity, in most instances, does not have any regular officiating priest and thus, mostly, no regular *puja* takes place, as in the case of village of Pataspur (Bankura) (Fig. 62) or in the village of Dhumkoro (Bankura) (Fig. 63), where the deity is worshipped by people to fulfil their personal needs. However, certain exceptions are there with regular officiating for priest *nitya puja*. In these instances, the duty was performed by a locally referred Brahman *purohit* (witnessed to be a non-Brahman and elevated to a status of Brahmanism through *nitya puja*). This practice was also accompanied by rice *bhog*—as befits the status of any mainstream Brahmanical deity. A typical example was observed with Billamani Thakur, of Chhilimpur (Bankura). The regular priest is from a local Pal family. Located amidst an open field, a special worship takes place on 1st of the month of *Magh*, with the offerings of *seddha chal* (par boiled rice) as *bhog*. In close lines of a similar example is the Bhairab of Patrahati, worshipped as a *grāmadevatā* with a local Brahman *purohit* from the neighbouring Jagmohanpur village, acting as the officiating priest. Located at the eastern end of the village, the deity is marked by votive offerings of terracotta horses and a special *puja* takes place on Gajan at the site, reflecting attempts to associate the deity with Śiva.

However, inspite of its association with the so-called lower classes of a village, it was observed during the course of the fieldwork that, often, any special or annual *puja prasad* is partaken by all the members of a village, as in the case of Village Tiliboni/Basantapur (Fig. 64). The Bhairab *sthan*, located on the south-western border of the village, along the banks of the Dwarakeshwar River, receives an annual *puja* on the 1st of the month of *Magh* by a priest from the local Bagish family. This *prasad* is distributed all over the village, irrespective of caste and creed. [21]

## Dharmaraj

The Dharmaraj *sthans* are mostly seen to be located at the peripheries of villages. At several instances, because of expanding village population, the present *para* of the village where the *sthan* is located has moved into the centre of the village from the peripheries, like, the village of Charra (Fig. 65). In this case the Dharmaraj *sthan* is located in the north-western part of the village, where the *puja* is managed by the Dom *para* of the village, and a three-day *mela* refered to as the Dharmaraj *mela* is held in the month of *Jaisthya*.

Mostly marked by votive offerings of terracotta horses and elephants, Dharmaraj is seen to have no *nitya puja* or any regular officiating priests, with some exceptions like the *sthan* in Charra. In places where no *nitya puja* takes place, the worship is prompted by occasional needs, on certain days, though mostly by people from so-called lower classes of the village. An example is that of the Dharmaraj *mela* of Gokulpur (West Mednipur), where the annual *puja* takes place on a certain date on the month of *Baisakh*. At several instances, the *grāmadevatā* status of the deity was also seen to be an important aspect in some villages, rendering devotion which is associated with any mainstream Puranic deity. This feature was noticed in the village of Charra as well as other places like, Kapistha (Bankura) (Figs. 66, 67). Here, the deity resides in a concrete temple in the centre of the village, and the idol is referred as a *salgram sila*, which is placed inside an earthen pot and only taken out when it is to be given a bath at the time of the annual *puja* in the month *Jaisthya* after *Akshay Tritiya*.

## Other Grāmadevatās under Varied Local Names

Several deities are worshipped as *grāmadevatās* in some of the villages, with many of them often associated with mainstream deities. On the other hand, there were many others, where the structure and architecture of the idols reflect the images of mainstream Brahmanical deities, but their present names are local ones that are famous within a village or in adjoining villages. In this reference, mention may be made of several Jain idols in the region of study, across the three districts, which are worshipped as local deities and often as *grāmadevatās* as well. This fact has also been mentioned in details under the sub-heading of Jainism in the current chapter earlier. Of these many examples, mention may be made of few, like Nangta Syamchand Thakur of Dharapat village (Bankura) (Fig. 36) or Kkhandarani of the village of Bheduasole (Bankura) (Fig. 38). The details of both deities have been mentioned above. While the former, which is worshipped as a male god, relates to blessings for the birth of a child, the latter is worshipped as a female deity and is worshipped for general well-being and protection against natural calamities. In a similar manner, several Śiva *lingas* were also often seen to be ascribed the role of a *grāmadevatā*, like, the Lohariya Śiva of Lohariya village (Purulia), that draws people from neighbouring villages or the idol of Pandabeswar Śiva of Pandua (Bankura)— referred to three laterite stones under a tree, that receives *manasik* from married women for fulfillment of desires for a progeny. In this reference, it is also significant to mention the religious syncretism noticed in various parts, between Brahmanical religion and Islam in several villages. At several places, it was seen to be associated with the popularity that of a local priest who is revered as a *pir*. Mention may be made of the villages of Dwarika, which has a large number of Muslim populations that trace their ancestry in the past as being *lathiyals*, who were brought over by the Malla royalty. The village narrates the lore associated with *pir* Musafir Saheb. Similarly, Pandua also narrates lore associated with Satya Pir Saheb and his burial ground is a worshipping site with votive offerings for both Brahmanical religion and Muslims (the site is not allowed to be photographed for religious reasons). The influence of Islamic architecture was also prominent at various parts, especially in West Mednipur and mention may be made of the Śiva Temple at Moghalmari (West Mednipur).

An interesting aspect noticed during the course of the fieldwork was the attempts to associate the names of mainstream deities with folk deities, rendering the touches of a *grāmadevatā*. One such important example was found in the village of Chhatna (Bankura), with reference to goddess Basali. She is referred to as Basanti, Basanti Durga and Dwibhuja Meenasurabadhini (the one with two arms who slayed Meena *asura* or demon). Her *nitya puja*, the offerings as well as the worshipping procedures are quite similar in manner to many mainstream Brahmanical goddess. The explanation of her names could also be found in the village folk lore, which reflects the importance to align the deity with a mainstream Brahmanical goddess. A similar importance associated with the deity Basuli was witnessed in Advaicandi (Bankura) (Figs. 68, 69), where she is the central figure of the village. Likewise, the deity of Ma Brahmani of Hadalnarayanpur (Bankura) (Fig. 25) is considered as a very important part of village life inspite of the presence of the local royal family and their various temples related to worship of mainstream gods and goddesses.

Moreover, often, the names of the villages were seen to have been derived from the names of the various *grāmadevatās* of respective villages, as was seen in case of the village of Hariatore (West Mednipur), which is named after the *grāmadevatā* Hariaburi. Another similar instance is the village of Pandua (Bankura), which got its name from the previously mentioned Pandabeswar Śiva.[22] An interesting feature of this village is the worship of Bagda Buro in the Bauri and Bagdi *para,* in the middle of a ploughing field. Though not considered as a *grāmadevatā,* yet the respect and adulation attached to the deity, as evident from the votive offerings of small-sized terracotta horses under a *kayet* tree, is similar in extent to that of a *grāmadevatā.*[23] Quite like Pandua, another example where the village is named after the *grāmadevatā* was noticed in Bisra (Bankura District), where the name of the village is related to the name of deity Bisahari of the village. This very aspect of the association of the names of villages with the *grāmadevatās* also reflects the significance attributed to the deities. Another attempt to associate a *grāmadevatā* with a mainstream goddess was seen in the worship of Dasohara in Ayodhya (Fig.70) or the Aswin *puja* of Bhairabpur (both in Bankura District)—both performed fifteen days prior to Durga *puja* with much grandeur.[24]

At several occasions during the course of the fieldwork, it was noticed that the popularity of certain festivals and fairs associated with few specific deities has cut across geographical boundaries, drawing people from several neighbouring regions, such as Deulghata (Purulia), where the festival and *mela* of *Palas Parban* draws a large crowd. (this feature has been mentioned earlier in the chapter). The annual festival involving the *puja* of Sarbamangala of Naricha (Bankura) and (Fig.71) *mela,* starting from the 1st of *Magh* for about ten days, also draws a large crowd from all over the district of Bankura.[25] In this context, mention can also be made of Hirimbeswari of Kharagpur (West Mednipur), who is worshipped on the *amavasya* (new moon) of the month of *Kartik* by the officiating Brahman priest. Another similar example is the annual worship and associated *mela* of the deity of Kalanjay of Patrasayer (Bankura) (Fig. 72), or the Baruni *mela* of Susunia (Bankura) on *Madhukrisna Trayodasi* on *Caitra* Gajan. Similarly, other important festivals which were seen popular in the region include the Baram *puja* and Bhang Singh *puja* of the village of Nutanbazar (West Mednipur). These are popular at other places in the district as well. A similar instance occurs as the seven festivals of the village of Suabasa (Bankura), including such festivities like Maghi *puja* and Nagordola (held in *Magh* and accompanied by fowl or goat sacrifice), Badna (in *Paus*), Salvi *puja* (at the time of Doljatra in *Caitra*), Ero Sim *puja* (in *Asad*), Hariyar Sim (in *Bhadra*, when the sowed rice plants are green), Chendera (spelled Che-de-ra) *puja* (in *Baisakh*, which marks the beginning of the hunting season, without which the locals are believed to avoid entering the jungle). Festivals like Salvi *puja*, Bandna or Maghi *puja* were seen famous in other villages of the region as well, e.g., the village of Jugunthol (Bankura). All these common festivals were seen to be accompanied by a merry celebration of *khichuri bhog* along with sacrifice of fowl or goat. Similarly, there are also other festivals associated with *grāmadevatās*, such as the worship of Bura Buri and Marang Buru in the months of *Kartik* and *Magh* respectively, which were seen to be worshipped over a large region spreading across the villages of Parashibona, Paharbedia, Suabasa and Biskodor. In this context, it is also important to mention the recent popularity of the Rani Sati *mandir* of Balarampur (Purulia) (Fig. 73) to the level of a *grāmadevatā*, where the annual *puja* coincides with the Manasa *puja* of *Sravan Sankranti.* Her popularity attracts several devotees, many of whom belong to the Marwari community, spreading all over the district of Purulia.

In contrast to the popularity of *grāmadevatās* within a specific region, are some festivals/*melas*, which are only limited to specific villages, such as the Eken *puja* in the village of Penchashimul, which takes place on *Paus Sankranti*, or the worship of the *grāmadevatā* Bamun Ma of Biskodor (Bankura) in the month of Baisakh, which is decided by the *Gram Sholoanna Committee*. The worship of Yamraj, within the Bauri *para* of *Para* (Purulia) (Fig. 26) is another occurrence of a village deity that is considered sacrosanct within a specific village. This place holds a seven-day *mela* during the time of Buddha *purnima* every year. Popular locally within the village is also the deity Nakti Durga of Burda village (Purulia) (Figs. 74, 75) or the Harup *mela* of Hatiya Sini in Harup village (Purulia), which has been mentioned before. Of similar types are the Mahotsaber *mela* of Moghalmari (West Mednipur), which is locally famous as Sasisenar *mela*, the Hauri mayer *puja* of Anandapur (West Mednipur) and the Bangathakur *mela* of Sarengagar (West Mednipur), which commences on the 3$^{rd}$ of the month of *Magh* every year and continues for the next seven days. Similarly, the Saharay *puja*, Safrat *utsav* of *Paus Sankranti* and Salui in the month of *Phalgun* of Betjharia (West Mednipur) are also important within specific villages.

Finally, it can be summed up from what has been mentioned earlier that the archaeological evidences are further complemented by different ethnographic details. Various excavations of microliths suggest that possibly the people were camping on the high grounds, with contacts amongst themselves and those of the Neolithic Culture (Banerjee, pp. 52-53) and that the excavations preceded the Chalcolithic Period. The later archaeological remains tell us about the rudimentary economy and the mode of subsistence from very ancient times, including maritime trade in historical period (prominent from Tamluk reports). However, it should be mentioned that none of the reports suggest a possible mention of rites, rituals or festivities. Instances of local worshipping, mostly patronised by royalty, are evident from Early-Later Historic times and the following Early/Medieval period, roughly corresponding to the Pre-Gupta, Gupta and Post-Gupta era, till the Early Medieval period. Stray finds in form of temple ruins and remains of idols and literature of a Later Historic era, confirm philosophical and religious beliefs of contemporary society. However, this evidence does not correspond to the portrayal of folk deities and religious beliefs in the region, but it mainly reflects the popular religion of the region from time-to-time, mostly patronised by the local royalty. On the other hand, the survival of folk rites, rituals and ceremonies in present times was evident through the fieldwork. In the light of non-availability of any written record to ascertain the antiquity of these ceremonies, it becomes extremely difficult to establish with surety the presence of the same in earlier times. However, the nature of their existence in modern times confirm their popularity and also attempts to complement the available archaeological and historical records, as they often include influence of Brahmanical, Jain and Buddhist pantheons. A major part of the local religious history is reconstructed through the art traditions of these religions. The main Brahmanical deities represented the cults of Visnu, Śiva, Sakti, Surya and Ganapati, while the so-called minor deities included Varahi, Parvati, Manasa, etc. The Jain images are those of Tirthankaras and Sasanadevis, and some of the Buddhist images comprise Mahayana Tantric divinities. Several of these deities are worshipped under various local names of local gods and goddesses. Apart from them, miniature votive shrines, medallions, decorative designs and motifs occurring on fragments of structural remains (*Ibid*:88-89) have also been reported from the region of study as important sources of archaeological information. Remains of temples, idols, possible suggestions of herostones, etc. which were seen to be worshipped in varied forms of folk deities do point towards the trend of continuity of rites and rituals. Most of these idols date from the Late Historic to Medieval periods and often also verify royal patronage. Their existence in transformed characters suggests the prominence of folk beliefs in the region, a final appreciation of which is attempted in the next chapter of the present work.

## ENDNOTES

1. Interestingly, West Bengal has evidences of human activities from very pre-historic times, especially reported from two different regions of the state : the Darjeeling Himalayas in the North and the Western Upland. Speaking in terms of cultural traditions, while the former showed examples of neoliths, the southwestern Bengal revealed information about all the important stages of pre-historic tool-traditions.
2. The proposed longer and larger concentration is along the River Dwarakeshwar, where resources could have been more diverse and abundant and the occurrence of few agrarian tools were needed to process agriculture, as found in the Gamidhya-Ayodhya area. All these speak of important emphasis on storable foods in the more sedentary segment of the annual cycle (Chattopadhyay *et al.* 2009, pp. 83-84).
3. Dasgupta, (pp. 16-20, 35-43).
4. Neolithic tools were also found in the Lower Ganga Valley, but these are debatable as often scholars argue that these could have been brought down in the present region by the river before their fall into the Ganges. Some excavated historical sites also yielded microlithic tools, including Bangarh (Dinajpur), where microliths were found below the Sunga level, and at Tamluk (West Mednipur), neoliths with ill-fired pottery belonged to the 2nd century BCE. Moveover, it has been proposed that these neoliths of "historical period were perhaps ritual objects" (Chattopadhyay, Op. cit. pp.89).
5. It is significant to mention here the site of Birbhanpur, which has yielded much information pertaining to the chronology and hydrographical condition prevailing in earlier times. The microliths of Birbhanpur have been assigned to pre-pottery stage, but a later date than most other places of India, such as the 4th millennium BCE. However, "there is no indication or evidence as to whether these people were actually associated in any way with the food-producing economy" (Ibid:pp.88).

6. It is also important to mention here the ample evidences of ground and polished stone tools in the Bishnupur/Vishnupur Sub-division of Bankura District, where, as mentioned by Chattopadhyay (Ibid et al. 2009:84-85) that a recognition of a true Neolithic horizon is yet to be established.
7. Banerjee, Amalendu (1997, Rock Shelters of Patina, pp. 51) speaks in reference to his trial trenches at Patina Village (on south bank of River Subarnarekha, situated 18 km east of the town of Gopiballavpur, on the south-west Midnapur District). Banerjee also mentions the caves and rock shelters explored by him about 300 ft from the bed of the River Subarnarekha and that these could have possibly been the used sites of the ancestors of the present populace of the Chhotanagpur Plateau of Singhbhum in Bihar, as well as the Mayurbhanj hill ranges of Odisha (Bannerjee,1997:16-17).
8. (After Dasgupta, 1975, p.5) According to Dr. Stella Kramrisch, the Oxford Figurine resembles the Apsara Panchachura of Mahabharata, who came after Lakshmi from the churning of the ocean, while Prof. Johnston mentioned her to be identical with goddess Maiya of the Oxyrhynchus Papyrus (no. 1820) of Egypt. There are also examples of explanations of stories from Jatakas on terracotta, like the Chhadanta Jataka and the Vassantara Jataka and various Buddha images of Mahayana association (Dasgupta,1975:7-8).
9. The Tarpandighī Copper plate of Lakshmansena speaks of a Buddhist monastery (Majumdar, Ibid., 102, 104, Maity and Mukherjee, Op cit. pp. 293) An important mention regarding the same is seen in the Paharpur Copper plate inscription that mentions a Brahman Nātha arman and his wife, in the village of Vatagohali, as having purchased or acquired the land gift for the worship and the maintenance of the Jaina Vihāra of Vatagoh ligrāma (Maity and Mukherjee, Ibid. pp. 55,57). considerable information of this nature about land grants to Buddhist monasteries is available from inscriptions of which many even record the names of the Āchārya (Ibid, 2009:85-86).
10. The Deopara inscription of Vijayasena talks about the "lofty houses of gods" or the high temples that were constructed, and one such temple by the name Pradyumnesvara, the abode of Lakshmi, is mentioned in the inscription. "A vivid description of this temple also provides 'A lofty edifice of Pradyumnesvara, the wings of the plinth and the main structure that occupied several quarters. On the top of the temple, a golden jar was placed" (tad -*Ghata...Suvar a-kumbhasya)*.
11. (Majumdar, pp. 49, 55 after Chhattopadhyay, 2002:84-85 from Maity and Mukherjee, p. 85). A temple of Visṇu is also referred to in the Bhuvanesvara inscription of Bhatta-Bhavadeva that refers to the installation of a stone image of Nārāyana along with Ananta and

Nisiha (Nārāyanān-tan si ha) in a temple and also of the engagement of one hundred damsels in the service of god (Maity and Mukherjee, *Op. cit.* pp. 353—after Chattopadhyay, Ibid:85). There is also a mention of a beautiful garden and a tank in front of the temple.

12. A similar reference to a temple is also seen in the Tarpandigh Copper plate of Lakshmansena.
13. The association of the family of Mallabhum royalty with Vaisṇavism was often so strong that it has even come under severe criticism with scholars suggesting possible deliberate attempts to impose the popularity on all subjects of Mallabhum (Ghosh:1976:336-337). This aspect was also clear from the words of several local educationists and teachers who are associated with writing local history in local journals.
14. The researcher was not allowed to take photographs of any of these temples within the town of Bishnupur by the present descendants of the Malla royal family, which, in their words, could only be completed after the payment of a certain sum of money. Having denied the precondition, the researcher could not get any recent photographs of these monuments.
15. At Jagmohanpur in Bankura District, across the Gosai para, within a walking distance of 2 kms across Shubhankari Canal is the Candi sthan at a Candi tala. A special puja takes place during the time of small pox in the months of Phalgun and Chaitra—toward off the evils of pox and cure those who are suffering. At this time, married women make offerigs of conch shell bangles and saree.
16. Nitya puja of the Manasa deity of Gamidhya Village (Bankura District) is performed with atop chal (parboiled rice), batasha (a type of sweetmeat), and various other sweets. On the days of special puja on Saturdays and Tuesdays, the prasad includes chewda, jaggery and milk. At Dasohara, this deity receives a special puja for two days on the panchami after the puja, which is also referred to as Pancami. The puja includes goat sacrifice.
17. This temple of Bisahari of Bisra Village in Bankura is located on the south-west part of the village. Previously nitya puja used to take place, which was officiated by a Brahman purohit. But now, it is only limited to twice a year on the day of Dasohara and on 1st Magh, which is looked after by the Gram Sholoanna Committee. This puja has elaborate khichuri, chatni, payasam and tarkari bhog, which are distributed throughout the village alongside holding goat sacrifices.
18. In the village of Bisra (Bankura District), the Śiva sthan is located within a distance of 20 ft from the place of the Bisahari sthan. This place also does not receive nitya puja, but is worshipped only on Śivaratri and on the days of the Dasohara puja.

19. The Chuasini of Indpur (Bankura District) has nitya puja as well as its annual puja on 28th Caitra which is officiated by one Swapan Chatterjee from the Brahman para. The annual festival has Ramayana path and Jatra, fireworks display and a mela. The place also receives special puja during the time of Gajan in Caitra. Apart from these pujas, a special bhog is prepared on a certain day of Bhadra, which is decided by the *Gram Sholoanna Committee.* This is a khichuri bhog and is distributed all over the village.
20. The Makra Sini sthan in Bankura District is located 14 kms from Bheduasole Village (Bankura District). The area was under Khhatra Police Station till 2007, but it now lies under Herbandh Police Station, on the bank of the River Silabati. The sthan is located within 20 mts of a cremation ground just on the banks of Silabati and has a Kali and a Śiva temple on its right. It has Deuli Village in south-east, Mulian in south-west and Junebedia in north.
21. In the village of Tiliboni/Basantapur in Bankura District, the Bhairab sthan does not receive nitya puja. The annual puja on the 1st of the month of Magh takes place by clearing the year-long deposited votive offerings of terracotta horses from the worshipping site. No sacrifices take place at the site. The votive offerings are of terracotta specimens of horses, which are procured at a price of Rs 200-250 a pair each (approx) from Bishnupur during the time of puja. The sthan belongs to a local Goswami family, who do not reside in the village at present, and the responsibility of the annual puja for the month of Magh is on a local Bagish family from Basantapur.
22. The officiating priest of Pandabeswar Śiva of the village of Pandua (Bankura District) is one Ramaprasad Chakrabarty from the local Brahman para, and annual puja takes place every Makar Sankranti, along with *khichuri bhog.*
23. At Pandua (Bankura), at the site of Bagda Buro, puja is performed by one from the so-called lower classes of the village-Tripura Digar (75) from the same para, especially on Makar Sankranti, during which khichuri bhog is served.
24. The Aswin puja of Bhairabpur (Bankura) is a bi-annual puja, and it also takes place at the time of Sravan Sankranti although it is much less in extent of its popularity as compared to the Dasohara of Ayodhya, which attracts people from several neighbouring states as well. Many people attend this puja for fulfillment of wishes, especially for birth of a progeny.
25. As a nitya puja offering, the Sarbamangala deity of Naricha receives a machh pora (which is a local pona or magur fish, wrapped in leaves and dry roasted in fire, where the fire is kept both on top and beneath the wrapped fish), along with rice bhog. This is a famous prasad of the deity, and devotees come thronging from all over the district for it.

# 5

# Discussion

The history of ancient Bengal and especially the region under study, presents a myriad reflection of beliefs and practices which developed through time and under the influences of different religious ideals. Locating the region of study as a geographic entity through various historical records, it is important to keep in mind the significance of the survival of religious traditions of the autochthones/*vratyas*, constituting the various social groups (tribals, sub-castes, castes/*antyaja* and other ethnic groups), who received special attention to reconstruct the regional religious historical tradition. Their survival strategy depends on the geo-physical specificities of their habitation and thus, the woodland areas in the plateau region, which has a large concentration of tribal population, with a subsistence pattern of fishing, hunting, etc. differs from the plain regions with an agro-pastoral economy (pastorals including Gop and, agriculturalists including Sadgop and other *antyaja* groups like, Dom, Bauri, Bagdi, Hari and others). The surviving pattern, in time, influenced the cognitive representation, reflected through various religious beliefs and practices in the region. Though the evidences pertaining to folk religious traditions is limited in nature with a lack of written sources, but various archaeological and historical records pertaining to various stages of settlement and economic activities in the region of study, provide valuable information about the introduction of different religious beliefs and practices. This is specifically evident from the Historic period onwards and thus, our interpretation about the same may not be necessarily explained by following a specific chrono-cultural sequence, but various archaeological, historical and ethnoarchaeological evidences as mentioned above. The history of the region, also traces the settlement pattern, which also saw the rise of local/feudatory powers or ruling authorities in the early medieval times and an influence of trading activities on the local religious traditions.

Beginning from the very prehistoric times, one can witness the elaborate use of stone tools and the gradual clearing of forests by the microlith-using hunter-gatherers, denoting exploration of newer settlements by the original inhabitants as they expanded into the plateau region with newer settlers filling in the plain regions. The manner of the abundant occurrence of prehistoric microliths on the river banks highlights the important aspect of the dependency of the inhabitant hunter-gatherers on fishing activities and also the fact that these microlith-users were "equally at home in the forested stretches like their Palaeolithic ancestors. The abundance of microlith occurrences in the entire *sal* forest zone of West Bengal from the north of Birbhum to the southwestern part of Mednipur is undoubtedly striking and emphasises, if anything, a great dependence on the part of the microlith-users on forest produce." (Chakrabarti, 1993:199). A possible strain of continuity of Palaeolithic culture is also suggested by scholars (*Ibid*), uptill $8^{th}$-$10^{th}$ centuries CE., or even till a little later date in the region, when there are well-documented historical ruins in the form of temples and images in the region of study, especially Purulia and some parts of Bankura. Though, it cannot be surmised that the socio-cultural and religious life of the people continued without a change from the Mesolithic stage, but there are assumed to "have been microlith-using hunter-gatherers outside the pale of the contemporary historical world, which must have interacted in various ways with the established historical communities of the plateau" (*Ibid*) and thus, there could also have been a wide prevalence of the use of microliths "among the Chalcolithic and Iron Age communities of the region in the 2nd and 1st half of the first millennia BCE." (*Ibid*). Such evidences can be cited from the sites of Mahisdal and Tulsipur. Though, interestingly, the polished tools (neoliths) could have formed integral parts of the microlithic assemblage in these areas, but unfortunately these remain undated and as a result, further postulation also remains static. However, it can be stated, that the time possibly witnessed agricultural operations to be first carried out in the region by the Neolithic people who practiced, perhaps a very rudimentary type of shifting cultivation. With growth of population and advancement of agricultural techniques, there was a natural rise in the demand of the requirement of lands for cultivation, and thus, the emergence of the Early Village Farming (EVF) sites. Thus, the water-logged areas, forests and waste-lands—all were exploited gradually for cultivation. This is an evident fact from various land grants, dating between c. 5th to 7th century CE. (Majumdar, 1971), which speaks variously about the purchase and donation of wastelands and also water-logged areas related to cultivation. Though in region of Bengal, there is no clear evidence to suggest the exact date of the introduction of iron, but it can be ascertained that in the post-Christian era, iron was in great use for agricultural operations and deforestation. These are also corroborated by archaeological facts from various sites and by 3rd and 4th century CE, there were wide areas in ancient Bengal which were being cultivated with the help of the iron plough.

Though the information pertaining to settlement pattern is available from various archaeological records, it is not until the Historical/Late Historical periods, that information pertaining to religious as well as developing economic activities are available. Though no records mention the religion and religious ceremonies/festivities of the autochthones/*vratyas*, yet a glimpse of this is available from the various records pertaining to the trade and commerce of the region, as well as the religions patronised by the royalty, both of which had everlasting effects on the religion of the autochthones. Socially, the assimilation of Puranic and Buddhist ideals and principles had already prepared the ground for a certain pattern of religious beliefs in Bengal, much before.

Buddhism was formally taken as a state religion under the rule of the Pala kings. The significance of such a process was immense, as is evident from the words of N.K. Bose, as he mentioned that this act (1959:9), "gave rise in later times in Bengal to a number of unorthodox sects, in which the human body itself is treated as the mystic temple of God, which had its origin in the treatment of humanity as the highest value, in contrast to Vedic ritualdom." Through time, the religious traditions of the *vratyas* assimilated within the orthodox order of the Puranic Brahmanical religious traditions and the latter also borrowed from time-to-time from the former, giving rise to a peculiarity of beliefs in the region of study (one can refer to the established ideas of upward mobilisation, i.e., universalisation and downward mobilization i.e., parochialisation here). Known by another name the influence of Buddhism and Jainism also continued through time and found a way of expression through the folk festivals of the region. This is apparent from evidences from neighbouring regions, as mentioned by Nagendranath Vasu (intro. ccxxxiv-ccxxxv:1911) about the forest tribes of Mayurbhanj (Odisha), where he mentioned the observance of Buddhists within the forests of Gadajats, and the fact that in "18$^{th}$ century, Buddhism was not altogether a lost creed—

the much honoured memory of Buddha was not altogether a lost thing in India." (*Ibid*).

The evidence of Radha is also available from Early Historic literary examples, including Jain texts *Acharanga Sutra* and *Kalpasutra* (which mentions the region in its Prakrit form as *Radha* i.e. *Ladha* and speaks of an earlier date, when Mahavir travelled through the region, especially Subbabhumi). From these texts, mention is also found of *Ladha*, to be comprised of two specific divisions—Vajjabhumi and Subbabhumi—which might have corresponded with the present southern, western and northern parts of the Radh country. Information from these texts also mention the region as a riverine, low-lying, flood-prone terrain, which is corroborated by archaeological findings of microliths, which are seen in easy abundance in forests and along riverbanks and along hill slopes. The archaeological references of Early Historic period of the region of study suggests a possible existence of hunter-gatherers and a rather primitive farming in the high plateau and effective agriculturists in the plain—where both were integrated within a network of resource distribution, like copper and tin, which could have come only from the high plateau. This could also suggest the existence of the original inhabitants in the high plateaus and the relatively new settlers to the region in the plains. However, further studies pertaining to the same is required since the West Bengal black-and-red ware sites in the areas which also have presence of "microlith-using hunter-gatherers, does not have any specific chronological or cultural significance" (Chakrabarti, *Op.cit*: 204-205). It also suggests that the agricultural subsistence pattern of modern pre-industrial Bengal, basically goes back to this period. (*Ibid*). Thus, it can also be surmised that associated with the agrarian pattern and the mode of living, much part of the folk beliefs, rites and rituals could also have had their continuity from this time. Similarly, the evidences of the agrarian festivals mentioned in the Asokan edicts of early historic age of Dhauli and Jaugad, could also have existed at this same period. From these Rock Edicts, it was ascertained that even at the time of Asoka, there used to take place local festivals, which corresponded with the modern-day period of Tusu festival in the region. It is possible that the time the edicts were written, these harvesting festivals were already popular amidst the locals of the region (under different names) and Asoka merely mentioned this popular winter harvest festival in his composition. Asoka is also said to have popularised another festival of the region, "which included the carrying of an image or idol, pompously decorated in a two or three-storied palanquin, that was in similar popularity of *Ratha Yatra* of modern times" (Sen:1991:16-17). Significantly, it can be mentioned that these rock edicts also suggest the region of study to have possibly been under the Magadhan empire at certain points in history. Dated earlier than the Asokan rock edict of Odisha, is the Mahasthan Rock inscription, which also suggests the region of study to have been under the influence of the Magadhan empire. Closely following is the evidence of Chandravarman of 4$^{th}$ century CE of the Susunia inscription. This is significant in various ways. Not only does it offer an insight into the territorial extent of the royalty in the region and the first mention of a royal power in the region, but it also suggests the earliest reference of Vaisṇavism in the region, with Chandravarman himself being a patron of the religion.

Further evidences of the Historic period in the region of study, are also available from the writings of Chinese pilgrims, including Fa-Hien, I-Tsing, Hiuen Tsang and others. From the accounts of Fa-Hien is known the importance of Buddhism, especially in the regions of Pataliputra and Tamralipti and the rise of the port at

Saptagram, especially from the time of Late Gupta Age. The socio-religious life of contemporary times is also available that mentions the importance of Buddhism during the time of 4th to 5th century CE. Though the existing monasteries were prosperous and were sponsored by rich merchants of the time, yet the importance of individual worship of Visṇu was also popular (Sen, *Op.cit*: 46-47). This is also an important time as the beginning of 7th century also saw the rise of Sasanka in Bengal, who is ascribed to provide the earliest royal patronage towards Śaivism in the region of study. It can also be surmised that the religion of Śaivism existed even before Sasanka patronised it with a royal emblem and the folk element prevailed through history in the form of Gajan and *ban phor*, the associated ceremonies of the festival of the puja of Śiva in *Caitra Sankranti* which are also evident in recent times in the region of study.

From an understanding of local history, the period of 4th-5th and 10th century CE. was important for the formation of Indian society (Chattopadhyay,1998:1-37). However, apart from the literary evidences, the paucity of other epigraphical, historical and archaeological records of the intervening period between the Mahasthan rock edicts of Asoka and the Susunia rock inscription, till the Gupta Age, makes it difficult to weave a continuous strain of history in the region of study, especially pertaining to the local inhabitants. The copper plate grants of the Gupta Age provide certain information about local inhabitants as well as local chiefs. These speak about purchase and sale of lands, unearthed from various places in Bengal, which range between mid-5th to 7th century CE. (Majumdar, *Op.cit.*, Sen, *Op. cit.*). In the socio-cultural scenario, there was much importance accorded to local chiefs, which is known from the land grant unearthed from the village Mallasarul (Burdwan). This feature also helps to perceive the appearance of small monarchies as having "emanated from new ruling families all of which emerged into history in what may have been peripheral areas of those times. Chronologically situated within the time-frame of the suzerain rule of the Gupta monarchs, they nevertheless represented the appearance of local monarchies from somewhat unascertainable backgrounds" (Chattopadhyay, 2005:182). So, the land grants also help to understand these local chiefs, and the local populace which were under them. The significance of these local chiefs were prominent even in later times, especially in the Early medieval time onwards (which has been mentioned later in the chapter). Such an understanding of the plates as well as the presence of the local chiefs also further assist in understanding the period to be associated to an early spread of Buddhism in Bengal. Though Puranic Brahmanical religion and the court language—Sanskrit, is said to have received royal patronage, yet the religion of Buddhism also received incentive to spread its preaching. Thus, time period for the early spread of Buddhism is ascertained to be 4$^{th}$-6$^{th}$ century CE. (Sen, *Op. cit.*), which mention certain areas to be under the influence of Buddhism, like Tamralipti, Mrigsthapan in Varendrabhumi, Samatata, etc. These are corroborated from findings of various Buddha images of different materials from such places within the region of West Bengal like, Panna (Mednipur District), Biharail (Rajshahi District), Mahasthangarh (Bagura District) and other artifacts including numismatic evidences (Maynamati, Tripura District) and copper inscription of Vainyagupta (Tripura District—506-7 CE.). All these evidences testify the importance of the religion of Buddhism, corresponding with the time of the Guptas in Bengal (Datta, *Op.cit.* 119-120). It is also essential to mention the perception of the period as a time which is associated with the "process of transformation to visibility of the goddess cults" through the very prominent visibility of the Brahmanas and their rituals" (Chattopadhyaya, 2005:181-182). This is further explained by the appearance of the "cult of goddesses from disparate geographical locations and at different points in time", taking place mainly because of the linkage established between such cults and emerging monarchies through the mediation of the Brahmanas and their rituals", which has further been postulated to represent the process of "Brahmanical mode of cult appropriation" (*Ibid*: 182). Thus, supplementing archaeological records with those from history, it can be surmised that the period witnessed the gradual development of various religious traditions, alongside the prevailing animistic religion of the *vratyas*, which ran as an under-current and alongside the religion that was patronised by royalty and different vassal chiefs. Thus, at a time when Buddhism, followed by Puranic religion and the principles of Saktaism and Śaivism were making their presence felt in the region of study, the religion of the masses continued alongside, obviously with strains of communication influencing and thereby assimilating their ethnic identity. Throughout the time of the Early and Late historical periods, the religions of Jainism and Buddhism gained popularity through royal patronage, as evident from the various relics of temples and idols, which are found till date in scattered manners across the region of study and were also evident from the various villages studied under the present research. Mention may be made of Parihati in Mednipur, Pakbira in Purulia and along the Kumari-Kangsabati region of Bankura where such evidences include Radhamohanpur as well as places like Ambikanagar, Chitragiri, Paresnath, Rudra and others. All these regions provide vital information (which have been incorporated within Appendix 4 and 5 of the present work) to throw light on the surviving evidences of Jain and Buddhist influences in the region. The field-work also incorporated significant information about the survival of Puranic Brahmanical religious traditions which incorporated various folk traditions within its fold, evident from places like Garraipur, Satpatta and Kechanda. Along the Damodar region, such places included Pakhanna, Jainagar, Hatasuria, Barjora, Sarakdihi—all of which had influences of Ganga Valley due to their close proximity and the presence of a strong Puranic-Brahmanical tradition within an agro-pastoral group, projecting elements of folk tradition. Thus, Saiva influences are seen to survive under the varied names of Siva, including Sarupnarayana, Rupnarayana, Dharmaraj, etc. It is also significant to mention here the prevalence of various regions which also reflected different survival of folk/tribal traditions as well. Mention may be made of such interior places of Purulia, including Ranipukur, Bundwan, or the adjoining regions of Susunia and Chhatna as well as Koro and Dhumkoro and different regions of Mednipur like Shilda, Mohanpur, Satbati and Jhargram. All these regions also reflected significant concentration of tribal religious traditions and the representation of orthodox Brahmanism by the reduction of rigidity within the traditions of the latter. It is also important to mention that the assimilation of these thought processes with that of the local folk traditions as well as the Puranic Brahmanical traditions cannot be put into a chronological sequence as cognitive representation through history is devoid of being measured with an yardstick. Yet, the present existence and survival of several of these deities under varied folk names/Brahmanical names as well as the reduction of rigid norms of Puranic Brahmanical traditions, all suggest towards the assimilation of thought processed through time—a fact which was also evident during the course of the present field-work. Thus, the various religious traditions did not leave the *vratyas* and the folk religion of the land out of its influence, even though the significance ascribed to Buddhism gradually seemed to have reduced through time, as evident from the writings of Chinese pilgrim I-tsing (671-695 CE.), who mentioned the presence of five or six Buddhist monasteries in Tamralipta, while Hiuen-Tsang mentioned nearly ten. As such, it can be ascertained that with the intervening time of about 30 years, there was a decline in the popularity of Buddhist religion in the region under study (Sen, *Op.cit.*:61). The Early Historic period also witnessed gradually opening up to the outside world through trade contacts and making the Ganga delta a very important zone. This development is evident from various historical records pertaining to the region of study, including, such examples as, Pokharna, Dihar, Tamluk, Tildah, as well as adjoining districts and also, Bangladesh. The significance of trade and commerce also had far-reaching effects on the socio-religious beliefs of the locals.

The post-Sasanka period saw an age of anarchy in Bengal, with various small administrative units fighting for survival and in the process, trying to conquer each other's territories. From an introductory piece in an administrative document (*sashon-patter upakramanika sloka*) of 9$^{th}$ century, it is known that the region of Bengal underwent several small divisions of kingdom after the death of Sasanka, from the time of the end of 8$^{th}$ century (Sen, *Op.cit*:69). Several kingdoms were busy in conflicts and fights within themselves throughout the time period, which were finally put to rest by the election of the King Gopala, whose son Dharmapala extended the importance of Bengal in the political map of the nation in years to come. The Pala Dynasty ruled for nearly 400 years henceforth. Though there are conflicting views pertaining to the process that entailed the appointment of Gopala as the ruling king, as well as the acceptance of Buddhism as the state religion needs to be corroborated further by other facts, yet it helps to highlight the need for stability in an anarchic socio-cultural and administrative condition in Bengal, which finally saw a termination in the rise of the Pala power in the region The assimilation of the religious spheres of Brahmanical religion and Buddhism also saw incorporation of the tenets of and Saktaism finally its rise.

The Pala rulers patronised Buddhism, which was their official religion and though they also encouraged Brahmanism, yet the strains of Vaisṇavism, under the royal emblem, started decreasing from earlier times as is found in the family names of the Pala Dynasty, since after Dharmapala, some non-Vaisṇavite names (*Ibid*) are noticed On the other hand, in a natural process, the popularity of Buddhism decreased under the subsequent Sena rulers, under whom, the socio-cultural scenario saw a resurgence of Brahmanical beliefs and practices by importing Brahmans from Kanauj. Consequently, acute casteism grew. Between $6^{th}$ and $7^{th}$ century CE, heterodoxy flourished in Bengal and the Puranic Brahmanical religion was imposed later in this region by ruling dynasties. It is important to mention here that the appropriation of various religious ideas and beliefs could do little to effect and influence or eradicate the local religious traditions, including various strains of Buddhism and Jainism, which continued to exist as an under-current and suffered a lasting blow under the attack of Bhaktiar Khilji, when several of the Buddhist monasteries besides those of the Radh region suffered severe damage and destruction (Datta *Op.cit*. 119-120). The invasion of Islam had far reaching consequences on the history of Bengal. Finally, the Mughal conquest of Bengal was completed by Man Singh under Akbar. By the time of reign of Bir Hambir, the Malla ruler of Bishnupur (1591-1616 CE) the region of study saw the rise of several local kingdoms. The period of Islamic invasion also saw important changes which had further socio-cultural and religious significance, since the time after the death of Aurangzeb in 1707 till 1757, the entire region of Bengal, including the region of study, suffered through unsettled times that can be variously perceived through the division of 13 *chaklas* by Murshid Quili Khan for administrative purposes, the intrusion of the Maratha *bargees* and finally the advent of the East India Company after which the region went under Mir Qasim in 1760. These administrative changes also had their effects on the local intermediaries and money-lenders, the local chiefs and vassals, who from time and again rose against the British rule, incited by their socially and financially changed circumstances. These resentments were as part a reflection of the want of a more satisfying culture in which religion had an important role to play.

It is also necessary to mention a significant character of the medieval times—the rise of several small kingdoms between 16$^{th}$ to 18$^{th}$ centuries. This led the region to inscribe a local history of its own, under the local chiefs and rulers, who often originated from the *vratyas* and patronsied the religion of the local inhabitants, rendering a royal emblem of approval. Thus, the formation of regional societies through regional lineage showed the reciprocation of local *dharma*/beliefs. This can also be explained in the words of Chattopadhyay (*Op.cit*), as mentioned earlier regarding the early medieval society, through the Brahmanical mode of appreciation appearing as one of the prime factors in societal formation as well as development of geo-political character of the region. With a number of small principalities in the region, including, Mallabhum, Gopabhum, Sikharabhum, Dhalabhum, Tungabhum, Brahmanabhum, etc., the local history of the region gained prominence through time. In this regard, the evidence can also be identified from the *Brahmananda* section of *Bhavishya Purana* which was compiled mostly between 15th-16th century, and speaks about Varahabhumi, Manbhumi, Tungabhum and Sikhara which are identified with Barabhum pargana, Purulia and Dhanbad, Raipur *thana* in the Bankura District and Panchet, respectively. (Hitesh Ranjan Sanyal:73). The *Dharmamangal Kavyas* also speak about *Dwadash Banga* or *Baro Bhuinya*, whose presence at the time of the coronation of the king of Bengal region was important. By 15th century Islam CE, during Islamic times in Bengal, these *Baro Bhuinya's* had become considerably significant and important and the strict rule of the Mughals did little to curb them completely. Time and again, several of them had their eyes set on acquiring the entire region of Bengal, and mention may be made of Isha Khan, Kedar Ray as well as Tripura's Dhanyamanikya and Bir Hambir of Ban-Bishnupur—who all wanted to declare open revolt against the Muslim power to get considerable control over the maximum of Bengal (Sen, *Op.cit*:13-15).

Socially, the region of Bengal saw important financial activities and a flourishing trade and commerce, which also influenced the religious beliefs. Bengal being a rich region, fed by alluvial rivers and their soils, has always been an important ground for cultivation and production of various food grains, which supplemented trade and commerce. This condition had an important influence on the socio-cultural life of the people of the region as well, which also partly influenced the popular religion of the region as is evident from the architectural influences of Greco-Roman styles in Tamluk of later historical times. The above development also brings to notice the importance of trade, resulting in prosperity that induced acculturation, which in turn also influenced variously the religious beliefs, practices and traditions of the region. Though ancient textual data on Chhotanagpur are virtually non-existent, but later Vaisnava literature helps to perceive a route from Odisha to the Ganges valley across 'Jharkhand'. In 1515 CE, Chaitanyadeva, the propagator of Gaudiya Vaisnavism, travelled through Jharkhanda/ Jharkhand on way to Mathura and Vrindavan. Though these routes are likely respectively have been in use in historical period, yet the specific dates cannot be substantiated precisely due to non-availability of continuous historic data (Chakrabarti, *Op.cit*:17). It should also be noted that the region of study occupies only a part of this route of communication, but it nevertheless contributed considerably in history towards connecting important geographic regions and, in course, also influenced the development of specific religious ideas, beliefs and practices. Mention may be made here of Bankura and Mednipur, which were used for traveling variously between Kolkata and Puri, where pilgrims used to frequent Kolkata for a dip in the holy water of river Ganga. This was also the reason for the birth of various *chotis*/rest houses in the region of study, including Gangajalghati or Durlovpur *choti*. The name of Gangajalghati is ascribed to the sacred river of Ganga, which is still described in local lore, to have been carried by pilgrims from Kolkata, who used to traverse the route. A similar picture is also available from the study of the votive offerings of terracotta horses and elephants pertaining to the worship of Sini in the region of study of D.K. Bhattacharya and R.K. Chattopadhyay. This account mentioned the impetus of the flourishing trade between Magadha in the north and Utkala in the south on the cognitive bearing of the locals, which gave rise to the specific terracotta horses and elephants with reins in later years, even after the frequency of the traders reduced considerably. The picture of the horses and elephants remained as metaphorical symbols in the cognitive bearing of the locals of a flourishing time. Such evidences of terracotta horses and elephants, which are offered as votive offerings, were seen in plenty during the course of study, especially by the so-called lower classes, in form of offerings to folk deities, including Sini.

The changing social influences and the intrusion of Islam also saw the gradual development of stringent Brahmanical rules and regulations in the society on the one hand and, on the other hand, it saw the rise of different religious influences like Bhakti/Chaitanya, Sufism, the emergence of several *pirs* as well as Tantrism, including the rise of neo-Vaisnavism. The rise of Tantrism also gradually started getting reflected through various literary works, including the Devi in *Markandeya Purana*, where "she is seen as the mother who gives birth to Brahma, Visnu and Śiva" (Roy, *Op.cit*:19). It is also mentioned that the present mode of worship of the Goddess Durga is in real terms the merger of various thought processes and beliefs, as mentioned by J.N. Banerje (1966:119)—"Several concepts, both Vedic, epic, Puranic influences seems to have merged along with various thought processes to give rise to the worship of Durga in its present form." The deity, as *Sakambhari* is stated to be the goddess of corn and she is worshipped at the time when the corn and harvest is ripe. An important feature of Durga puja is the worship of *Navapatrika* or the ritual of *navapatrika-pravesa* or the worship of the nine plants, and the goddess is worshipped as the personification of vegetation spirit (Roy, *Op. cit.*). With changing social rules, new castes and classes also developed, pointing towards the rising impetus of social and religious syncretism. Apart from the four-fold divisions of Muslims— the Syeda, Mughals, Pathans and local inhabitants, new occupational groups emerged, including the Pithari (cake-seller), Kabari (fish seller) and Rangrej (cloth dyer). The time also saw a gradual increase in the process of absorption of the *vratyas* or the autochthones, considered previously as so called low castes by the Puranic Brahmanical tradition and society, which continued through time and through various changing socio-cultural and religious circumstances even through the Muslim rule. Thus, various religious thought processes, often borrowing from folk religious beliefs, merged with one another, giving rise to several divinities that gradually came to be worshipped in line with the traditional Puranic/Brahmanical deities of the society and one such important example "is that of goddess Candi, who is also referred to as non-Puranic" (Roy:20), whose folk association is corroborated through various lore and mythologies. The association of the deity to the autochthones was also evident during the course of fieldwork of the present research work, with several theriomorphic representations of the goddess worshipped in various villages as *gramadevatas*, especially by the so-called lower classes. The influence of Candi, Sitala and other goddesses reveal the importance of magical cults of Tantra on later Brahmanical life. The evidences of these religions, especially Tantra, on the folk life of Bengal is also evident from the various *rupkathas* of Bengal, where there is several mention of sages who posses magical powers and could easily 'bring alive dead people'. The availability of these tales in their transcripted form dates to a recent period of only a century ago, but they have been existing in oral traditions, through generations, reflecting the various beliefs and ideals. In a similar manner, the *bratakathas* also refer to several deities, unknown to the Puranic-Brahmanical tradition, whose modes of worship are also nontraditional, like Itu, Bonbibi, Olaichandi, Jwarasur, Maghmangal, Punyi-Pukur, etc. (*Ibid*: 21). Even in present times, the prevalence and popularity of these deities as well as the *bratakathas* reflect the popularity of these beliefs and religious traditions, which was also evident during the course of fieldwork, including the influences of Sufi as well as Tantrism. The different village deities were seen to be worshipped under varying importance, ranging from fertility deities, gods or goddesses who cure specific diseases like small pox, chicken pox, measles or diarrhoaea, or deities who are worshipped for general and overall well-being of the village. However, it is also important to mention the prominent assimilation of thought processes evident during the course of the fieldwork—ranging from Jainism, Buddhism, Vaisṇavism and Śaivism and Tantrism, with local religious traditions. These religious ideas also seem to have borrowed from time-to-time from each other and thus, in turn, they left their influences on the socio-cultural environs of the region and its inhabitants. Different examples were evident during the course of the fieldwork to suggest this aspect, including the idol of Jain Tirthankara at the temple of Dharapat (Bankura), which is at present worshipped as the village fertility deity Nangta Shyamchand Thakur. The idol bears evidence of having been transformed into an idol of Visnu from a Jain Tirthankara (with two additional hands sculpted within the background) in later times in history. In course of time, the deity is finally worshipped as a village deity. Several such evidences reflect the transformation through time, incorporating the beliefs, ceremonies and religious practices of the *vratyas*/local inhabitants within the Puranic Brahmanical rules and regulations, which dominated all norms and customs of society prevalent till then. The invasion of the Portugese and still later, the British helped to further add to the variety in the life of the inhabitants, variously reflected in myriad nature through ceremonies, rites, rituals and festivals, including certain typical stringent Brahmanical rules and regulations of the society. These are variously available from different records of English merchants and mention may be made of the accounts of

East India Company merchant Thomas Bowrey, who visited the region much before the Battle of Plassey. These accounts mention the importance of the Brahmans in socio-religious and cultural spheres, albeit seen from the eyes of a Westerner who was new to the thoughts and environs of the region. The Brahmans (spelled as *Brachmans)*, are mentioned to be respected by all, including the so-called low castes of a region. The Brahmans were especially noted for their powers of setting rules of the society, like the order of *sati.* The Brahmans of Bengal region were also regarded as being "great students on the magic art", and make their "sorceries more apparent than they of any other kingdom in Asia." They were also regarded as the ones with knowledge, being "Reputed to be very wise philosophers and with great zeal study the Pithagorean Philosophy. They are alsoe great students in the art of Poyson soe much in esteem among the Eastern inhabitants. In fine, they are reverenced by the common natives more like Gods than men." (Temple:204-205). In this respect, Bowrey also mentioned the worship of the locals, mostly supported by the Brahmans of the society as well. Bowrey observed Bengal being the home of "Bengalas—the idolatrous people of the countrey, having very strange ways of worshipping their Gods (or rather Devils) which they set up in their Pagodas, as also in their own houses, images are mostly of hideous shape that these poor ignorant souls doe soe much deifie, and torture theire owne persons for the silly humors they hold of adoreinge them, one of which was the festival of Gajan." 'Bowrey's accounts, like many accounts from colonial times, penned by the colonials, have to be analysed carefully as the objectification and representation of local culture often take a distorted platform, as analysed through colonial and tainted eyes. Nevertheless, Bowrey's accounts, upto a certain extent, can help to ascertain the importance of the segmented social order and the ethnic worship of various deities in the region in the late medieval ages, which had the acceptance as well as the consent of the rigid Brahmanical society. A similar picture of a rigidly partitioned society is also mentioned in the *Mangal Kavyas* of medieval times. Varna Ratnakara of Mithila, in the medieval times, speaks of *bhadra* and *mand jatis* amidst Brahmanical religion There is no mention of any Kshatriyas or substantial Rajput castes and even after the Muslim conquests, the Kayasthas are recognised as semi-independent chiefs, called as *bhuinyas* who ruled over 12 kingdoms, as mentioned above.

Finally, it is also important to mention the close bond that existed between the local inhabitants with the local chiefs, especially with the gradual increase and spread of pluralism from the time of the intrusion of Islam in the region and thereafter the Portugese and the British, binding the independent and semi-independent principalities and the locals together. With particular socio-cultural traits, their sense of homogeneity helped them to bind themselves together inspite of the spread of such religious thought processes like Jainism, Buddhism and Tantric influences, Brahmanism, Śaivism or Saktaism and also the liberal Bhakti cult. The cultural interactions changed the beliefs and practices of the people to a certain extent and also the cultural life of the original inhabitants, resulting in the important survival of folk and mainstream religion within the same milieu. Thus, several of the erstwhile idols of religions like Jainism, Buddhism or the different facets of Brahmanism survived through time in the folk religion of the region of study in a transformed manner, and in the present area of study, several Jain and Buddhist idols of possible deities and Tirthankaras were observed to be worshipped as different folk gods and goddesses, including Dharmaraj/ Yama, Bhairab, Manasa, Candi, Sini, Sitala and others. A similar fact of the association and subsequent survival of Jainism was also echoed by Dr. Roy as he spoke about the association of Jain idols with the folk culture of the region that left a long-lasting impression on the local religion, but it is always the association with the folk religion that stands as an important character of the idols in recent times, which was also variously evident during the course of fieldwork from all the three districts of study. Thus, the patronised religion by the royalty often differed from the popular beliefs of the locals/*vratyas*; yet, the folk ceremonies, festivals and religious ideals survived as an under-current throughout history and often merged with the former. Interestingly enough, these folk beliefs seemed to have survived with or without royal patronage and are reflected in present times through such evidences of the local royalty of Bishnupur, Hadalnarayanpur, Jaykrisnanagar, Jamkuri, Panchkot, etc. Though various gods and goddesses exist as their family deities, yet their association and patronage of local Gajan/ Charak, Manasa puja, Dharmaraj or Sini puja is evident even in modern times. A similar trend also continued with the *bratas* of the region, including Tusu, Bhadu and others, which could have received the involvement of local chiefs from time-to-time, but never depended on a royal order to appropriate their significance and existence. Handed down through generations, these beliefs survived through time through cognitive representation of human civilization, which rendered the region its specific cultural ethos. Beliefs and rituals, especially in peasant societies need to be viewed as a part of a larger ideological order, and the religious traditions, especially in peasant societies, bind them to the larger social order. McKim Marriot (1955) explained how two processes of explanation and ritual action exist side by side, interpenetrating and complimenting each other. The assimilation process can also be viewed as a two way procedure, explained by Redfield's mention of the Great Tradition and the Little Tradition of which the former can be explained by so-called Pan Indian Sanskritic Puranic religion, and the latter is considered to possess the beliefs and practices commonly obtained among Indian peasant societies. Such processes of assimilation of ideas can also be further elaborated from the explanations of universalisation and parochialisation of Marriot, where by the former he meant a downward devolution of the elements of the Greater Tradition and its integration with elements of the Little Tradition and by the latter, he meant a process of localisation, of limitation upon the scope of intelligibility, of deprivation of literary form and reduction to less systematic and less reflective dimensions. At the same time, much part of these approaches and their understandings are outdated at present and border on measures, which are no longer acceptable to communicate ideas and ideologies as they rather segregate many marginalised voices in isolation, which in no way can be ascertained through lesser or greater perspectives. It is also important to keep in mind that this explains a rather colonial picture of understanding socio-cultural changes and is also cliched and outdated in respect to recent theories and assessments of anthropology, it is also important to understand that while these two processes are operative, there are new traditions being built on accounts of influences from outside of a specific geographical region or location. Regarding this aspect mention may be made of the development of economic activities, trade and commerce too, which finally lend the region of study, its specific socio-cultural and religious character. Socially, the assimilation of Brahmanical and Buddhist ideals and principles had already prepared the ground for a certain pattern of religious beliefs in Bengal, much before Buddhism was formally taken as a state religion under the rule of the Pala kings. This early spread of the religion can be attributed to trade activities. These two religious orders also are significantly important in the life of Bengal, as well as the region of study as "In these two religious systems, there is a moral approach to the problems of life by their emphasis on the primacy of human spirit" (Roy:102-103). Thus, the various religious sects assimilated within the folds of the broader purview of folk culture give rise to several local ceremonies, fairs, rites and rituals, which complimented and supplemented the broader picture to render a discrete character to the region of study.

Though tentative and suggestive, yet as a concluding remark, it should also be mentioned that this study is an initial attempt to comprehend these many processes concerning local festivals, *melas* and ceremonies and would benefit significantly from various future researches pertaining to the understanding of a continuous process of historical development of religious ideas through archaeological assemblages, as well as the continuous development of socio-cultural elements including settlement patterns, royal patronages and geographical boundaries in reference to local festivals. The fieldwork undertaken, though not an exhaustive one, was intensive in nature and could have benefitted if the region was not facing a serious social crisis due to political reasons which hampered much of the process of the collection of data from various villages, especially Purulia and West Mednipur. Nevertheless, the data gathered with much effort and provided within the present research paper, attempts to represent a scenario of village and rural communities, which have undergone important processes of assimilation of thought processes and ideas, rendering them a distinct identity. Traversing several historical processes, prompted by socio-economic needs, this activity brought many of them to a lasting assimilation scene and slowly initiated a steady process of interaction in various ways, thereby exposing them to many transformational conditions.

# Appendices

## Appendix 1

A brief preview of various population groups and their specific ceremonies, seen prominent in the region of study (After K.S. Singh ed. People of India series Vol. XXXXIII).

### Bagdi

They are an indigenous agrarian community of the scheduled caste category of West Bengal, also known by the synonym of *Byagrakshatriya*. They have such titles like Roy, Mullick, Tentule, Kushmete, Kansaikule and Duley. According to Mitra from *Brahmavaivarta Purana*, it is known that they originated from a Kshatriya father and Vaishya mother. In recent times, several are landless agriculturists and some are also share-croppers. Several are also involved in other daily-wage activities like rickshaw pulling, masonry, etc. They worship Nabagraha, Kula Candi and others. Important festivals of the Bagdi include Manasa puja, apart from the mainstream Puranic festivals like Durga puja and Gajan.

### Baidya

They use such titles like Roy, Chowdhury. The very word 'Baidya' is a Sanskrit term denoting a medical practitioner. They refer to two social divisions- Kulin and Bhanga and two geographical divisions-Rarhi and Barendra. Several legends surround about their migration history. According to some, they came from Karnataka as physicians, while others say, they came to India from Nepal or Tibet as Buddhist Sraman and served people as medical practitioners. Traditionally physicians, with the spread of education, several have also shifted to other occupations like- business, service, etc. and many also have agricultural lands as well. Their major concentration is in the plains of West Bengal. Traditionally they are considered all as so-called low castes apart from the Brahmans. They belong to the Vaisnava, Sakta or Saiva sects of the Puranic religion. At the family level, they worship Lakshmi, Madangopal, Satima, etc. Kali and Siva are their village deities Narahari thakur and Gouranga Mahaprabhu are their regional deities

**Bairagi**

The sub-group Ramayut or Ramanujis and Acharya can be seen in Jhalda and Bagmundi Police Stations of Purulia. Their family deities are Lakshmi, Radha-Gobindo and Manasa. Their village deities are also Radha-Gobindo and worship takes place on the day of Gour Paurnima and again in the month of Vaisakha (April-May) for three days. Apart from the festivals of the mainstream Puranic Gods and Goddess, they also celebrate Jita Ashtami, Radha Ashtami, Paus Parban, Sital Sasti, etc. For them, important fairs include the one in Ayodhya Hills on Ram Navami, Harup mela in the month of *Jaishthya* (May-June), Sati mela, Satighat mela and Parsa mela.

**Baishya**

A small community of West Bengal, Bashhi is their synonym. They use such surnames like Deshmukh, Senapati, Layek, Mallick, Thakur, Haldar, Poira, etc. The term is derived from the word Vaishya or trader. They claim to have come from Maharashtra with Bhaskar Pandit of the Bargees and their surnames- Deshmukh and Senapati also prove this. Some are followers of Saivism, Saktaim and also Vaishnavism. Thus, they worship all important

Puranic deities and attend all fairs and festivals related to the worship of these Gods and Goddesses.

**Bajkar**

They are a semi-nomadic Muslim community with the synonym of Bejkar and the entire nomadic and semi-nomadic group is referred to as Gulgulia by the locals of Purulia and Bankura. They are found in Purulia, Bankura, Mednipur and Burdwan. Participate in the *Jumma namaj* on Fridays only. They go to the *Pirer mela* at Dishergarh in the month of *Pausa*.

**Bauri**

They are amongst the earliest settlers of Mednipur, Bankura, Birbhum and Howrah. They are the original priests of Dharmaraj or Dharam deity- a vestige of the early mixed Jin-Buddhist cult of Bihar and Bengal. Later, after the rise of Brahmanical supremacy and Muslim rulers, they were pushed to the so-called lower rungs of the existing Brahmanical *jati-varna* hierarchy as untouchables. A landless community, they are mostly engaged as rickshaw-pullers and manual workers or share-croppers. They worship such deities as Rankini, Baram, Sitala and Manasa. Their festivals include Tusu, Bandna and Karam.

**Bedia**

They are considered as untouchables or *jalachal* by most so-called higher castes like Brahmans, Karmas, Vaisnavas, Benes, Khandaits, Tambolis and Sunris, but are treated as equal by others. They are landless marginal farmers and cultivation is their main occupation, but they also work as wage labourers in the fields of rich peasants and also sell leaves from forests. They observe Karam, Jita, Dhangra, Sarhul, Bandna and Tusu and worship Kudra, Bhan Singh, Ind, Garam, Barpahar, Baghut, Kali, Manasa, Mahadani,

Burha Burhi and Dharam puja, apart from attending and observing the pujas of traditional Puranic Gods and Goddesses.

**Bhumij**

Listed under the scheduled tribe list of the Indian constitution, etymologically they are referred to as the sons of the soil. They mostly still live by working as wage-labourers in agricultural fields and several still ensnare birds and animals from jungles. They worship Baram, Dharam (god of righteousness), Singbonga and Jahuburu. The Bhumij's also observe important festivals, like Bandna, Tusu and Karam.

**Birhor**

Their traditional occupation includes collecting tihore fibre and all family members make ropes from tihore. They also collect wood for fuel and catch wild animals. The religion of the Birhors reflects aniministoc worship. Their deities include- Singbonga, Lagu Haram Burima apart from several big and small deities throughout the year.

**Brahman**

The most common synonyms are Bamun, Dwija, Thakur, Dev-Sharma, Pandit and Masoi and also Baman, Sarma, Bhudana, Bhusur, Agraja, Dwija, Maharajji, Badaji and Goasinji (Risley). Most of them are quite well educated and well placed in life. They follow Puranic religion and worship Lakshmi, Narayan and Siva as their family and main deities. Village deities are Kali, Panchanan, as well as Manasa and Sitala. Their important socio-religious ceremonies include- Itu, Kulimongolbar, Joymongolbar, Bipadtarini, Sitala Sashti, Chapra Sashti, Asoke Sashti, Nil Soni puja or Baralha Kumer puja, Jamai Sashti, Vishwakarma puja, Durga Ashtami and Sashti, Bhagabati puja, Ghara (watering the tulsi plant in Vaisakha), Bastu puja and Boubhojan.

**Chitrakar**

They belong to the list of Other Backward Classes (OBC) category and are a caste of *patuas* of West Bengal. They are landless and their traditional occupation included painting and the most important profession was *chitra prodarshan* (exhibiting painted scrolls for money) which are miniature paintings on cloth or paper, depicting stories from the Ramayana and Manasa Mangal Kavya. However, in recent times, they are also seen to do other jobs as daily wage-labourers and in government offices or schools. They are also adept in making earthen dolls, like *hingul-putul, jo-putul* and *sashti-putul* and earthen decorated pots or *gatha-chitra* and Lakshmi-pat. The religion of the Chitrakars portrays an important feature of two simultaneous religions occupying same space of performance and existing within the same social paraphernalia without a scuffle. They obey Qazi and Islamic rules and yet worship Puranic gods and goddesses. Thus they consider themselves as traditionally belonging to Brahmanical religion, but it is interesting to note that they possess two names- one is Hindu and another is Mohameddan. They follow the customs and rituals of both the religions as well. They worship all major Brahmanical gods and goddesses and consider all important Brahmanical sacred places as sacrosanct with the same fervor as they observe the daily *namaz* or observe Islamic festivals.

**Dandachhatra Majhi**

Their community name is Dandachhatra Majhi and they do not have any sub-groups. They are mostly landless labourers and marginal farmers and at times work as agricultural labourers apart from selling ropes and *sabui* and *babui* grass. They used to worship the forest deities under the feudal chiefs of Mayurbhanj. Their household deity includes Mangala Thakur, which is common to all.

They observe the Bandna festival and also the Rajja *Parab* and apart from taking part and observing all major Puranic mainstream ceremonies and festivals, they also worship Manasa, Brahmi and Barun.

**Deshwali Majhi**

Listed under the scheduled tribe list, they have an oral tradition that mentions the term Deshwali Majhi to have appeared out of the Santals from after the Santal rebellion of 1855-56 (Mahto:378). Mostly marginal farmers and landless labourers, they work for wages and are mostly self-employed workers or brick-kiln workers. They also sell dishes and plates made of stone and *chira*. Amongst their important festivals is the annual hunting festival- Disum Sindra in the Ayodhya hills of Purulia, only limited to the men and young boys. Girls take part in the Chata *Parab* of Chakoltor of Purulia. They mostly worship elements of tribal religion- nature, trees, stones, etc. and their major deities include, Baghut, Jhira, Kudra, Ghar-Kudra, Dara-garha, Bachchi-Burhi, Barpahar, Basant Kumari, Bankumari, Maghai, Charkasini, Rangahari, Bisai Candi, Goroya-Jita, Tusu, Karam, Jantal and Sarhul.

**Dhoba**

They are the washerman community of West Bengal and are of the status of the scheduled caste in the state. Mostly landless agricultural labourers, they worship all conventional Puranic deities as well.

**Dusadh**

An educationally backward class, they were traditionally the original settlers of this land, especially of Manbhum area of Purulia district and are now found mainly in the Sonathali, Pokaband, Para, Kinutar and Gahyra villages of Purulia district. They worship Kudra, Babu Thakur, Gram,

Hari, Panchbahini and Satbahini, Tangi-Tanga and Baram. Their festivals are Tusu, Karam, Jawa, Jita, Ind, Chata, Sarhui, Ashari and Rohan. They also observe the Bandna and Karam rituals.

**Gandhabanik**

They are a business community of West Bengal, having such surnames like- Gandhabania, Putuli Bene and Bania. They carry such surnames like Samajbandhu, Roybahadur, Baisyaratna and Kabisekhar. They hold an important festival on *Pausa Sankranti* and observe a *parab* and make *pithas* (cakes prepared from rice, molasses and coconut), *payesh-* not only for the family but also visitors as well. Gandeshwari Mata is their *kuladevata*.

**Ghasi**

Ghasis are a scheduled caste community. The Bhumij tribal chiefs of Bagmundi, Jhalda and Begun-Kodars brought them from Chhotanagpur areas of Bihar to work as midwives. They are also called as Machaowar. The community follows folk religion, including Manasa and Sitala, they also worship Rajapokhar, who is the lineage protector god. They also worship Kudra, Baba Thakur, Garam Hari, Panchbahini, Satbahini, Tangitanga and Baram. Their festivals are Tusu, Karam, Jawa, Jita, Ind, Chata, Sarhul, Asharia and Rohan.

Listed under the scheduled tribe list of the Indian constitution, they have synonyms like Kol, Larka Kolh, etc. They worship Singbonga, Gurubonga as their gods and also organise Baram and Karm pujas. They follow such festivals like Tusu, Karam, Bandna and Pausa mela, etc. They do not have any specific songs, dances or handicraft, but have a number of folktales and folklores that speak about their origin. They have a folklore describing the creation of the worlds.

### Jalia-Kaibarta

They are a fishing caste of West Bengal, having several synonyms like Jele, Jalo, Jalia, Jali, etc. Amongst their pujas, Ganga, Satyanarayan and Mahakal are especially important since Mahakal puja is organised at the time they move out in the high seas for fishing and Satyanarayan puja is performed after they return to their abode after fishing in the seas. An important festival is the Jalpai festival or the laying of the net, which begins on the first of *Magha* (January-February). They also worship the Gram devata and Bura-Buri. The Brahman priest performs religious functions for them. Many members of the community have taken to Vaishnavism and often perform *Harinaam Sankirtan.*

### Kalu

They are a community belonging to OBC in Bengal, engaged in extraction of oil from seeds, which was also their traditional business. Now several are also engaged in agriculture and grocery and other works. They do not exude any separate identity of their own in the sphere of religious beliefs. Several have adopted Vaishnavism, Saktaism as well as Vaishnavism.

### Kamar

The Kamars belong to OBC category in West Bengal and is a cast who work with metals. They are also known as Karmakars. They follow Vaishnavism and also Saktaism. Their family deity is Vishwakarma, worshipped on the last day of *Badra* with offerings of sweet, parched rice, fruits, flowers, sandalwood paste and water from Ganga, clothes and silver ornaments.

### Kayastha

They are referred to as the writer caste of Bengal and have such synonyms like Kaet, Kayath, Kaya and Kastha.

The *Yajnavalka* gives an account of their origin, which says that they were writers and village accountants. King Ballal Sen is said to have divided the Kayasthas into four subcastes according to their places of residence, i.e. Uttar Radhi, Dakshin Radhi, Bangaja and Barendra. Religionwise, they do not portray any different characteristic features, but the same as is present in neighbouring classes who also profess Brahmanical religion, including ceremonies, fairs and festivals. The Brahman priest performs their rites and rituals.

**Kharia (Hill)**

A recognised scheduled tribe in the state, they live in West Bengal (mostly Purulia and also in Mednipur and Bankura), Odisha (in Mayurbhanj district) and in Bihar (Singhbhum and Dhalbhum districts). Each family has its own spirit and the locality were a particular group resides also has its own spirit that acts as a guardian angel. The forest is ruled by several spirits and their food supply is guarded by a female spirit- Bankumari.

**Kumhar**

With a constitutional status of another backward class, they are a potter community and have such synonyms like- Kumar, Kumbhakar, Rudra Pal and Kumore. They worship Sashti, Agni, Brahma, Indra and Pavana. On the first day of *Jaistya*, special services are held by them at the same time, when the festival of Vishwakarma is held. They have the Khamar puja in *Pausa*, when fresh paddy is brought into the house, and also the *Caitra-Sankranti* puja.

**Lodha**

Under the Indian Constitution, they are considered as Primitive Tribal Group (PTG) and are listed under the scheduled tribes list since 1956, before which they were a scheduled caste. Unfortunately, age-old government data referred them as a criminal tribe, owing its origin to the epic literature, Savara. They have such village deities like- Garam, Baram, Sitala, Candi and Yugini. All are propitiated with animal sacrifices by a special person who helps the priest in performing these rituals. They have their own music, dance, folklore and riddles.

**Lohar**

They claim to have been originally Karmakars who were ostracised due to overindulgence in liquor. They do not have any special art or craft to their credit and claim to have an aesthetic touch in the weaving of fishing nets and kanthas which women sew.

**Mahishya**

They are a landowner and cultivator class and have the status of clean Sudras in the *varna* order (Bhowmick:827). They are also sometimes equated with Kaivartyas, which is a generic geographical term signifying a group living in water-logged areas as *ke* means water. Though traditionally a landowning and cultivator class, they also at times, work as wage-labourers. They worship all Puranic gods and goddess, along with local ones. Several have also adopted Vaishnavism.

**Malhar**

They are locally called as Dokras or Dhokras and they call themselves Malhars or Marals. Migrated from Odisha and Bastar, they are said to have settled in Bankura, Burdwan, Mednipur districts of West Bengal, Gaya district of Bihar and Bastar district of Madhya Pradesh and also in some parts of Odisha. Apart from taking part in and worshipping all important Puranic deities, they worship the *Siva-tala* and the *Raksha Kali-tala* as their sacred centres of worship. They also perform the Vishwakarma puja.

**Marwari**

They are the community who are said to have migrated from Rajasthan. They have sub-groups based on occupation as well as their region of origin in Rajasthan like, Srimali (Brahman by caste and name is derived from Srimal in Rajasthan), Rajput (Kshatriya by caste), Oswal (Vaishya by caste), Pushkarna (derived from lake Pushkar in Ajmer), Parikh, Maheshwari (they believe Lord Siva or Maheshwar was their ancestor) and Agrawala (believed to be the descendents of king Agrasena). They profess Brahmanical religion however there are many who have adopted Jainism.

**Mayara**

A caste of sweetmakers of West Bengal and have such synonyms like Modak, Madak and Madhunapit. They consider the worship of Tulsi, Lakshmi and Narayan as important. They open the *hal-khata* on the *Poila*-Vaisakha day. Their village deities are Raksha Kali, Kalachand, Dharmaraj and Manasa.

**Mete**

They are considered as autochthones of the region and are said to have been formed from the *mati* or soil of his body and thus, the name. They are a fishing community and have such synonyms like- Metia and Malla Bagdi and claim to be a branch of Bagdi. Traditionally, they are fishermen and women, however, they also work in agrarian fields.

Manasa puja, is performed by local priest *deghure* and she is worshipped on *Sravana-Sankranti* and *Manasa-tala* is an important sacred place in the village. They also observe the Dharmarajer mela and Gajaner mela.

### Muchi

They have such surnames like- Ruidas, Chamar, Das, Charmakar, Rishi and Rabidas. They worship Lakshmi, Narayana, Gopinath and Tulsi as family deities, apart from worshipping traditional Puranic mainstream deities and Didima or Sitalama as regional deities.

### Mundas

They are a well known tribe of West Bengal and are listed in the scheduled tribe list. They have various sub groups, including Kharia, Majhi, Kol, Bhumij, Mahali, Nagbangshi, Savar and Manki. Their festivals include- Dhuria puja, performed in May-June for rains, Ashari in July to make agricultural operations trouble-free and for better crop, Karam in August and Garam in January, Sitala in February, Bandna *parab*, in October-November, which is a cattle caressing festival and Shirur in March or April. They also have a rich tradition of folk songs and lores and both men and women take part in festivals.

### Napit

Counted amongst Other Backward Class in the state, they are a *nabasakha* group of West Bengal.Their family deities are Damodar, Lakshmi and Sashti and regional deities are Sitala, Basundhara, Siva, Mahamaya, Hari, etc. Some also observe Viswakarma puja.

### Oraon

Though they are found all over the state and are included in the list of scheduled tribe. Their major concentration is in the areas of Jalpaiguri and the western fringes of the state, including Mednipur, Purulia and Bankura and also in Sundarbans and adjoining 24 Parganas. They profess faith in tribal religion as well as Brahmanical religion and in most rites and rituals, the priest from their locality- *pahan* presides over matters. Their main deity is Dharma- who is the supreme one. They also believe in other spirits like- Chala, Pacho, Kalmai or Candi. Sarnaburia or spirit of the sacred bush, Mahadania bunga, Devi Mai, Gaon-deoti, Bir-belas, Cando-belas, Bura Buri, Panch balar, etc. Their important festivals are- Sarhul, Karma, Phagu, Sohurai, Dussehra, Asri, Nawakhani, etc. They also offer *Harir loot* (offer in the name of Hari).

**Oriya**

The name of the community if Oriya and synonyms are Odra and Uriya. They are mostly agriculturists and marginal farmers. In recent times, they are also seen to be engaged in other occupations like, chef, carpentry, vegetable and fruit selling, etc. Some even work as industrial labourers. They worship Baram, Rankini, Siva, Durga, Kali, Kothari, Radhakrishna, Gramthan, Kalnagini, Manasa, etc. They sing Tusu, Bhadu, Karam, Jhumur songs and participate in Bandna, Jitua, Sarhul festivals.

**Rajput**

The community is also known by its synonyms like- Rajput Khatriya, Chhatri or Chhetri. Traditionally a landholding caste, in recent times, they also are engaged in jobs in governmental and non-governmental offices. Professing Brahmanical religion, they worship, apart from other deities, Shani on Saturdays, called as *Barathakurerbaar,* Bipadtarini, Itu, Kali, Mangal Candi, Sibratri, etc. They also worship Sitala and Manasa.

**Rajput Solanki**

They were traditionally landowners and landed aristocrats of the Kshtariya order. They profess Brahmanical religion but do not have any specific separate features pertaining to their rites and rituals, apart from the worship of Siva, by the name of Kedareshwar or Chapaleshwar, which is of importance to them.

**Rajwar**

Inhabiting the Chhotanagpur plateau, and listed under the list of scheduled caste, they live in the three states of Bengal (found in mainly Purulia, apart from Bankura, Birbhum and Mednipur), Bihar (found in Singbhum and Ranchi districts) and Odisha (found in Banai, Gangpur, Jashpur, Sarguja, Udaipur, etc). Though professing Puranic religion, they worship and follow all rituals common to the district of Purulia, like Bandna, Jita, Bhadu, Tusu, Gajan, Rohin, etc. Barhula puja is done on the last day of *Magha* (January-February). On Rohin puja, they do ancestor worship. They dance the Chho and also sing Bhadu and Tusu.

**Savar/Sabar**

They are a community of snake charmers. They also have their own local spirits who needs propitiation for peace and prosperity. Their oral traditions are stories, mainly borrowed from *Manasa Mangal* text and almost always focus on Behula and Lakhindar. These songs are sung at the time of snake charming.

**Sadgop**

They are a cultivating class of West Bengal, having such surnames like, Sarkar, Roy, Mondal, etc. They claim descendant from Gopala of the Pala dynasty. They are mostly a landed class and do agriculture. In recent times, many are also seen to have other occupations like business, wage-labourer, etc. They are mostly found in the districts of Burdwan, Hooghly, Bankura, Birbhum, Mednipur, 24 Parganas and Murshidabad. They are mainly Vaisnavas and also Saktas and worship Hari, Narayan and Lakshmi.

They attend Dharmaraj and Gajan pirer mela. They have the Brahman as their priest.

**Sahis**

They claim to have their origin in some Maratha stock who visited Bengal to look after horses of the then kings. They slowly settled in the villages and assimilated within the cultures. Their main festivals include the cattle-caressing festival or Bandna and also Tusu.

**Sankhakara**

They are mainly a landless community, however, many also practice agriculture. They are mainly found in Bankura, Hooghly, Kolkata, Burdwan, Nadia, Birbhum and 24 Parganas. They worship all deities of Puranic pantheon. Agastya muni is their family deity and a puja is done on $28^{th}$ of *Badra*, which is important for them.

**Santal**

Their highest concentration is in the Rajmahal hills and the neighbouring areas. Their major concentration in West Bengal is in Mednipur. They are a migratory community. (Bhattacharya) They speak the Santali language- a non-Aryan, Austro-Asiatic family of language, related to the Mundari group of languages. They profess tribal religion/ animism. The gods they worship are represented in nature, like mountain, trees and stones. It is believed that *Thakur jiu* or the creator, created all and everything on earth, including them. The lesser god or *Mararan buru*, meaning big mountain, acting as the behest of the *Thakur jiu*, guided the Santals in their journey to find their own land.

**Swarnakar**

Their traditional occupation is working with gold and silver. Though they own lands and some do agriculture, yet making jewelleries, etc. is their primary occupation. They also lend money sometimes. Several of them have accepted Vaishnavism and they also worship Vishwakarma. The art of jewellery-making is a distinctive craft of the caste.

**Tambuli**

They are a landowning community and most of them are agriculturists, but in recent items, several have taken to various business occupations, including selling groceries and other such items. Most of the Tambulis are Vaisnavas and a few are worshippers of Sakti and Siva. Dharmaraj is an important deity of the village and the Gopal and Pirtala are sacred centers within the village.

**Tanti**

They are also known as Tantubaya and the name '*tantu*' means natural fibre or *ansh*. They are both a landowning and landless community and many have left the profession of weaving and taken to agriculture. They profess Puranic religion. The Aswini Tantis perform *kulo pujo*- which is a tribute to the family deity- Siva. The Purandari Tantis worship Vishwakarma as they consider themselves as an artisan class.

**Tili**

They are an oil trading community of Bengal and constitutionally belong to Other Backward Classes categories. Cultivation is their main source of income and several have their own lands. There are still others who are seen to work as wage labourers or in grocery shops. Several of the Tantis have adopted Vaishnavism and have Narayan, Tulsi and Lakshmi as their family deities and have a Tulsi plant in their courtyards. They also worship Sankhani Manasa (to save from snake bites), Dharmaraj (to save the villagers from cholera) and Didithakurun.

# Appendix 2

Brief account of the database so far published of excavations that correspond to the region of study, especially to the Early Village Farming period. (after-Chattopadhyay, R.K. *et al.*2007). There are as many as twenty excavated sites bearing traces of BRW occupation in varying geographical niches. Of the many sites described below, Dihar and Pakhanna experienced fresh excavations recently. The overall view of the sites corresponding to the region of study include-

| Hat Ikra | Charul | Pakhanna |
|---|---|---|
| (23$^{0}$49/25//N/87035/42//E) situated on the left bank of river Bakreswar which flows about 1km west of the present village. On behalf of the Dept of Ancient Indian History, Culture and Archaeology, Visva Bharati University, N.C. Ghosh and A.K. Nag excavated the site in 1985-86. The total occupation deposit of the excavated mound of Hat Ikra has been divided into two periods, i.e. 'Chalcolithic' and 'Ferro- Chalcolithic'. While the IAR (IAR 1986-87: 94) report claims that a maximum deposit of 2.40m has been revealed at Hat Ikra, the Puratatttva report (Ghosh and Nag 1984-85: 117) suggests | The Directorate of Archaeology and Museums, Govt. of West Bengal has conducted trial diggings at Charul (23030/N/88015/E) in the year 2003. The site is located on the Brahmani in the Katwa subdivision. Sporadic occurrence of BRW has been reported at a depth between 1.20 and 2.00m.<br>**Dihar**<br>(23007/10//N/87021/) is situated on the left bank of river Dwarakeswar in Bankura district, Police Station Bishnupur, about 6 km north of Bishnupur town. | (23 24 45 N/87 22 40 E) is situated on the southern bank of Damodar, in the Barjora Police Station of the district of Bankura. The site was excavated by the Dept. of Archaeology, University of Calcutta, under the general supervision of. Chitrarekha Gupta, A.C. Pal, M. Mitra, A. Datta and R.K. Chattopadhyay from 1996-97 to 1999-2000 and again in 2001-02. Five main areas, viz. Bhairabdanga, Satbardanga, Garer-danga, Itapara and Kalyanpur were excavated, of which only Bhairabdanga and Satbardanga have yielded evidence of |

that it is a 2.55m thick deposit. The Chalcolithic period at the site is about 78cm thick on average and has a maximum thickness of 1.30m. Only one $C^{14}$ date, 2950̃120 (1000 BCE) from the beginning of Period II, is available from Hat Ikra.

### Tulsipur

(22 56N 86 46 25"E), located on the right bank of river Kangsavati below its confluence with the Kumari near Kangsavati reservoir. Chakrabarti (Chakrabarti 1993: 130) estimated size of 1 acre for the site. Before her excavation at the site in 1967-68, J. Birmingham (University of Sydney in collaboration with the Eastern Circle of ASI) explored extensively the region near Tulsipur-Ambikanagar (IAR 1965-66: 57- 8) and identified site as a BRW bearing one.- but no detailed report (Birmingham 1972: 1-23), but ceramic assemblages study in details. Further exploration at the site by R.K. Chattopadhyay (Chattopadhyay 1989: 171-3) at the site has revealed the occurrence of coarse BRW representing the shapes like angular shallow bowl, red ware, fine textured grey ware and a good number of late historic red slipped ware.

The site was excavated twice for the first time from 1983-84 to 1984-85 and for the second time from 1990-91 to 1994-95 by the Dept.of Archaeology, University of Calcutta under the general supervision of A.C. Pal (Pal 1992: 101-6). The total cultural deposit of the site is divided by the excavator into two broad Periods viz. Chalcolithic and Early historic. Since both painted and plain BRW occur together at Dihar, the excavator believed that the occupation belonged to a comparatively late Chalcolithic horizon. The site has also been recently excavated by the same department in the field sessions of 2008-2009. Technologically, the neoliths of Dihar are all well developed and show remarkable chipping-pecking and polishing. (after Chattopadhyay et al. 2009:84-86)

EVF occupation. The site is highly disturbed in context due to continued human intervention and modern settlement growth. Regular fluvial activities of the Damodar have also acted as a major element of destruction. However, both the Bhairabdangaand Satbardanga area have yielded the evidence of EVF phase of culture (IAR 1996-97:177-8, 1997-98:200-3). The 2001-02 excavation on the mound of Bhairabdanga confirmed the earlier finds. On the basis of the plant remains collected from the site, the Chalcolithic level of Pakhanna has been dated to 3320̃400 years BP (Ghosh et. al. 2005: 221-32).

| Sijua | Moghalmari |
|---|---|
| ($23^0 37^/$N/$88^0 02^/$E) is a small village located on the left bank of Kasai or Kangsabati near Bamal, the famous 'Neolithic' site of Medinipur district. It is about 7 km from Ramgarh. The site is located within an undulating landscape near the modern village of the same name but outside it. Test diggings at the site by the Directorate of Archaeology and Museums, Government of West Bengal, revealed the existence of Chalcolithic Culture at the site. The mound has been irretrievably damaged by regular erosion. The total occupational deposit of the site measures 1.50m and is divided into two distinct periods: Period I: Chalcolithic; Period II: Early historic. | ($21^0 57^/$N/$87^0 16^/$E) is located in the district of Paschim [West] Medinipur, in the Police Station of Dantan. The site is located on the left bank of the Subarnarekha about 5.4km north of Dantan town. The site was excavated by the Dept. of Archaeology, University of Calcutta, under the direction of Asok Datta in the field seasons of 2003-04 and 2006-07 to identify the proper location of ancient Danda bhukti (Datta: 2004) and resulted into a twofold cultural sequence from 'Chalcolithic' to an early mediaeval. The Chalcolithic remains were found at a locality called MGM 2 and is represented by a deposit of 1.48m.The main pottery types discovered from the Chalcolithic period were BRW (both plain and painted varieties), red ware, black-on-red ware and black ware. Major shapes in pottery type included bowls, basins and handi along with different types of vessels. |

# Appendix 3

The following are excavated sites of early village farming settlements in adjoining areas of the region of study, corresponding to the BRW culture period. This information is also from available published data. In order to understand the cultural pattern of the region, the following is an attempt to bring to notice a holistic picture.

| Tamluk | Kotasur | Haraipur |
|---|---|---|
| ($22^0 22'$N/$87^0 55'$E) is situated on the right bank of river Rupnarayan in Purva [East] Medinipur district. The site was excavated twice: first by M.N. Deshpande of the Eastern circle of ASI in 1954-55 (IAR 1954-55: 19-20 and Ghosh 1989 [vol. II]: 430) and again in 1973-74 by the Eastern Circle of ASI under the guidance of S.K. Mukherji and others (IAR 1973-74: 33). As a result of the second phase of excavation a four-fold sequence of the site was established. Of the four cultural periods, the first two revealed the existence of EVF settlements at the site. Period I: The excavation besides confirming the earlier known cultural sequence brought to light new evidence about the cultural phase of the pre-NBPW horizon. BRW in its characteristic shapes | ($23^0 58'$N/$87^0 45'$E) is located on the left bank of Mayurakshi in the Birbhum district about 5 km northeast of Sainthia Railway Station. The site was excavated by the Dept. of Ancient Indian History, Culture and Archaeology, Visva Bharati University,under the general supervision of N.C.Ghosh and A.K. Nag from1986-88. The total 3.60m excavated occupational deposit was broadly divided by the excavators into three levels i.e. upper, middle and lower in the first year of excavation. In the second year, however, a fivefoldchronology hasbeen suggested. Excavations at the site did not yield BRW, although later explorations by various authorities have resulted into the discovery ofBRW and related assemblages from the site (IAR 1975-76: 58). | ($23^0$ $52'$N/$87^0 35'$E) is a small village by the side of the Bolpur-Siuri Road. In 1964-65 the Eastern circle of Archaeological Survey of India (ASI hereinafter) has conducted a small scale excavation at the site under the supervision of R.C. Kar, R.G Pandya and Amir Singh. The excavation revealed a 3.5m thick occupation deposit, which has been divided by the excavators into six layers. The Chalcolithic habitation deposit is about 2.6m thick. No clear cut chronocultural sequence has yet been published. The chronology of the site is also yet to be established. The most important discovery from the site is ten child burials. Besides, plain and painted BRW were found between the layers 6 and 3. Other ceramics of the |

| are found in this period. No regular habitation deposit could be traced owing to the limited scale of excavation. Neolithic celts and a variety of bone tools are the other finds of the period. The C$^{14}$date of Period I of Tamluk is 1350-1000 BCE (?) based on the half life of 5730Ĩ40. Period II: The use of iron started at the site without any break. BRW of degenerated variety continued to occur. | | site are Black-on-Red Ware, white painted red ware and a dull red ware. Burnt clay nodules with reed impression and a charred wooden pole (4cm in diameter) have been discovered. Other finds from the site include short beads, ground and polished stone celts, a stone pestle, and bone points. |
|---|---|---|
| **Mahisdal** | **Bahiri** | **Nanur** |
| (23$^{0}$42$^{\prime}$N/87$^{0}$42$^{\prime}$E) is situated in the southern part of district Birbhum on the left bank of river Kopai. A small scale excavation was conducted at the site by shri R.P. Das on behalf of the Eastern Circle of ASI in 1963-64. The mound is located about 0.25km south west of the modern village near the railway bridge. A maximum deposit of 2m has been exposed. The total cultural deposit was divided into two periods by the excavator of which the first one has been termed Chalcolithic. Four C$^{14}$ dates are available from Mahisdal: three from Period I and one from Period II. The three C$^{14}$ dates from period I are 1380 BCE, 1085 BCE and 855 BCE According to Chakrabarti the earliest calibrated date range of Mahisdal | (23$^{0}$39$^{\prime}$N/87$^{0}$40$^{\prime}$E) was first identified as a BRW bearing site in 1971-72 through the exploration conducted by the Eastern Circle of the ASI (IAR 1971-72: 81). The site is situated in the flood plain of river Ajay on the Bolpur-Palitpur road about 7 km east of Bolpur in the district of Birbhum. Dilip.K. Chakrabarti and S. Jamal Hasan's works on the mounds of Chandra Hazrar Danga on behalf of the Dept. of History, University of Delhi, unearthed cultural remains divisible into the following three periods: Period I: c. 1000+ BCE-c.500 BCE; Period II: c. 500 BCE†200 BCE; Period III: c. 4$^{th}$†6$^{th}$ centuries CE (Chakrabarti and Hassan 1982: 111-49). Period I has been identified on the basis of the occurrence | (23$^{0}$42$^{\prime}$N/87$^{0}$57$^{\prime}$E) is located in the south eastern part of the district of Birbhum about 20 km northeast of Bolpur on the Bolpur Kirnahar road. The mound was first excavated by K.G. Goswami on behalf of Asutosh Museum, University of Calcutta in 1945-46, followed by an excavation by the Eastern Circle of ASI in 1964 that resulted into a BRW bearing occupation horizon. From the excavation it is revealed that the site was under occupation from Protohistoric to modern times intervening through the historic and mediaeval periods. The lower levels of the site are comparatively undisturbed and have been divided into two periods. Periods I and II of the later phase of excavation have been taken to represent two segments of the Chalcolithic cultural phase. |

| | | |
|---|---|---|
| is 1619-1415 BCE. The $C^{14}$ date from 'Early Iron Age' Mahisdal is 690 BCE (Chakrabarti 1999: 242). | of plain and painted BRW and associated ceramics. Iron is found right from the beginning of this period. The above mentioned dating of Period I was further substantiated by three radio-carbon dates[18a] which are 900 BCE, 660 BCE and 610 BCE respectively. The recent calibrated date range from Bahiri, Period I is 1112-803 BCE (Chakrabarti, 1999: 242) | |

| **Pandurajardhibi** | **Mangalkote** |
|---|---|
| ($23^{0}25^{\prime}$N/$87^{0}39^{\prime}$E) is situated in the village of Panduk, Police Station Ausgram in the district of Barddhaman on the right bank of river Ajay. It is the first excavated EVF site of Eastern India. The mound is both extensive and a high one compared to the other mounds of the region. It is about 5m high and occupies an area measuring approximately 8 acres. The site was excavated twice, for the first time from 1962-65 and in 1985 for the second time. After preliminary exploration of the site, excavation started from 1961-62.The excavation was conducted under the supervision of P.C. Dasgupta, assisted by D.K. Chakrabarty and S.C. Mukherji on behalf of Directorate of Archaeology, Government of West Bengal. The first phase of digging confirmed a five-fold chronology of which the Periods I, II and II yielded BRW and related assemblages. However, a modified chronology has offered a four-fold division of the cultural assemblages. Period I: Chalcolithic; Period II: Prosperous Chalcolithic; Period III: Iron Age with an overlap with the preceding culture (Phase a) and Period IV: Early historic and Medieval (Phase b). Only one $C^{14}$ date is available for period II of Pandurajardhibi from the excavation of sixties. It is 101-2ĩ20 BCE (not calibrated). | ($23^{0}31^{\prime}$N/$87^{0}56^{\prime}$E) is situated in the district of Barddhaman on the eastern bank of Kunur, near its confluence with Ajay. The site was excavated from 1986-90 by the Dept. of Archaeology, University of Calcutta under the general supervision of. A Ray, C. Gupta, A. C. Pal, S.K. Mukherjee and colleagues, followed by a second phase of digging in 2005-06 by R.K. Chattopadhyay. Excavations at the site were conducted in a limited scale on four mounds of the locality. These are Vikramadityerdhibi (Sarkaridanga), Manumiyardanga (near Madrasah), Kacharidanga (near the confluence of Kunur and Ajay) and Kolubaridanga. The excavation produced the evidence of an average habitation layer of 6.50m (Ray and Mukherjee, 1992: 109), which was 5.20m-5.50m in slope areas. The whole occupational deposit has been divided into 5 consecutive periods. The last excavation of 2005-06 at Kolubaridanga, aimed at focusingearlymediaeval-mediaeval archaeology of the site, revealed no BRW bearing horizon (Chattopadhyay, Sanyal and Saha 2006: 119-21). Period I: Chalcolithic (1200-600 BCE). Only one $C^{14}$date is available for period I. It is 2870ĩ15/110 BP corresponding to 940 BCE. On the basis of this radiocarbon date theexcavatorshavedatedthe |

| | |
|---|---|
| | Chalcolithic period of Mangalkote between1200-600 BCE. The calibrated $C^{14}$ date range of Mangalkote is at par with Bahiri, i.e.1112-803 BCE (Chakrabarti, 1999: 242). All the later periods havc been dated to the historical eras, although BRW remained a steady element in the succeeding Periods II and III. |

| **Bharatpur** | **Natsal** |
|---|---|
| ($23^{0}24^{/}$N/$87^{0}27^{/}$E) is a small village in the district of Barddhaman on the left bank of Damodar. The site is located about 7 km southeast of Panagarh station. The site was jointly excavated by the Eastern Circle of Archaeological Survey of India and the University of Burdwan under the direction of S.C. Roy, assisted by others.Digging continued from 1971-72 to 1974-75, revealing a fourfold cultural sequence from 'Chalcolithic' to 'Late Historic' (Ghosh1989 [vol. II]: 66-7): Periodd I: Chalcolithic; Periodd II: Early historic; Period III: Could not be dated firmly owing to the lack of datable materials; Period IV: c. CE $9^{th}$ -$10^{th}$ centuries. Three $C^{14}$ dates (IAR 1974-75: 77) are available for Period I of Bharatpur. The earliest of them comes from the mid level of the Chalcolithic phase and counts for c. 1435 BCE. The two other dates from Bharatpur are 1180 BCE and 900 BCE respectively. | ($22^{0}11^{/}59^{//}$N/$88^{0}02^{/}47^{//}$E) is located on the right bank of Rupnarayan, 2.5km east of Mahishadal of Purva [East] Medinipur district. The site has yielded BRW (Ghosh 1989, [vol. I]: 237). The Directorate of Archaeology, under the direction of Amal Roy, superintendent of Archaeology, Directorate of Archaeology and Museums, Government of West Bengal has conducted excavation at the site in 1999-2000. In the light of the small trial excavation, the excavator has tentatively divided the material remains from the site into three periods i.e. Protohistoric/ Chalcolithic (layer 5), Early historic (layers 3 and 4) and Mediaeval and Late Mediaeval period (Layers 1 and 2). Layer (5) starts from a depth of 2.10m and it is composed of black sticky soil. From layer (5) have been recovered BRW, Black Ware, Red Ware, bone tools etc. |

# Appendix 4

Information from field data from places explored during ethnographic fieldwork in the region of study. (Reference- B=Bankura, P=Purulia, M=West Mednipur)

| Name of Village | Location | Information About Fairs/Festivals/*Pujas* And Bratas | Local Lore About History, Culture |
|---|---|---|---|
| Bālsi (B) | 23. 07'10°°N/8721°E P.O.- Bālsi, Police Station- Patrasayer, Block- Bishnupur | Siddeshwari Kali *mandir*, Balleshwar Jiu & Lakkhinarayan Jiu *mandir*. Balleshwar & Lakkhinarayan- are considered *gramdevata*. Lakkhinarayan- *nitya puja* & special *puja* from early hours of *Makar Sankrānti*, along with a *mela* held outside the temple. On the first day of *Māgh*, *Harinaam-sankirtan* takes place. The other important festivals-*Rath Yatra*/ Lakkhinarayanjiur *Rath* (*Asad*)-,- famous even in adjoining villages. *Ban Utsav* (*Chanchor*- a day before Dol Yatra) with *bhog*, *nagar kirtan* in the *atchala* in front of the temple and idol *pradakshins* around the village in his *palki*, accompanied by *dhak-dhol* and *khol-kasha*. Balleshwar- *nitya puja* & Gajan on *Caitra Sankranti*, as well as *Harinaam-Sankirtan* and *Raamkatha*. Important bratas- Janmashtami, Radhashtami and Śivaratri | Local legend- name of Bālsi= Ba= Balleshwar, La = Lakkhinarayan and Si= Siddheswari. Lakkhinarayan Jiu- legend of installation of the *shila* by a *sadhu* and the *raja* getting divine orders to construct temple. Assumed locally to be 450 yrs old. Also verified by official records of donation of temple property by the then raja of Bishnupur- Gopal Singha, (1094 *bangabda*),preserved documents in the Choudhury family who were bestowed with the responsibility of construction as well as looking after the temple and has eversince been the *sebayat* of the temple. |

| Name of Village | Location | Information About Fairs/Festivals/*Pujas* And Bratas | Local Lore About History, Culture |
|---|---|---|---|
| Muninagar (B) | P.O.- Muninagar, Police station- Bishnupur, Block- Bishnupur | Sri Sri Radhkanta Jiu Narayan temple with, within Tamboli *para*- made by Bir Singha Thakur of the Malla royal family. Brahman priest performs *nitya puja* as well as *Raas Utsav* for three days, including *Kirtan*. Shiv temple in front of Narayan Jiu temple. Basuli *Mandir*- east of village, within Bagdi *para*, also locally called Chhinnamasta or Basulimata. Locals aware about the idol being of a possible Jain Tirthankara. The temple receives *nitya puja* and an annual Manasa *puja*, in the month of *Sravan*. A Bhairab and Śiva *sthans* next to Basuli. Important *bratas*- Janmashtami, Radhashtami and Śivaratri | The village did not yield any significant lore associated with festivals rites and rituals or about the past history of the village. |
| Hadanarayan- pur (B) | P.O.- Hadalnarayanpur, Police station- Patrashayer, Block- Patrashayer | Important-The Narayan temple, Durga *daalan*, Laxmi temples of local royal family, referred to as *baro, mejo* and *chhoto taraf*. Important- a *Raasmancha* of *bara taraf*- with 17 peaks, a spiral staircase leading to the top and 11 doors aligned *para*llel for proper ventilation. Ma Brahmani temple in the southern part of the village, with 2nd *Magh* special *puja* with a *khichuri bhog*. The temple also has Nareshwar Śiva, with *Gajan* on 14th day before *purnima* of *Shuklapaksha*, supervised by *Gram Sholoanna Committee*. A Manasa mandir stands in Rui Das *para*, also supervised by *Sholoanna Committee.* | Brahmani idol- possible Jain origin, as well as an idol, resembling a male and female pair, placed within the temple. According to local lore, the original name-Narayanpur. The prefix was after the royal family of Hadal, who came to settle about 150 years back, from across the Bodai river. |

| | | | |
|---|---|---|---|
| Hatkrisnanagar (B) | P.O.- Haatkrishnanagar, Police station- Patrashayer, Block- Patrashayer | Krishnachandra temple of Narayan- south of village- of the Chunchor royal family, under the Malla kings. The deity is carried out to the present *Raajbari* in Chunchor on *Ulta Rath* and kept till *Raas Utsav*. Local Brahman priest conducts *nitya puja* and special *puja* on Janmastami. A *daalan*- a recent cement structure for worshipping of Annapurna, Durga, Laxmi and Saraswati in village centre. Important *bratas*- Janmastami and Śivaratri | The name of village- after Krishnachandra. |
| Dwarika (B) | P.O.- Dwarika, Police station- Bishnupur, Block-Bishnupur | The village is divided between eastern and western *paras*, of which the former is a Muslim *para* and latter has a mixed population of Brahmins, Kayasthas and Tamli, Teli, Bauri and Bagdi. The Muslim *para* has *Pirer Majar*, Bara Masjid and a Darga. Other temples are of Laxmi Janardan Jiu, Pashan Kali, Durga and Manasa temples. Important *bratas*- several Muslim festivals throughout the year, as well as Śivaratri, Durgashtami, etc | The local lore tries to explain the reasons for the first Muslim settlements here- being brought over as *lathiyals*, who were given lands to settle down by the Malla kings. Local lore also mentions- a *pir*- Musafir Saheb, whose death (1986 or 1386 *Bangabda*, on 6th *Baisakh* at 11.25 a.m.) anniversary on 6th *Baisakh* is observed with a feast.. |
| Uliara (B) | P.O.- Muninagar, Police station- Bishnupur, Block- Bishnupur | Eastern side of temple has a Śiva temple, with a two-day long *mela*- on *Phalgun Sankranti* and 1st *Baisakh*. Officiating priest is a Brahman. Other temples include- Damodar mandir in front of Śiva temple, Manasa *sthan* (within Bagdi *para*) and a Kali temple behind it. Also a masjid. Important *bratas*- *Narayan Raas, Maghi Purnima,Chabbish Prahar kirtan* | The village did not yield any significant lore associated with festivals rites and rituals or about the past history of the village. |

| | | | |
|---|---|---|---|
| Pandua (B) | P.O.- Pandua, Police station- Patrashayer, Block- Patrashayer | The village has a eastern and western *paras* and both has a Muslim population and a masjid each. Also important is the cemetery of Satya Pir. The rest of the population includes- Tamli, Kolu, Napit, Majhi, Brahmins, Teli, Bauri and Bagdi. The Teli's refer to themselves as Vaisnava-Brahmans and attend all *naam sankirtan sabhas* in the village. Important *pujas*- The Manasa, called as Kaliburi or Kanoniburi, and is worshipped as Dasohara (Mete *para*). Along with Manasa, is also placed idols of Kali and Dharmaraj and the worship is officiated by the same non- Brahman priest. Bagda Buro (Bauri and Bagdi *para*), in the middle of a ploughing field. No image, only votive offerings of small sized terracotta horses. Priest is one Tripura Digar (75) from the same *para*. *Puja* takes place on *Makar Sankranti* with *khichuri bhog* | According to lore- name of village from the *gramdevata*- Pandabeshwar (from Pandabeshwar to Pero to Pandua). It also describes the association of Satya Pir, who breathed his last here, and is revered by the Hindus more than the local Muslim population. |
| Penara (B) | P.O.- Uliara, Police station- Bishnupur, Block- Bishnupur | In western section, close to the Brahman *para* stands an idol, worshipped as Kali (2'6"l X 1'6"w X 8' h)-heavily eroded and possibly a male, Jain idol. Same Brahman *para also* has Bipadtarini, Singhabashini Durga and Sankattarini, (respectively from the left) temple with votive offerings and annual *puja* during Durga *puja*. On northern side, within Bagdi *para* is Basudeb or Bishnu temple, but officiating priest is from Brahman *para*. | The village did not yield any significant lore associated with festivals rites and rituals or about the past history of the village. |

| | | | |
|---|---|---|---|
| | | Radha-Damodar next to Basi Hari Pukur and periphery of Brahman *para*. Has Brahman priest and special *Raas puja.* Important *bratas*- Durga and Kali *upavass*, Nabanna, Jitashtami, Baipadtarini (just before Durga *puja*), Sankattarini and Makar Sankranti. | |
| Radha- mohanpur (B) | P.O.- Radhamohanpur, Police station- Sonamukhi, Block- Sonamukhi | Four main *paras*, but important - the worship of the laterite male idol, locally referred to as Buddhadev (Madhyam *para*/Mondol *para*). Apart from *nitya puja*, a six-day festival with a *mela*, from *Maghi purnima* (*Magh*). An old Visṇu temple and another *mandir* (a *samadhi mandir*) of Gobindochand or Gobindchand. | The Buddhadev idol was used as a washing platform in a face-down manner. It was discovered in 1328 *bangabda* and established in the temple on *Maghi purnima* in 1329. |

| Bishnupur town (B) | 2305'N/8723'E P.O.- Bishnupur, Police station- Bishnupur, Block- Bishnupur P.O.- Uliara, Police station- Bishnupur, Block- Bishnupur | Capital city of the royalty of Mallabhum. Has several temples with fine examples of terracotta- the Shyamray *mandir* (estd.1643, Raghunath Singha), Madanmohan *mandir* (estd.1698, Durjan Singha), the Jor *mandir* (a set of three temples estd., Krishna Singha, son of Gopal Singha,1726), *Nandalal mandir* (possible date of construction being later half of 17th century, though the exact year and the name of the king is unknown under whom it was built), Radhamadhab *mandir* (estd.1737, Churamanidevi, the daughter-in-law of Gopal Singha),Kalachand *mandir* (estd.1656,Raghunath Singha), Radhagobindo *mandir* (estd.1729 by king Krishna Singha), Krishnabalaram *mandir* (possible time of estd. is 16th century), the Radhashyam *mandir* (estd.1758, Chaitanya Singha), Jorbangla *mandir* (estd.1655, Raghunath Singha), Mrinmayee *mandir* (referred to as the oldest in Bishnupur as the date popularly noted in 997 CE. by Jagatmalla, who was supposedly instructed by the goddess in his sleep), Sarbamangala *mandir* (though the exact date is not ascertained, yet assumed it's not a recent construction. Radhalaljiu *mandir* (estd.1658, Bir Singha) or the *Chhinnamasta mandir* (a comparatively recent construction of 1973, though the idol dates to earlier times and was a part of the Bishnupur royal family treasure). The place also has several remains of splendid architecture, including Pathar Darja (or the supposedly main gateway of Bishnupur), the *Gar Darja* (small gateway of Bishnupur), the stone chariot (possibly constructed by end of 17th century), Raasmancha (established in 1587 by king Bir Hambir), even the Dalmadal Kaman or cannon. | Several lore about royal family and their accession to the throne. Also a lore about Sri Ramkrishna visiting the place and after a bath in the adjoining Laalbandh *pukur*, he is stated to have experienced strange overwhelming smell that captivated him. |
|---|---|---|---|

| Antra (B) | | Being close to Dihar, people attend the temple of Shanreshwar at Dihar (3 kms away). The village by itself does not have any village deity, but a recently bult Kali temple within the Bagdi *para*, by the people of the same community, is revered quite as much. Apart from this, *baroari* Saraswati *puja* takes place on behalf of 20 families, consisting of about 70 people. Important *brata*- Ashtami, Bipadtarini and Śivaratri. | The village did not yield any significant lore associated with festivals rites and rituals or about the past history of the village. |
|---|---|---|---|
| Tiliboni/ Basantapur (B) | P.O.- Uliara, Police station- Bishnupur, Block- Bishnupur | Only the western part of Tiliboni is referred to as Basantapur, of which much has been reclaimed by Dwarakeshwar. Thus, many former ruins of temples and idols, including the major part of the palace of Saileswar *raja* have disappeared. These were first spotted by local teacher and educationist- Maniklal Singha. The village deity-Bhuteshwar Śiva within Brahman *para*, (south of the village)- presided over by a Bhattacharya family. Other temples in same *para* are- five Śiva temples of *chouchala* roof, a Radhamohan Jiu temple and a Raasmancha. Bhairav *sthan*(south- western border). Officiating priest- Krishnakanto Bagish (75). No *nitya puja*, but on 1st *Magh* with *Prasad* Important *bratas*- Mangalchandi (*Jaishthya*), Bipadtarini, Jagattarini, Janmasjtami, Sankattarini, Kojagori Laxmi *Puja* and Durga *Puja* and Gurupurnima, as well as during Narayan *puja* on every *purnima* (full moon) at the household *tulsitala*. | Local lore mentions Raja Bir Hambir- of Malla royal family-attending Bansanti *puja* here via Dwarakeshwar, which also saw a *mela* taking place. Thus the name of village. Local lore also mentions the Rajput clan to have been established here by royalty with the profession of *lathiyals*. Quite interestingly, a local lore describes the local Bhuteshwar Śiva to one of the seven brothers of Shanreshwar Śiva (Dihar). Another lore describes how a local Bandopadhyay family was gifted the surname of Bhattacharya by Veer Hambir to look after Bhuteshwar Śiva. |

| | | | |
|---|---|---|---|
| Bisra (B) | P.O.- Uliara, Police station- Bishnupur, Block- Bishnupur | The name of village- after Bishahari (south- west part). Earlier had *nitya puja* by Brahman priest, now only on the day of Dasohhara *puja* (with goat sacrifice) and 1st *Magh*, (*khichuri, chatni, payasam* and *tarkari bhog*. A Śivalinga, on the left of Bishahari- worshipped on Śivaratri. Important *bratas*- Tusu (majorly celebrated by Bauris). Others- Durgastami, Laxmi and Śivratri. | Local lore explains the installation of Bisahari deity, which is represented by a stone by a local Brahman, who was instructed by Devi in his sleep. She was installed on the day of Dasohara. |
| Prakasghat & Chhilimpur (both are located within 100 mts of each other) (B) | P.O.- Uliara, Police station- Bishnupur, Block- Bishnupur | Prakasghat and Chhilimpur- together constitutes few important *pujas*- as Prakasghat has Śiva at Shinipur Śiva *mandir*, Chhilimpur has Bisahari, Manasa and Bhairab (north-western border) as well as Kekai Candi *sthan* (western outskirts). This is a heavily eroded laterite stone, placed loosely on a niche in a broken brick wall of a house along the main road. Attempts of association with Laxmi is clear- from the Laxmi feet *alpana* drawn near the base of stone and receives *nitya puja* every Tuesday of *Caitra* and *Bhadra*. Billamani Thakur or Dharmaraj *sthan* (on way towards Chhlimpur, amidst open field)- *puja* 1st of *Magh* by a priest from local Pal family from Prakashghat. *Puja prasad* has *seddha chal* (par boiled rice) *bhog*. | The village did not yield any significant lore associated with festivals rites and rituals or about the past history of the village. |
| Bhara (B) | P.O.- Muninagar, Police station- Bishnupur, Block- Bishnupur | Important *paras* are- Kayastha, *Mussalman*, Bagdi and Bauri, apart from others. Rathtala, with *Raas mandir* (village centre, Mondol *para*). Next to this mandir is a 300 yr old Durga *puja* tradition with a *dalaan*. A Radhamohan Jui temple (in south within Brahman/Chakraborty *para*), apart from 14 | The idols which are referred as Hanuman are locally called as the relics of ancient Jain idols. However, due to indistinct and broken structure, this |

| | | | |
|---|---|---|---|
| Kusadwip (B) | P.O.- Pandua, Police station- Patrasayer, Block- | The eastern side has a miscellaneous *para* and main population include- Tili, Datta, Bauri, Bagdi and Muslim *para*, with a Pir *sthan*, attended to only by Muslims. Deuleswar *mandir* (west within Kayastha *para*). Priest from Bagdi *para*, with Gajan & *Chabbish Prahar Naam Sankirtan*. Temple is in ruins at present of heavily eroded laterite stone blocks, but original temple could have been large (24'l X 23'b and surrounding *dalaan*- 8'). Mahamaya *mandir* (Tili *para*), with *nitya puja*, twice daily, officiated by a Brahman (*prasad- chewda*, one *poa seddha chal*, one *poa* milk and seasonal fruits). Many new temples- in Bazaar area (central part)- Bhairab, Kalanjoy, Dakkhineswar and a Durga *daalaan*, adjoining the Harisayer *pukur*. Important *bratas*- Durgastami, Bipadtarini, Janmastami and Radhastami. | The village did not yield any significant lore associated with festivals rites and rituals or about the past history of the village, though the archaeological significance of the village have been earlier established through various excavations by the archaeology department (Kolkata). Several of the reports have been published under the categories of stone tools, lithic assemblages or mettalurgy details of the artifacts available. Similar stone tools and few metal artifacts were also seen in the personal collection of local teacher and ex- teacher- the Late Sudhir Duari. |
| Pataspur (B) | P.O.- Hadalnarayanpur, Police station- Patrasayer, Block- Patrasayer | Small village (2 ½ kms l X ½ km b), referred to as village of *utbastu* or refugees. According to official records of the SDO of Bishnupur, they are from across the Bodai river from Bangladesh and about 86 % of the population consists of scheduled tribe. No caste division within the three *paras*- south, east and west. People aware about the existence of three temples, which stand in half-submerged manner near the river Damodar- Visnu, Sitala, Durga and Damodar. (All located within an area of ½ acre). Another temple of Durga has completely vanished into the soft bed/mud. Deuleswar Śiva (eastern end) as well as a Dharmaraj *sthan*. Recent *pujas* include- Sarbojanin Durgotsav, Kali, Manasa and Saraswati and Laxmi, which is considered to be a continuation of Bangladeshi tradition. The local *bratas* observed include, Laxmi *puja*, Durgastami and *Makar Sankranti*. | They claim to be from various parts of Bangladesh like, Decca, Faridpur, Khulna, Pabna and Noakhali. Locals refer to have collected various terracotta items from the mounds of the three half- submerged temples. |

| | | | |
|---|---|---|---|
| Jagmohanpur (B) | P.O.- Nabasur, Police station- Sonamukhi, Block- Sonamukhi | Also referred to as the village of refugees, the village has four main *paras*- Roy, Bagdi, Morol/ Mondol and Gosai. Recent temple- Manasa within Mondol *para*. Apart from these, others are *baroari pujas* like Durga, Kartik and Kali. Candi *sthan* at a *Candi tala* across Gosai *para*, within a walking distance of 2 kms across Shubhankari Canal. Revered for protection against small pox in the months of *Phalgun* and *Caitra*. Officiating priest- a Roy from Roy *para* | The village name is after a resident- Jagamohan Goswami of the Goswami *para*- referred to as original inhabitants of the place. Locals mention the time of resettlement during a time of flood in Bodai river in 1920 in Ishabpur. |
| Patrahati (B) | P.O.- Radhamohanpur, Police station- Sonamukhi, Block- | Bhairab *sthan*- (east-end of the village in Ghosh *para*) and next to Bhairab *pukur*. *Puja- nitya puja* and also Gajan officiated by a Brahman priest from Jagmohanpur. Manasa | The village did not yield any significant lore associated with festivals rites and rituals or about |

| | | | |
|---|---|---|---|
| | Sonamukhi | *Puja*- special *puja* in *Sravana* on a specific date determined by the *Gram Sholoanna Committee.* | the past history of the village. |
| Patrasayer (B) | P.O.- Patrasayer, Police station- Patrasayer, Block- Patrasayer | The village constitute of a fair concentration of so-called upper caste Brahmanical religion and a large section of Bauri, Bagdi, Hari, Mochi, Kaibarta and Dihar classes who were mainly employed as agricultural labours in the fields and were very poor, however, recent employments in various sectors like, construction workers, drivers, etc, have resulted in the employment of several people. *Gr madevat s of the village*- Basanta Candi and Kalanjay. The Kalanjay Śiva- has Gajan & *mela*, beginning on Aksay Tritiya and ending on *Baisak*. The Basanta Candi *mandir*- Kenduli *mela* (*Paus Sankranti*) and a special *bhog* prepared till 22 of *Magh*. A Bhairab *sthan* on the left of the temple has votive offerings of terracotta horses where no *nitya puja* takes place. *Puja*- annual six-day *puja* on 9th *Magh*, accompanied by a *mela*. | Local legends relate the village to be ruled by Daman Singh, a scion of the Malla royal family of Bishnupur and the ruins of whose fort can still be seen at Dumnigarh, 9.7 kms west of Patrasayer. Various lore associate the construction of the Kalanjay Śiva templewith royalty- by Raja Chaitanya Singh of Bishnupur. |

| | | | |
|---|---|---|---|
| Bamira (B) | P.O.- Bamira, Police station- Patrasayer, Block- Patrasayer | Majority of Brahman families and few of Bagdi and Bauri communities who reside at the end of the village with several open-air Manasa *sthans.* in open air. A significant portion of the so-called lower communities are still employed in the lands as labourers. Important within the village is a terracotta Śiva *mandir* in the south of the village, a Raashmancha in the north and a Raam *mandir* in north-east corner. Here mention may be made of the *Caitra* Gajan, followed by a three-day *mela.* Important *bratas-* Durgastami, Tusu and a *Paus mela.* | The village did not yield any significant lore associated with festivals rites and rituals or about the past history of the village. |
| Jamkuri (B) | P.O.- Jamkuri, Police station- Patrasayer, Block- Patrasayer | Archaeologically, the village is significant because of several small stone images of Jain pontiffs (Tirthankaras) and Visnu- several of which are preserved at the Bangiya Sahitya Parishad museum at Bishnupur. Important to witness were also the several *patuas* who still, though on the decline, but finds an important place of mention, especially during the *mela* of Raam Nabami in the village, associated with the goddess Radharajrani. They are traditionally called *sutradhars* and specialise in manufacturing traditional Durga *pats* or scroll paintings, which they also sell in village fairs and *melas.* | Local lore associate the local royal family with Mallabhum royalty. Even the family deities are explained as related with the Radharajrani deity of Jamkuri considered to be the elder sister of Mrinmayee of Bishnupur royal family. |
| Jaykrisnapur (B) | P.O.- Jaykrisnapur, Police station- Bishnupur, Block- Bishnupur | Manasa *mandir* (centre of village in Rai *para*). *Puja- nitya* and also during *Paus* on the Saturday and Tuesday, after 20 *Paus.* Śiva temple (*Purana Chowmatha*). *Puja-* Gajan on *Caitra Sankranti,* and *mela* for a week starting from 25th of *Caitra* and also 15 days of rice *bhog.* | According to local belief, the very name of the village associates itself with the Vaisnava Malla kings. |
| Dharāpāt (B) | P.O.-Jaykrishapur, Police station- Bishnupur, Block- Bishnupur | Deity of Nangta Syāmchānd/Nangta Thakur/ Syāmchānd Thakur- at the outside wall of an old temple. *Puja-* no *nitya puja,* but annual *puja* on 20-25th of the month of *Sravan* every year and also on *Naag pancami.* Across | Interesting to note the possible idol of Jain Tirthankara Parsvanath, who is worshipped as Manasa. The Jain deity |

| | | | |
|---|---|---|---|
| | | the road to Syāmchānd is a Manasa temple with a deity inside. *Puja*- special *puja* on Nag *pancami*. The idol receives votive offerings as well- of terracotta horses and elephants. Priest is from Brahman *para*. | was first transformed into a Visṇu image and now it is worshipped as Manasa Local lore also mentions the Syāmchānd idol to be constructed by local *raja*- Advesh- a vassal of the Malla royal family. the structure is of neatly plastered laterite, about 18.3 mts (60 ft) high and constructed, according to an inscription over the front arch, in 1616 or 1626 *Saka*, corresponding to 1694 or 1704 CE. This discrepancy in ascertaining the date is attributed to the mutilation of the third digit of the figure, signifying the year of foundation, which could be either read as 1 or 2. |
| Ayodhya (B) | P.O.-Radhanagar, Police station- Radhanagar Outpost Police Station, Block- Radhanagar | Main puja of the village is Dasohara. Worshipped in a theriomorphic representation, in *Aswin*, she is considered very *jagrata* by the locals | Several lore associated with the blessing giving power of Dasohara |
| Radhanagar (B) | P.O.-Radhanagar, Police station- Radhanagar Outpost Police Station, Block- Radhanagar | Original inhabitants of village are Brahmans, Sadgops, Kayastha, Bagdi and Bauri and on west reside- Santhals, Bauri and Sadgops. Village has 22 *paras* with Manasa *mandir* in each. Manasa Mandir of Lohar *para* is referred to as Ratan Muni by the so-called upper classes of the village and has *nitya puja* from *purohit* Mohan Lohar with special *puja* every Saturday and Tuesday. Important *baroari* festivals are Śiva, Durga and Manasa temples (Sarma *para*) & Kali Mandir (Bhattacharya *para*). Bhairab Thakur in Sayer *para* (near Lohar *para*), with few votive offerings of terracotta horses and elephants and does not have *nitya puja*. Gangadhar Jiu Śiva *mandir* and its adjacent Bhairab Mandir in the Chatterjee *para*- with *nitya puja* also has Gajan. | The village did not yield any significant lore associated with festivals rites and rituals or about the past history of the village. |

| Naricha (B) | P.O.-Dihar, Police station- Bishnupur, Block- Bishnupur | The village has a majority number of Sadgops, apart from other castes. Important- is the annual festival and *puja* of Sarbamangala (pl.90), starting from the 1st of *Magh* for about ten days. Big crowd attends it from all over Bankura. For *nitya puja*, the *machh pora* (local *pona* or *magur* fish wrapped in leaves and dry roasted in fire from both sides) along with rice *bhog* is also a famous *prasad* all over Bankura | The deity is considered to be very *jagrata* and an incarnation of goddess Durga. |
|---|---|---|---|
| Rautkhanda (B) | P.O.-Dihar, Police station- Bishnupur, Block- Bishnupur | Significant is the *puja* and festival associated with the deity Jagatgouri- who is considered to be *gramdevata*. She is worshipped daily as Manasa and Durga. The deity draws crowd from all over Bankura. | A lore mentions the find of the idol in a nearby ploughing field. |
| Dihar (B) | P.O.-Dihar, Police station- Bishnupur, Block- Bishnupur | An archaeologically important site, it had received explorations and excavations on behalf of the Department of Archaeology, University of Calcutta for 6 seasons, dating from 1981-1987 and again in 2008. The main area of importance is a celebrated centre for Saivite worship- two laterite temples, dedicated to Sandeswara and Saileswara (locally also famous as Salleswar)- variant names of Śiva, on the banks of Kana Nadi. *Puja- nitya* as well as Gajan *mela*, from 2nd *Caitra* till 1st *Baisakh*. The place has several annual *melas* like, the last Monday of *Baisakh*, *Paus Sankranti*- famous as *Makar Mela* and the *Saptami* after Saraswati *puja* in *Magh*, when there is another *mela- Bankuri mela*. | Locally, both the temples are considered as *jagrata* and are respected by all across Bankura district, as well as outside. Locally believed the temples to have been built by Prithvi Malla, the king of Bishnupur in 1346 CE. |

| | | | |
|---|---|---|---|
| Bhenduasole (B) | P.O.-Bheduasole, Police station- Indpur, Block-Indpur | The settlement has a large number of Utkal Brahmans, apart from other classes, including a very small settlement of Bauris and Tambolis. The *baroari puja* includes Durga, Visṇu, Śiva, as well as Manasa within the Bauri *para*. The temple of Khkhandarani is important, with an idol (35″l X 16″b X 8″w) of a possible Jain origin- of probably Tirthankara Parsvanath. It is within a cultivable land between Bheduasole and Panchpukur village. On the south-eastern part of the village, the idol is located within a broken temple. The temple ruin also had a broken *Amalaka* (circumference 3 ft and height 1 and a-half ft) about three metres from the temple. The *brata* rites of the village consists of Bhadu, observed mostly by the Utkal Brahmans. | The village has several lores about the relation of Khhandarani to Jain religion. The Utkal Brahmans also has lores about their association to their original homeland and stories of their migrations generations ago. |
| Indpur (B) | 2310.2′N/8655.8′E P.O.-Indpur, Police station-Indpur, Block- Indpur | The village has an admixture of Utkal Brahmans, Kayasthas and Bauris.The village has a *gramdevata*, as well as Śiva temples | The village did not yield any significant lore associated with festivals rites and rituals or about the past history of the village. |
| Advaicandi (B) | P.O.-Advaicandi, Police station- Indpur, Block-Indpur | Like adjoining villages, the *baroari puja* of the village constitutes of Candi *puja*, *Harinaam Sankirtan*, Śiva, Visṇu *pujas*, which are all managed by the *Gram Sholoanna Committees*. An important deity of the village is Basuli, which is protected by the Archaological Survey of India, Kolkata Chapter. The village also has a substantial number of people belonging to Tantubai community. The village also has a *gramdevata*, placed under a tree within the Tantubai *para* at one end of the village. The officiating *purohit* is a non-Brahman from the same *para* and no specific offerings or special annual *puja* takes place. The deity is | The village did not yield any significant lore associated with festivals rites and rituals or about the past history of the village. |

| | | | |
|---|---|---|---|
| | | worshipped occasionally by locals. About 300 mts from the village, stands the Chukai Sini *sthan* under a tamarind tree and surrounded by cultivating fields. The worship being a collective effort of the Bauris, the *purohit* is also from the same community- Ajit Bauri. The annual worship takes place on the day after *Makar Sankranti*. | |
| Baner bandh (B) | P.O.- , Police station- Indpur, Block- Indpur Next to Baner Bandh | From the village of Indpur, travelling via the villages of Chokra (2 kms from Indpur), Krishnanagar (another 1 km) and Halukmari (another 1 km), the area of Bandh Sini is located at the rear end of the village of Halukmari and in the north of the adjoining village of Purushottampur. | The village did not yield any significant lore associated with festivals rites and rituals or about the past history of the village. |
| Heer bandh Thana (B) | P.O.- , Police station- Heerbandh, Block- Heerbandh | The Makra Sini temple is located on the bank of the river Silabati. The area is located within 20 mts of a cremation ground just on the banks of Silabati. The site also has a Kali and a Śiva temple on its right. Though there is no regular *puja*, but the site has a four-day long *Paus Sankranti mela*. | The village did not yield any significant lore associated with festivals rites and rituals or about the past history of the village. |

| | | | |
|---|---|---|---|
| Koro (B) | P.O.-Amarkanan, Police station- Gangajalghati, Block- Gangajalghati | Important within the village is the Manasa temple within the Rajput *para*, which has important *puja* during the month of *Sravan Srankanti*, which also witnessed goat sacrifices of a about 40 in number. Apart from this, the deity also receives special *puja* every *Sankranti* by an officiating Brahman *purohit*. Significantly, a broken piece of *amalaka* (3 ½' X 2') was seen lying on the right side of the temple, near the Gamariya pond. An *atchala* in front of the temple also has *Harinaam Sankirtan Chabbish Prahar*. A Bhairab *sthan* was seen about ½ km from the village centre, which only has *puja* on *Makar Sankranti*. The National Highway No. 60, lies between the ploughing field where the Bhairab *sthan* is located and the main village of Koro. | The village did not yield any significant lore associated with festivals rites and rituals or about the past history of the village, excepting the fact that the *amalaka*, which is situated in front of the Manasa temple within the village at present, was discovered next to the Bhairab *sthan* by farmers while ploughing fields about 48 years ago. |
| Kapistha (B) | 2322.8'N/878.2'E P.O.-Kapistha, Police station-Gangajalghati, Block-Gangajalghati | Important within the village is the Dharmaraj, which is referred to as the centre of the village and consist of a *shalgram shila*, kept inside an earthen pot. This is brought out at the time of the annual *puja* in the month of *Jaisthya*, after *Aksay Tritiya* and given a bath in the adjoining Roybandh *pukur*. The deity is worshipped by married women for blessings. On the north of the temple stands the Dom *para* and the *puja* of the temple is also managed by a priest from the Dom *para*. Apart from the regular *baroari pujas* of Durga, Kali, Saraswati, the village also has two Manasa temples- one within the eastern *para* and the other is near the Dharmaraj *mandir* in the Dom *para*. Interstingly enough, this deity of the Dom *para* carries an idol all year round, that closely resembles the deity Parvati. The image is also portrayed with Siva as its consort. Important bratas of the village include- Sasti, Itu, Durgastami, Laxmi. | There is a local lore associated with the discovery of the *shila*, which is worshipped as Dharmaraj. Local lore has it that the stone was discovered in the adjoining Sedo *pukur* or pond about 200 years back, at the time of the Samanta kings. |

| | | | |
|---|---|---|---|
| Lohardanga (B) | P.O.-Kapistha, Police station- Gangajalghati, Block- Amarkanan | A very small village with a small population, the village does not have any *para* division. Significant is the Candi *sthan*, which is located between the north and south of the village. The deity has worshipping taking place on the day of Saraswati *puja* in the month of *Magh*. The time also witnesses *kirtan* singing. Apart from this, Durga *puja* takes place in *Aswin*. A Kalir *sthan* is located next to the bandh of the village. | The village did not yield any significant lore associated with festivals rites and rituals or about the past history of the village. |
| Gangajalghati (B) | 2325.1'N/877.0'E P.O.- Gangajalghati, Police station- Gangajalghati, Block- Gangajalghati | A large village with several *paras*, like, Kali (with goat sacrifice) and Durga *pujas*. The Kali *puja* is accompanied by goat sacrifice. Several Manasa temples, within the Dhibor, Tanti, Keor, Bauri and Bagdi *paras*. Important bratas of the village constitute of Śivaratri, Sasti, Tusu and Bhadu. | Road was supposedly used by pilgrims between Puri to Kolkata, taking Gangajal with them. The place was used as a resting place or a *choti*. Thus, the name of the place. |
| Bhairabpur (B) | P.O.- Amarkanan, Police station- Gangajalghati, Block- Gangajalghati | Important festival of *Aswin puja* at the time of *Sravan Sankranti* and *Bhadra-* fifteen days prior to Durga *puja* in the month of *Aswin*. The village also has Manasa *puja* in the Bauri *para*. | The village was supposed to have been under Chandravarman (4 th century CE, Pakhanna) and later under Panchkot royalty. The Malla kings introduced local zamindari with Muslim *ghatals* ($12^{th}$- 13th) |

| | | | |
|---|---|---|---|
| Amarkanan (B) | P.O.- Amarkanan, Police station- Gangajalghati, Block- Gangajalghati | In recent times famous for Sri Ramkrisna Sebadal Asram. Historically famous for participation at the time of Subhas Chandra Bose for freedom struggle. Gandhiji is also said to have visited the place. The entire region, till date, has a predominantly large section of Kshatriya and amongst the so-called lower classes, the village has a large number of Bauris. Apart from this asram, the village, at present, did not seem to yield any important information regarding any other festivals, *melas*, or worships. The regular *pujas* of Durga, Kali and Saraswati is patronisedby the*GramSholoanna Committee.* | The local lore relates to the region being under the Bishnupur Malla kings, who gave it to four *ghatal*. The local lore, quite like Gangajalghati, also relates the region to be on the transit road for pilgrims in ancient times, who would travel to Puri, especially from Burdwan, as the region was under Burdwan zilla. |
| Dhumkoro (B) | P.O.- Amarkanan, Police station- Gangajalghati, Block- Gangajalghati | Archaeologically significant site with several remains in the form of possible herostones, *amalaks* or broken idol ruins. Typical example, of a possible herostone- on the eastern side of the *bandh*. There is a local lore about the *raja* and *rani* going to *shikar* associated with this herostone. Broken, male idol seen next to Bhangagaria pond (northern part. Head=1'17"Lx1'17"Wx4 ½'H: lower torso, with the legs=1'16"Lx1'14" Wx8"Depth of base). A series of broken steps noticed under the mound where this idol was located, leading to the pond. Several possible herostones located near the *bandh* with several immersed into soft mud. Six could be seen at the time of fieldwork | The village did not yield any significant lore associated with festivals rites and rituals or about the past history of the village, but the villagers were seen to be aware about the area being under royalty being evident from the flight of steps near Bahangagoria pond and the discover of several idols and remains of pillars. |

| | | | |
|---|---|---|---|
| | | which were also half-submerged. (from left are 1½′ in diameter and 2 ½′H for the first round one. The next one with a sculpted figure with bow and arrow is 5′Hx6 ½′). Bhairab *sthan* next to *bandh* with no *nitya puja* or officiating priest, nor does it have any officiating priest. Broken idols found near Bhairab *sthan*.(1½′Hx6″ W), as well as several possible herostones (5′ above ground). Quite close to the Bhairav *sthan* and few lying submerged as well. There is an old Dharmaraj temple and a recently built Manasa temple in the Bauri *para* (north-eastern part), with special *puja* on *Bhadra Sankranti*] accompanied with *khichuri bhog*. *Harinaam Sankirtan* is a regular phenomenon that takes place annually. | |
| Metla (B) | P.O.- Kesiara, Police station- Gangajalghati, Block- Amarkanan | Lakkhinarayan Jiu temple important. *Puja- nitya* as well as 30th *Caitra* Gajan -1st *Baisakh*, with rice, milk and jaggery *bhog*. Manasa temples- eight present within various *paras*. Important *bratas*- Tusu and Bhadu- where all the males of the village participate. | Temple stated to be built in 1718 (approx). Large number of village claims Rajput lineage and also how they came here under the local vassal of Bishnupur and Burdwan royalties. |
| Durlovpur (B) | P.O.- Durlovpur, Police station- Gangajalghati, Block- Amarkanan | No significant *pujas*, excepting *baroari* Manasa, Kali, Durga as well as *Harinaam Sankirtan Chabbis Prahar* on the recently constructed *atchala* of the village. Important *bratas*- Bipadtarini. Bhadu and Tusu are almost extinct. | Like Gangajalghati *choti*, this area too, was a resting place for pilgrims traveling between Kolkata & Puri. Thus Durlovpur *choti* (northern part). |
| Chayanpur (B) | P.O.- Gobindodham, Police station- Gangajalghati, Block- Gangajalghati | The village did not yield any significant important festivals, apart from the ones organised by the *Gram Sholoanna Committee*, including Kali and Laxmi *pujas*. Important *bratas*- Jitastami and Śivaratri. Both Bhadu and Tusu were seen to be extinct. | Believed the name of village to be after king Chayan Singha. No other traces of significant lore associated with festivals, rites seen. |

| | | | |
|---|---|---|---|
| Banasuria (B) | P.O.- Gangajalghati, Police station- Gangajalghati, Block- Gangajalghati | The village has mostly inhabitants of Santals and other so-called lower classes. They follow various local festivals and ceremonies | The village did not yield any significant lore associated with festivals rites and rituals or about the past history of the village. |
| Chhatna (B) | 23 1̣8.4'N / 86 5̣7.8'E P.O.- Chhatna, Police station- Chhatna, Block- Chhatna, Gram Panchayat- Chhatna | Important for Badu Candidas, who is supposed to have resided here and was a devotee of the local deity- Basali. Basali- (centre of village) and main deity. There is a Bhairab *sthan*, close to the temple of Basali, with no *nitya puja*. Manasa *sthans*- several within Bauri *paras* of the village. | The village has a lot of local lore describing the association of goddess Basali with the royalty and her establishment at the present place. |
| Deuli (B) | P.O.- Gangajalghati, Police station- Gangajalghati, Block- Gangajalghati | The village has few local and village deities. | The village did not yield any significant lore associated with festivals rites and rituals or about the past history of the village. |

| | | | |
|---|---|---|---|
| Susunia (B) | 23 2̣1.5′N / 86 5̣9.2′E P.O.- Susunia, Police station- Chhatna, Block- Chhatna | Rich archaeological ground for ancient and palaeolithic remains. Information available from published reports. The main caste of the village is Karmakar (one group makes copper utensils and the other includes an assortment of occupations- bell-metal workers, stone- carvers and sculptors as well as bamboo artisans). Others are- Brahmans, Kshatriyas, Vaisnavas, Bauris and Mondols. The mainstay is crafts and associated fields. Tourism is still in incipient stages of development. The agricultural gounds are in the south, which produces once year agriculture. An important aspect is the Narasingha idol on the north- eastern part as well as the non-stop flow of water that issues from the mouth of the idol Most significant is the *Caitra mela*- the Baruni *mela* on Madhukrisna Trayodasi on *Caitra* Gajan. Manasa temples across the village, including the Bauri, Chowdhury and Singha *paras*. At all of these, annual *puja* takes place on *Sravan Sankranti*. Important *bratas*- Bhadu and Tusu, Jitastami, Bipadtarini, Laxmi and Durastami. | Several lores are associated with the ancient findings of Susunia, including the inscriptions on top of the hill of king Chandravarma, dated to 4th century CE. Locally, it is also believed that the perennial water fountain has spitirual association. The water is also believed to have curative powers and thus, bathing people in the site is a very common site to behold. Interestingly enough, prominent through various lore collected from across Bankura, Susunia is perceived to be the local representation of the mighty Himalayas as the abode of Śiva. |
| Jugunthol (B) | P.O.- Susunia, Police station- Chhatna, Block- Chhatna | Important are the Salvi *puja* (*Caitra*), Maghi *puja* (*Magh*), Bandna *puja* (*Paus*). All of them have *khichuri bhog* and fowl sacrifice. | No significant information about past history of the village. |

| | | | |
|---|---|---|---|
| Penchasimul (B) | P.O.- Susunia, Police station- Chhatna, Block-Chhatna | Important- Eken *puja* (*Paus Sankranti)* as well as the Candi *puja* (7th of *Baisakh)*. Both the Eken and Manasa as well as Bhairab *sthans* are in the western part of the village. *Harinaam Sankirtan Chabbis Prahar* takes place for three days. (*Caitra* in the village *atchala)*. Important *bratas*- Jitastami, Radhastami, Śivaratri, Bhadu and Tusu. | There is a local lore about the name of the village. Unfortunately, as was seen during the course of fieldwork, it is only limited to a hand few elders in the village, who can remember the poem and could pen it down for the researcher. *Sarva srehstha hai gaja jar sahodar Tahar bahan jeba diba andhabor Nai budh majhe jeba bharater rajan Je tarute sedhechhilen bhuter sadhan Ei dui milonete je palli hoi Sei khanate bari mor janibe nischoi* |
| Biskodor (B) | P.O.- Susunia, Police station- Chhatna, Block-Chhatna | *Chabbis Prahar Naam Sankirtan* in *atchala* during the months of *Baisakh/Jaisthy*a. There are considered three village deities or *gramdevatas* Candi (western part), Bamun Ma (there is no fixed date, but the annual worship takes place in a decided date in the month of *Baisakh*, apart from the regular worship every Saturday and Tuesday) and Gournitai Mahaprabhu. (reflecting significance associated with the religion of Vaisnavism). Important *bratas*-Special *puja* on *Baisakh Sankranti*, Bipadtarini, Bhadu and Tusu. | The village did not yield any significant lore associated with festivals rites and rituals or about the past history of the village. |

| Paharbedia (B) | P.O.- Susunia, Police station- Chhatna, Block- Chhatna | Only two *paras* in the village, of which one is relatively earlier and is the *adivasi para.* Important also is *Harinaam Sankirtan* as well as the respect associated to the local Sanyasi *sthan.* Important *bratas*- Sanyasi *puja brata*, Bipadtarini, Śivaratri. | The village did not yield any significant lore associated with festivals rites and rituals or about the past history of the village. |
|---|---|---|---|
| Parasibona (B) | P.O.- Susunia, Police station- Chhatna, Block- Chhatna | No special *puja* takes place, excepting the local ones arranged by the *Gram Sholoanna Committee.* Important local festivals are of Bura Buri, Marangburu (*Kartik* and *Magh*) Dolyatra (*Caitra*) | The village did not yield any significant lore associated with festivals rites and rituals or about the past history of the village. |
| Suabasa (B) | P.O.- Lakkhanpur, Police station- Gangajalghati, Block- Amarkanan | A village of *adivasis*, there were mentioned to be seven important festivals throughout the year, apart from which some houses have personal Laxmi, Manasa *pujas*,-limited to families. At the village level, the seven important *pujas* are- Maghi *puja* and Nagordola (*Magh*, where the Nagordola festival is accompanied by fowl or goat sacrifice), Badna (*Paus*), Salvi *puja* (Doljatra, *Caitra*), Ero Sim *puja* (*Asad*), Hariyar Sim (*Bhadra*, when the sowed rice plants are green), Chendera (spelled Che-de-ra) *puja* (*Baisakh*, which marks the beginning of the hunting season, without these offerings the locals cannot enter the jungle, according to the villagers). | Villagers belief to worship all gods in the western side. Besides this, no other lore about the past history of the village. |

| | | | |
|---|---|---|---|
| Debogram (M) | 2237'N/8718'E (approx) P.O.- Goaltor, Police station- Shalboni, Block-Shalboni | Important- Śiva temple, *puja* in *Phalgun* for a month and a seven-day long *mela* associated with it. Apart from this, the village has Manasa temples, besides this, the regular *pujas* are arranged by the *Gram Sholoanna Committee* including, Durga, Kali, Laxmi. | The village did not yield any significant lore associated with festivals rites and rituals or about the past history of the village. |
| Jalahari (M) | 22 38'N / 87 18.5'E (approx) P.O.- Moupal, Police station- Shalboni, Block- Shalboni | Important is the annual Gajan of Bura Śiva of the temple by the same name. The festival is also associated with a seven-day long festival. | According to popular lore, there used to be two *bandhs* in the village, which used to be full of water all year round because of which, the villagers never experienced water scarcity. Thus, is the name of the village- Jalahari. |
| Deuli (M) | 22 38.9'N / 87 19.9'E (approx) | Significant is the festival of Kalsandar Parba in the month of *Magh* for one day. The deity is | Importance of Kalsanda states- several years ago, few cowherds while playing |
| | P.O.- Moupal, Police station- Shalboni, Block-Shalboni | located under a banyan tree in the village. | 'fake human sacrifice to a local god who demands humans', took a leaf and pretending it to be a sharp weapon, gently struck the neck of a boy who was pretending to be the one who is being sacrificed. Strangely enough, the head of the boy got cut with the stroke of the leaf and came apart from the rest of the body. It was only with the blessings of Kalsanda that he was infused with new life. |

| | | | |
|---|---|---|---|
| Bishnupur (M) | 22 39′N / 87 17.8′E (approx) Post Office- Jatra Bishnupur, Police station- Shalboni, Block- Shalboni | The village has Sadgops, Kumar, Goyala, Layek, Majhi and Santhals. The main occupation of the villagers are agriculture as well as fishing. Few decades back, the Bhim *puja* has started in the village in the month of *Magh* with a week-long *mela*. | The village did not yield any significant lore associated with festivals rites and rituals or about the past history of the village. |
| Dangarpara (M) | 22 36.5′N / 87 19.5′E (approx) Post Office- Dhangarpara, Police station- Shalboni, Block- Shalboni | The village has Tili, Layek, Subarnabanik, Santhals, Bairagi and others. Important- Śiva Gajan during *Baisakh,* with week-long Gajan *mela* and Saraswati *puja* in *Magh,* with four- day long *mela*. The village has a murti of Trailokyanath Śiva. Important is also the bi- annual Sitala *puja* and the annual *Harinaam Sankirtan Chabbis Prahar*. The village also has important recognition for a *Pirer sthan*, as well as a various village deities | Popularly believed the Gajan festival is nearly 200 years old. |
| Karnagarh (M) | 22 37.8′N / 87 19.3′E (approx) Post Office- Karnagarh Bishnupur, Police station- Shalboni, Block- Shalboni | Mostly Majhi and others are Brahmans, Mahisya, Santals and others. Significant are the Dandaswer Śiva and Mahamaya temples of which the former is bigger in size than the latter. Both receive *nitya puja*, apart from which they also receive special *puja*. Gajan is held with *mela* for Śiva during *Caitra*. Mahamaya receives special *puja* from Saradiya Saptami till Dasami with goat sacrifice, as well as a specific date at the end of *Baisakh* with *anna bhog*- referred to as Desh *puja*. Other temples are of Sitala and Jagannath. Sitala has *nitya puja*, as well as during the month of *Baisakh* and the Jagannath temple receives *puja* during *Rathyatra* | Popular lore has it that Saivite and author of *Sivayana*- Rameswar Bhattacharya, left his birthplace- Jadupur village,after being tortured by king of Ghatal- Sobha Singha. He attained *siddha* (the supreme knowledge) at the Mahamaya temple, along with the king of Karnagarh- Jasobanta Singha. |

| | | | |
|---|---|---|---|
| Sankrui (M) | 2233′N/8727′E (approx) Post Office-, Police station- Keshpur, Block- Keshpur | The village has Sadgop, Kamar, Majhi and the important *puja* is Sitala and Harinaam Sankirtan in *Jaisthya* and Manasa in *Bhadra*. | The village did not yield any significant lore associated with festivals rites and rituals or about the past history of the village. |
| Kana Sol (M) | 22 33.5′N / 87 27.8′E (approx) | The village consists of Sadgops, Brahmans, Kamar Majhi. Important is Jhareswar Śiva Gajan, which is stated to be 300 year old. This | The village did not yield any significant lore associated with festivals |
| | Post Office- Kana Sol, Police station- Keshpur, Block- Keshpur | receives *nitya puja* as well as Gajan *mela*. The village also has a Sitala temple | rites and rituals or about the past history of the village. |
| Parulia (M) | 2234′N/8726′E (approx) Post Office- Parsura, Police station- Keshpur, Block- Keshpur | The village has Sadgop, Majhi, Santal, Layek, Bagdi, etc. Important festivals include the *Harinaam Sankirtan* in every five years. The village also has a Damodar Jiu temple of Śiva, which also houses a Sitala and a Manasa idols. | The village did not yield any significant lore associated with festivals rites and rituals or about the past history of the village. |
| Nera Deul (M) | 22 33.8′N / 87 26.5′E (approx) Post Office- , Police station- Keshpur, Block- Keshpur | The village consists of both so-called higher and lower classes and important is the Lakkhijnardan Jiu temple, which has Raasutsav and the other is the Kameswarnath Jiu, which is a Śiva temple with a Gajan in *Caitra*. This temple of Śiva also has three idols of Sitala. The village also has Saraswati *puja*, | It is believed that a local king- Umapati Debbhatta constructed the temple of Kameswarnath Jiu, but due to some unknown reason, the top of the temple remained incomplete, thus, the name of the village. |
| Anandapur (M) | 2235′N/8726′E (approx) Post Office- Anandapur, Police station- Keshpur, Block- Keshpur | The village includes Brahman, Sadgop, Karmakar, Dom, Bauri, Hari and others. Important in the village is Harinaam Sankirtan. Apart from other *baroari pujas*, the village also has Haurimayer *puja* and Bir Jhapat utsav- both of which are locally considered as tribal festivals. The Bir Jhapat also has a *mela* for a day during *Paus Sankranti*. The deity receives pig, goat, fowl sacrifices. | There is a lore associated with the Utsav of Bir Jhapat, where one cannot begin the *puja*, until granted permission by the deity. |

| | | | |
|---|---|---|---|
| Dhalahara (M) | 22 3̣4.9′N / 87 2̣6.5′E (approx) Post Office-Parsura, Police station-Keshpur, Block-Keshpur | The village consists of Brahmans, Kayasthas, Bagdi, Dom, Layek and others. The important deity of the place is Bateswar Śiva, which receives two important Gajan *pujas*- one at the time of *Caitra Sankranti*, and another one at the time of *Baisakh Sankranti*. Both have week-long *melas*. Another important temple is that of Paglimata- referred to a Gouri deity. She receives special *puja* with aninmal sacrifice during Kali *puja*. | For maintaining the temple of Bateswar Śiva, the king of Karnagargh-Jasobant Singha had donated a land of 108 *beegha* zamin. It is popularly believed that the *pujas* of Śiva started in 1330 *bangabda* |
| Nutanbazaar (M) | 22 3̣3.8′N / 87 2̣5.6′E (approx) Post Office-Nutanbazaar, Police station- Keshpur, Block-Keshpur | The village consists of Brahmans, Tili, Majhi, Sadgops and Mahisya. Important *pujas* of the month are- Ambubachi (*Asad*), Manasa *puja* (*Sravana*), Saraswati (*Magh*), Dolyatra and *Harinaam Sankirtan* (*Phalgun*) and Sitala (*Caitra*). Apart from these, certain other festivals also take place, which are referred to as tribal ceremonies by rest of the villagers and are only attended by selected few of the so-called lower classes. These are- Baram *puja* and Bhangsingh *puja* (in *Magh*)- both of which has *mela*. The Bhangsingh *mela* is for a day. | The name of the village is recent one-derived from a new bazaar in the place. The old name was Nayagram. |
| Garbeta (M) | 225̣1.8′N/872̣0.9′E Post Office- Garbeta, Police station- Garbeta, Block-Garbeta | Important is the temple of Sarbamangala-referred to as a *dasabhuja*, *singhabahini* Durga. The deity has important *nitya puja* with rice *bhog* and festival of Durga *puja* (Aswin). Also important are Kameswar Śiva temple, (*nitya puja* and a three-day *puja* and festival during *Caitra Sankranti*and Gajan), Radhaballab Jiu temple of Visṇu (*nitya puja* | Locally several lore associated with devi Sarbamangala. One is a popular belief that there is a *yup-kastha* or sacrificial alter hidden within a pond-Pathgeria- close to the temple. several villagers, |

| | | | |
|---|---|---|---|
| | | and three day *mela* during *dolyatra* in *Phalgun*), Lakkhijanardan Jiu and 12 Śiva temples in the bazaar area of the village | or their ancestors are supposed to have witnessed it at some point. |
| Ruparghagra (M) | 2252′N/8719′E (approx) Post Office- Patharpara, Police station- Garbeta, Block- Garbeta | The main residents include- Brahmans, Bagdi, Kudmi, Kalu, Mal and Santals. Important are the festivals of Durga *puja* and Laxmi *puja* (*Aswin*) and Rupasini (4 th *Magh*)- marked by votive offerings of terracotta horses and elephants and also Sitala and Śiva. | Locally believed that Rupasini is supposed to cure illness and save from evil spirits and evil eyes. |
| Sarengagar (M) | 2251′N/8720′E (approx) Post Office- Garbeta, Police station- Garbeta, Block- Garbeta | The main habitation includes- Brahmans, Sadgops, Goyala, Tambuli, Santals and others. Important festivals of the village include the worship of Radhagobindo Jiu, the worship of Dasohara (*Jaisthya*). Another important festival, which is especially important for the Santals is the worship of Banga Thakur or the Sargar Jat Utsab. A week-long *mela* and festival accompany | Locally the festival of Banga Thakur is believed to be over 200 years old. |
| Nachanjam (M) | 2250′N/8720′E (approx) Post Office- Piardoba, Police station- Garbeta, Block- Garbeta | The village has Sadgop, Tili, Majhi, Kumar, Santals, etc. Important is the two-day festival and *puja* of village deity- Nachanjamsini, who is also considered to be a *Banbibi*- from the day of *Makar Sankranti*. Votive offerings mark the spot with terracotta horses and elephants. The other deities of village include- Mahaprabhu, Manasa, Candi | Previously, the village was known as Jamnagar. It is also believed that at a nearby village, named Ekchakranagar- the five Pandava brothers of Mahabharata were hiding during their anonymous stay away from the palace. |
| Khadikasuli (M) | 2249′N/8721′E (approx) Post Office- Bankadaha, Police station- Garbeta, Block- Garbeta | The village contains Brahmans, Bauri, Kamar, Santals, etc. Important festivals of the village are- three-day long *Harinaam Sankirtan*, starting from *Baisakhi purnima*, Laxmi *puja (Aswin)*, Machaisini (1st *Magh)* and Balibilasini (*Makar Sankranti*). Both the festivals receive goat sacrifices. | The festivals are believed to be nearly 200 years old. |

| | | | |
|---|---|---|---|
| Tildaganj (M) | Post Office- , Police station- Pingla, Block- Pingla | Within the village resides both Hindus and Muslims. Important is the annual Tileswar Śiva Gajan and three-day long *mela* during the month of *Baisakh*. The village also has four Śiva temples and three Sitala temples | The Tileswar Śiva is considered to be the *gramdevata* and the village is supposed to have been named after him. |
| Kharagpur (M) | 22 1̣9.3′N / 87 1̣9.2′E Post Office- Kharagpur , Police station- Kharagpur, Block- Kharagpur | The important deity is Khargeswar Śiva, who receives *nitya puja*, as well as special *puja* during the Śivachaturdasi in *Phalgun*, as well as during *Caitra Sankranti* during Gajan. Another deity- Hirimbeswari is located nearby to the Śiva temple, who receives *puja* on *amavasya* in *Kartik*. The officiating priest is a Brahman. Kharagpur also has a *samadhi* of one Pir Lohani Saheb, who is also revered for his magical as well as healing touches in the past. | Popularly it is believed that the local king- Khargasingha of Dharenda built the temple of Khargeswar, but there is another belief which states it to have been built by Khargamalla of Malla royal family of Bishnupur (Bankura). It is also locally believed that Hirimbeswari is after the name of Hirimba of Mahabharata. |
| Gokulpur (M) | 22 2̣0′N / 87 1̣8′E (approx) Post Office- Bar Gokulpur , Police station- Kharagpur, Block- Kharagpur | The inhabitants include- Brahmans, Solanki, Hari, Muchi, Dhopa, Napit, Dom, Santals and others. Important *pujas* of the village include- Dharmaraj (every *Baisakh*), Sasti (*Jaisthya*), Bhim *puja* on *Bhimekadasi* (*Bhadra*), Gosto utsab (*Aghrayana*), Saraswati (*Magh*), and also Sitala, Śiva, Kali and Durga *pujas*. | The village did not yield any significant lore associated with festivals rites and rituals or about the past history of the village. |
| Gharaigerra (M) | 22 2̣2′N / 87 1̣7′E (approx) Post Office- Jakpur, Police station- Kharagpur, Block- Kharagpur | The village is mainly of Bagdi and Sabar. Important *puja*- Raksa Kali *puja*- every *Caitra*, which also follows a *mela*. There is also a Raksa Kali temple in the village, along with Sitala. | The village did not yield any significant lore associated with festivals rites and rituals or about the past history of the village. |

| | | | |
|---|---|---|---|
| Hariatara (M) | 22 20'N / 87 18'E (approx) Post Office- Rakhajungle, Police station- Kharagpur, Block- Kharagpur | The village has primarily people of so-called lower classes, including Santals, Tanti, Napit, Dhopa, etc. Important *puja*- every year- during the months of *Asad, Caitra* and *Paus* celebrates with pomp and splendor the worship of the *gramdevata* - Hariaburi. | The name of the village is from the village deity. |
| Kanthra (M) | 22 20.3'N / 87 18.6'E (approx) Post Office- Salua, Police station- Kharagpur, Block- Kharagpur | The village has Kayastha, Sadgop, Bairagi, Napit and Santals. Important festivals of the village are- Radhagobindo Jiu's *Rathyatra* (*Asad*), Jhulanhyatra and Janmastami (*Bhadra*), Raasutsav (*Aghrayana*), and Dolyatra (*Maghi purnima*). The village also has Radhagobindo Jiu temple as well as Manasa. A significant utsav is concerning cattle, which takes place after Diwali. The cattles are bathed, painted and groomed and tied to a stump within a field. They are provoked to get excited by noisemaking with various metal objects, like ghanta as well as *dhol*. | The cattle utsav, bears a good resemblance to a similar festival that takes place in Bihar- Chhotanagpur plateau region. |
| Aandar Suda (M) | 22 10'N / 87 21'E (approx) Post Office- Dhibarpanda, Police station- Narayangarh, Block- Narayangarh | The village has Brahmans, Kayastha, Tanti, Lodha, Malakar, Kamar, Swarnakar, etc. Important is the festival of Basanti *puja*. The brass idol of the deity resides within a temple in the village. The village also has Candi and Sitala stone images. | Locally, the festival of Basanti *puja* is referred to be more than 200 years old. |

| | | | |
|---|---|---|---|
| Kasba Narayangarh (M) | 229.6′N/8723′E Post Office- Narayangarh, Police station- Narayangarh, Block- Narayangarh | The village has Muslim population, apart from Brahmans, Sadgops, Mahisya, Lodhas, etc. Important festivals of the village include- Rathyatra (*Asad*), with a four-day long *mela*, Durga *pujai* and also Brahmani devi's *puja* and *mela* (*Aswin*)- which is taken to be more than 400 years old, Kali *puja (Kartik)*, *Maghi purnima snanyatra (Magh)*, Dolyatra *(Phalgun)* and Sitala (*Caitra*), apart from other recent festivities of Saraswati *puja* and Laxmi *puja*. | Popularly believed that Brahmani devi was established as she instructed king Gandharba Pal (a vassal under the Ganga dynasty of rulers of Odisha) in his sleep to do so. This family of rulers were Sadgops. He got the instructions while sleeping at a local inn, on his way to Puri. |
| Asada (M) | 22 9.9′N/87 25′E (approx) Post Office- , Police station- Narayangarh, Block- Narayangarh | The village mainly consist of Brahmans, Kayastha, Mahisya, Solankis, etc. Important *pujas* of the village are Dharmathakur (*Jaisthya*), Manasa (*Sravan*), Viswakarma (*Bhadra*), Janmastami, Indra *puja*, Laxmi *puja* and Madammohan (*Kartik*)- which is a festival that takes place within the temple and the adjoining *Raasmancha*. Also important is the beheaded idol, worshipped as Candi, which is referred to as being destroyed by Kalapahar. | The deity of Madammohan was established by the local royalty and is still revered by several people all across region. Though the idol of Candi is referred to as female deity, yet it resembles a male deity, with another person lying on his lap- and finally resembling- *Narsimha avatar*. |
| Danton (M) | 2156′N / 8716′ E Post Office- Danton, Police station- Danton, Block- Danton | Important are the Jagannath temple and the Syamaleswar Śiva, which has both *nitya* and *puja* during Gajan every year. | Locally believed the place got its name from Sri Chaitanya who, while traveling through the region, had used a *danton*- referred to a thin slice of raw wood from a tree, which is used to clean and scrub teeth. According to many, the ancient name of the place is Dantapur. There are also various lore associated with Sarasanka pond. |

| | | | |
|---|---|---|---|
| Rautarapur (M) | 2156.8'N / 8716.8' E (approx) Post Office- Sukabol, Police station- Danton, Block- Danton | The village has Teli, Brahman, Goyala, Dhopa and others. Important *pujas* are the Sitala *puja* (*Baisakh*), Basuli *puja* and Rathyatra (*Asad*), and Important are the *puja* and *mela* of Iswar Jiu Narayana. The village also has Harinaam Sankirtan during *Phalgun* and *Caitra.* | The village did not yield any significant lore associated with festivals rites and rituals or about the past history of the village. |
| Palasiya (M) | 2155'N / 8715' E (approx) Post Office- , Police station- Danton, Block- Danton | Important to notice the prevalence of both Hindus and Muslims in village. The main classes are- Brahmans, Mahisya, Rajak, Kumar, Dule, Hari, Napit and others. Important festivals and *pujas* are all connected with Vaisnavism, including such festivals like, Jhulan (*Sravan*), Chaitanya Mahaprabhu Raasyatra with a one-day *mela* (*Bhadra*), Chaitanya Mahaprabu Giriyatra utsav (*Kartik*), Dolyatra (*Phalgun*)- which has a week-long *mela* and Mukteswar Śiva *puja* and Gajan (*Caitra*). | The village did not yield any significant lore associated with festivals rites and rituals or about the past history of the village. |
| Moghalmari (M) | 2155.3'N / 8714.8' E (approx) Post Office- Nekurseni, Police station- Danton, Block- Danton | Important classes of the village includes Brahmans, Dhopa, Majhi, Kamar, Santals, etc. Important is the Gajan (*Caitra-Baisakh*). The village also has Sitala and the temple of the Śiva is considered to be inspired by Muslim architecture. The village is also historically significant being the area for the battle of Moghalmari in 1576 CE, when the army of Daud Shah- the son of Suleiman Karrani, was defeated at thehands of the Mughal army, led by Todar Mal. Though the latter won, yet many soldiers lost their lives and thus, the name of the village | The Gajan *mela* is locally considered to be nearly 200 years old. Locally, the *Sasisenar Pathsala* is also important, which is only marked by a lithic symbol in present times. It is believed that Sasisena/Sakhisena- the daughter of the king of Amravati- Bikram Kesari, used to study here, in the same *pathsala* (school) as Ahimanik- the son of a farmer. A love story evolved, resulting in their elopement. This is also narrated in *Sakhisena* by Fakirram. |

| | | | |
|---|---|---|---|
| Khandarui (M) | 2154'N / 8714' E (approx) Post Office- Turkagarh, Police station- Danton, Block- Danton | The village has Brahman, Bairagi, Kayastha, Bhumij, Kol, Chhutor, Tanti, Kadma, Teli, Santals and others, apart from Muslims. Every year has Durga *puja* (*Aswin*), Sitala (*Baisakh*), Kali *puja* and Raasyatra (*Kartik*), Saraswati *puja* (*Magh*) and Gajan (*Caitra*). The village also has temple of Bhagyeswari devi and Kali. | The Bhagyeswari devi and Kali temples are mentioned to have been built by the migrants from Telenga region and thus, the architecture do not resemble any other of the area. Several Telengi Brahmans used to work under the Samanta kings for a period of time and later declared themselves as independent. Several lore speak about the possible skirmish between the two. |
| Sukarol (M) | 22'N/87'E (approx) Post Office, Police station- Kesiari | The village consists of Brahman, Bairagi, Rajak, Kalandi, Tanti, Mahisya and Santals. Important are the Śiva, Sitala and Candi temples of the village. The festivals of the village includes, apart from Durga *puja* and Saraswati *puja*, a *mela* held in *Aswin*. The itala is worshipped in Baisakh every year. | It is popularly mentioned that the Sitala idol was discovered in a local pond- Gopal Sagar |
| Buraburi Kalupur (M) | 22'N/87'E (approx) Post Office, Gopinathpur, Police station- Bhagabanpur | The village includes- Mahisya and Rajbangsi. Important festivals include Sitala (*Baisakh*), Raasutsav (*Kartik*) and Saraswati *puja* (*Magh*) and the worship of Buraburi. | A local lore ascribes the name of the village to two stone idols which were found within a forest which covered the present east region of the village. The whole village was under the Samanta royalty. Finally, these idols were established within a temple in the village and eversince the worship continues. Thus, the name of the village. |

| | | | |
|---|---|---|---|
| Biswanathpur (M) | 22′Ṇ/87′Ẹ (approx) Post Office- Naipur , Police station- Pataspur | The village consists of Brahmans, Sadgops, Mahisya, Dhopa and others. Important festivals include- Chandan Yatra (*Baisakh*), Jhulanyatra (*Saravan*), Janmastami and Radhastami (*Bhadra*), Gobardhanyatra and the following annakut utsav and Radhagopal Jiu Raasyatra (*Kartik*), and Dolyatra and Śivachaturdasi (*Phalgun*). The important tempels of the village are- Radhagopal Jiu temple, Krisnabalaram Jiu and a Śiva temple | It is popularly believed that the name of the village is after the name of the Śiva temple- Biswanath Śiva. |
| Teparpara (M) | 22′Ṇ/87′Ẹ (approx) Post Office- Pataspur, Police station- Pataspur | The village consists of Brahmans, Namahsudra, Mahisya, Kamar, Rajak, Dolui, Kodma and Tili. Every year, the important festivals consist of Ratyatra (*Asad*) and Kartik *purnima* has Raasyatra. The Rathyatra has a week-long *mela* and the Raasyatra has a six- day long *mela*. The village also has a temple dedicated to Lakkhijanardan, a Śiva temple and Sitala temple. | Both the festivals are considered to be 500 years old and the Raas utsab was started by the king of Panchetgarh and the temple stands within the donated land of the royalty. It is also locally believed that Sri Chaitanya had passed through the village on his way to Puri. |
| Naipur (M) | 22′Ṇ/87′Ẹ (approx) Post Office- , Police station- Pataspur | The village consists of Brahmans, Tili, Subarnabanik, Rajput, Solanki, Mathar, Jele. The important festivals include- Gajan (*Baisakh*), Madamohan Jiu's Rathyatra (*Asad* and *Magh*), Jhulanyatra (*Sravan*), Durga *puja* (*Aswin*), Bhim ekadasi (*Magh*) and Dolyatra | It is locally explained that excepting the Gajan and the Durga *puja*, the rest of the *pujas* were started by the local royalty by the name- Kanungo |

| | | | |
|---|---|---|---|
| | | (*Phalgun*). The Gajan *mela* takes place for a month in *Baisakh*. The Rathyatra has a *mela* for a week. The Bhim ekadasi also has a *mela* for a day. The village also has Śiva, Sitala and Madanmohan Jiu. The idol of Sitala is locally referred to as representing an image of a *raksasa*. | zamindars. The name of the village is also after the zamindars, who are said to have come from Rajputana (King Jyanadananda of Kanungo family in 1602) and settled in a new place. Thus the original name Nayapur, from which is the name Naipur. The Rathyatra and the Bhim ekadasi *melai* are both considered to be at least 300 year old. |
| Egra (M) | 2154'N / 8732.0' E Post Office- Egra, Police station- Egra | An old Śiva temple at Egra Itangarh- referred to as Itangarh Mahadev, which has architectural similarities with the *deul* of Odisha. Apart from *nitya puja*, the temple receives Gajan during Śivacaturdasi every year, which begins from the Sri Pancmi of *Magh*. A *melai* takes palce for eight days from the day of Śivacaturdasi. Jagannath temple within the Brahman *para*, which has Rathyatraevery *Baisakh*andevery Aksaytritiya, the images of Śiva and Durga are taken for a boatride in the Krisnasagar pond in the village, which continues for 21 days in the afternoon. | Regarding the construction of the Śiva temple of Egra Itangarh, there lies a dichotomy as according to some, it was built by the independent king of Odisha- Gajapti Mukundabed and others say it was done by a Samanta king of Utkal with the title of Mahapatra. |
| Chandri (M) | 2225'N/87'E Post Office- Chandri, Police station- Jhargram | The population of the village consists of Brahmans, Bairagi, Khandait, Majhi, Bhuj and others. Important is the Chandasekhar Śiva Gajan in Baisakh every year. Besides, the other deities are Sitala, Sabitri, Saatbhagini and other tribal deities, including Dakuiburi and Charamburi | Chandasekhar Śiva Gajan has a *mela* which is considered to be 200 years old and the temple of Chandasekhar Śiva is said to be constructed by the king of Jhargram. The name of the village is after the name of the deity. |

| | | | |
|---|---|---|---|
| Jhargram (M) | 2226.9'N/870.5'E Post Office- Chandri, Police station- Jhargram | The deity of the royalty is Sabitri. There is no idol and the rituals are performed on a chest/storage box and a *kharga* (a type of sharp weapon). The box is considered to contain a lump of hair of the goddess herself. | Interstingly enough, the village has several successors of the Malla royal family of Bishnupur. There is a story about the establishment of the goddess Sabitri, who was considered as a mortal. |
| Baliyat (M) | 2211'N/8652'E (approx) Post Office- , Police station- Gopiballabpur | The village consists of Brahman, Bairagi, Mahisya, Bagdi, Tili and others. Important is the Baliyat annual utsav and one-day *mela-* on *Caitra Sankranti*. People from far off place, from all over Mednipur as well as Odisha and Bihar often visit at this time. | Pandava brothers of Mahabharat, is believed to have bathed and offered prayers on *Caitra Sankranti,* while in hiding. |
| Kanpur (M) | 22 13'N/86 53'E (approx) Post Office- Tapasiya, Police station- Gopiballabpur. | The village consists of Kayastha, Goyala, Tanti, Namahsudra and Bagal. Important festivals are Makarsnan in *Paus*, Sitala in *Magh* and Dolyatra in *Phalgun*. Both are very old ceremonies. The Makarsnan has people coming from all over Mednipur as well as adjoining regions. There is another temple of Syamsundar Jiu, dedicated to Radhakrisna. | The village did not yield any significant lore associated with festivals rites and rituals or about the past history of the village. |

| | | | |
|---|---|---|---|
| Gopiballabpur (M) | 2212.3'N/8654.1'E Post Office- Gopiballabpur, Police station- Gopiballabpur. | The village has Brahman, Bairagi, Kshatriya, Vaisya and Sudra. Important *pujas* of the village is the Danda Mahotsav of Radhagobindo Jiu (*Jaisthya*). The other temples of the village are- Jagannath and Hanuman Jiu. There are some other temples, which are locally referred to belong to tribals, including- Saatbhogi, Talbetal, Duliaburi, Gungunia- which are all village deities. | Danda Mahotsav of Radhagobindo Jiu is considered to be more than 300 years old. |

| | | | |
|---|---|---|---|
| Nayagram (M) | 2202'08.24"N / 8710'57.58" E (approx) Post Office- Nayagram, Police station- Nayagram | The village has Karan, Kunar, Lodha, Majhi and Sadgop. Important festivals, apart from the Durga *puja*, is the Sitala and Kali *pujas*. The village also has historical value, with the Khelargarh fort, started by king Pratap Chandra Singha (1490 CE.), but was completed by his son Balabhadra Singha. | The Kali *puja* is stated to have been started by the royalty of Nayagram. There is also a Śiva temple, stated to have been established by local royalty. The royalty was an independent one. |
| Deulghat (P) | Post Office - Arsa, Police Station- Arsa | The place is historically famous for the two magnificent terracotta temples of Śiva. *Nitya puja* as well as Gajan still takes place. There is also special *puja* every Monday. The place also has several *melas*, which are famous and draws huge crowd from far off places like, Kolkata- including- Makar *mela* (*Paus*), Baruni *mela* (*Caitra*) and the Dolyatra *mela*- also referred to as Palas Parban. | Though a modern asram has been established at the site, about 30 years back, yet the historical importance of the site, with several relics of idols (possible Jain deities as well as Puranic deities) were seen to be preserved. |
| Palpal (P) | Post Office - Arsa, Police Station- Arsa | Important is the Hari *mandir*, Śiva temple, which has a *mela* for three days during *Baisakh* Gajan. | The village did not yield any significant lore associated with festivals rites and rituals or about the past history of the village. |
| Sirkabad (P) | Post Office- Sirkabad, Police Station- Arsa | Important is the Manasa deity in the Laya *para* (southern part of village) which has the anthropomorphic form of the deity,that is worshipped throughout the year and special *puja* on *Sravan Sankranti*, with animal sacrifice. There are total of seven Manasa temples of the village and excepting the one in Laya *para*, which belongs to a certain family, the rest are managed by *Gram Sholoanna Committee*. The Hari *mandir* (of Gaurange Mahaprabhu) of the village also receives daily *puja*. The other temples are all located in the bazaar area, with a Durga *dalaan* and Mahavir temple | The village did not yield any significant lore associated with festivals rites and rituals or about the past history of the village. |

| | | | |
|---|---|---|---|
| Open field,1km before Charra (P) | Post Office- Charra, Police Station- Charra, Block- Charra (on right side of Barakar Road from Purulia. Distance from Purulia is 8 kms and Mauja- Charra) | Several herostones within an area measuring (approx) 14½′ in diameter. A total of 11 herostones could be see, with varying lengths visible above the round | The village did not yield any significant lore associated with festivals rites and rituals or about the past history of the village. |
| Charra (P) | Post Office- Charra, Police Station- | Important is the Dharmaraj *mandir* within the Dom *para* (north-western part of village). This has special *puja*, apart from *nitya puja*- on | The villagers were aware about the significant importance of the various |

| | | | |
|---|---|---|---|
| | Charra, Block- Charra | Ram Nabami and three days of *mela* during *Jaisthya*- called- Dharmaraj *mela*. The other temple is of Basanti goddess. Both the temples contain various images which can possibly be of Jain origin. Even the entrance of the Basanti *mandir* has another idol of a possible Jain Tirthankara | idols within the village and that some of them can have possible Jain origins as well. But apart from this, the village did not yield any lore about past history, etc. |
| Deulbhita (P) | Horoktol-Udaypur Gram Panchayat- on the banks of Harai river and located next to Angarkhuli bandh. | The village consists of Rajuar *para*, Misra *para* as well as Bauri *para*, which has several Manasa *mandirs* and *puja* takes place on *Sravan Sankranti*. Within the Misra *para* lies an open ground at a slight elevation of 6 ft from the road (approx) where lies several remains of broken Śiva lingas (the biggest one amongst them measuring 4½′ L x 1′ W x 1′ H). Across the road, is located the Haragouri *mandir*. This is an encosed recent structure which houses several idols of Brahmanical as well as possible Jain deities. The temple is located on the western bank of the Harai river | The village did not yield any significant lore associated with festivals rites and rituals or about the past history of the village. |

| | | | |
|---|---|---|---|
| Para (P) | 23.52N 86.52E Post Office- *Para*, Police Station- *Para*, Block- *Para* | The village significantly has Kayastha, Muchi, Moira, Bagdi, Bauri, Dom and Brahmans. There are seven Durga and six Kali *mandirs* all across the village. Important within the village is the Yamraj *sthan*, within the Bauri *para* of the village and at one end of the village. This receives special *puja* on Buddha *purnima* and a seven-day *mela* follows. The Bauri *para* has Manasa special *puja* on Sravan Sankranti, apart from daily rites. At the eastern side of the village stands two terracotta temples, of which one is referred to as Candi mandir, where daily *puja* takes place, but the other one, though is referred to as Laxmi *mandir*, it is discarded. Important are also the Raghunath and Radharaman *mandirs*. The village also has a *Chabbis Prahar Harinaam Sankirtan atchala*. | It is popularly believed that the sanskar of the Radharaman *mandir* was done by Raja Mansingha, as he went to the 2nd conquest of Odisha via Telkupi. There are local lore associated to the royalty and the establishment of the deity and worship. |
| Cheliama (P) | 23.31.7N 86.41.4E Post Office- , Police Station- Raghunathpur, Block- Raghunathpur Block- 1 | In front of village is a Ram *mandir dalaan* and a Durga *dalaan*. Both do not have any idol, which is only present in the terracotta Raghunath *mandir*, which is stated to be built by local king- Raghunath, according to a plaque at the entrance of the temples | The village did not yield any significant lore associated with festivals rites and rituals or about the past history of the village. |
| Banda (P) | 23.52N 86.52E Post Office- , Police Station- Raghunathpur- Mangalda-Moutorh, Block- Raghunathpur Block-2 | The village is very small with only one *para*- Bauri. The village contains the ruins of a temple, possible Jain origin. This does not have any *puja* in recent times and stands protected by the Archaeological Survey of India (ASI) | The locals are aware about the temple being of historical importance. No other local lore available. |

| | | | |
|---|---|---|---|
| Mangalda (P) | Post Office- , Police Station- Raghunathpur, Block- Raghunathpur Blck-2 | Important is the Śiva Gajan and *mela* for three days which draws people fom all adjoining villages | The locals are aware about the temple being of historical importance. No other local lore available. |
| Gobrandha (P) | Post Office- , Police Station- Raghunathpur, Block- Raghunathpur Block- 2 | Important is the Śiva Gajan and *mela* for three days which draws people fom all adjoining villages | The locals are aware about the temple being of historical importance. No other local lore available. |
| Moutorh (P) | Post Office- , Police Station- Raghunathpur, Block- Raghunathpur Block- 2 | Important is the Kali *puja* and *mela* for a day. The *puja* has goat sacrifice amounting to few hundred and attracting crowd from all over Purulia. | The locals are aware about the temple being of historical importance. No other local lore available. |
| Dumurkola (P) | Post Office- , Police Station- Raghunathpur, Block- Raghunathpur Block- 2 | Important was the Visṇu temple, which is at present not visible. This was made by the local royalty, who were related to the Panchkot royal family (through the maternal side) | Popular lore has it that a fight ensued between the two royal families. The local family, then left for Bandi in Jharkhand and left the Visṇu temple in the village destroyed and vacant. |
| Panchkot (P) | 23.6N 86.76667E Post Office- Panchkot, Police Station- Panchkot, Panchayet- Panchkot | The place is famous for the remains/relics of the temples, as well as the palace of the erstwhile royalty of Panchkot. This is an important site for archaeological and historical assemblages and studies. | Various local lore concerning the royal family and the deities and temples of the family. |

| | | | |
|---|---|---|---|
| Talajudi (P) | 23.25.5N 86.46.4E Post Office- Talajudi, Police Station- Kasipur, Panchayet- Barandi | The village has five *paras*- Karmakar, Deogharia, Poddar, Sarak and Bauri. Important is the Baruneswar Śiva *puja* and three-day long *mela*- 27 , 28 at the time of *Caitra* Gajan. Within the same temple premise stands a Manasa *sthan*, which receives special *puja* on 1st *Magh*, along with goat sacrifice. This is also considered the *gramdevata* of the village. The village also yielded information regarding herostones near the temple of Baruneswar Śiva. | According to local lore, the name of the village is after the 108 *pukur* (pond) which used to be located within the village. The name has been derived from *Talab* + *Judi*. These waterbodies were considered to be the *Prasad* of Baruneswar Śiva |
| Kasipur (P) | 23.43N 86.67E Post Office-Kasipur, Police Station- Kasipur, Panchayet- Kasipur | Famous for Rajrajeswari *mandir*- the family deity of the local royalty of Kasipur by the title of Singha Deo. The temple bears a plaque, according to which it was established by king Jyotiprasad Singha Deo Bahadur in 1331 *Bangabda* (1924 CE.) | There are local lore about the establishemdent of the deity and its annual *puja* |
| Balarampur (P) | 236.1'N/8613.0'E Post Office- Balarampur, Police Station- Balarampur, Panchayet- Balarampur | The original inhabitants of the village are referred to Kaivartyas. At present, the residents include the *aadi* or the ancient *para* of the Kaivartya on the right side of the village and Kumor *para* on the left. The viilage is important for Jagannath, Śiva, Durga and Rani Sati *mandirs*. There are also many Manasa *mandirs* where annual *puja* takes place during *Sravan Sankranti*, with a *mela* and *chhou* dance and *jatra*. The Rani Sati mandir has an annual *puja* which coincides with the Manasa *puja* of *Sravan Sankranti* | Popularly believed that the village got its name from a Kaivartya named Balaram. The Durga *mandir* is considered to be 100 years old. Locally, the Rani Sati *mandir* is supposed to have many lore, but the people of the Marwari community, who looks after the temple, were not available for comments during fieldwork. |
| Gobindopur & Bagmundi (P) | 2310.7'N/863.7'E Post Office- Bagmundi, Police | Gobindopur has Kaivartyas, Karmakar, Brahmans, Das, Vaisnavas. It has Manasa *puja* in about five houses, who are referred to as *Sakha*- or people who have spiritual | The present king of the local royal family- Bhabani Prasad Singha Deo is much revered and |

| | | | |
|---|---|---|---|
| | Station- Bagmundi, Panchayet- Bagmundi | powers. The name Bagmundi is derived from a tiger head, which was hunted by local royalty about 500 years ago. Important religious activities of the village include- Raasmancha with 11 peaks and made of terracotta. Apart from this, a recent festival is to celebrate the birth anniversary of Subhas Chandra Bose, which is accompanied by a *mela* from 17th January till 23rd January. The village also has an *asram* and an idol of Bose. Bagmundi also has Manasa idols in almost every house and the worship entails goat and fowl sacrifices. | respected by all. |
| Ekra & Lohariya (P) | 234'N/8611'E (approx) Post Office- Bagmundi, Police Station- Bagmundi, Panchayet- Bagmundi (Lohariya is located 4 kms east of Gobindopur. Ekra is located 2 kms before Gobindopur) | This is famous for the worship of Śiva- referred to as Lohariya Śiva, which has Gajan and *mela* in *Caitra-Baisakh* for three days. The village mainly has Mahato population, who are also the worshippers. | Locally it is mentioned that the Lohariya Śiva temple of Lohariya is constructed at a site, where a cow was seen standing with milk issuing from its udder uninterruptedly. This was spotted by the Mahatos, who built the temple. |
| Burda (P) | 2310.9'N/861'E Post Office-Burda, Police Station- Burda, Panchayet- Burda | The village has Mahato- who are considered to be the oldest inhabitants of the village. Others are Kumor, Garai, Dhopa, Mura and others. The important deities of the village include- Śiva, Kali as well a Harinaam Sankirtan. An important tribal deity of the village is Nakti Durga (located on the right at the very entrance of the village). This is in the middle of the *Mahato para*. Important is also the Matha Buru *puja*. | Locally the Mehtos are believed to be from Punjab and the present generation is referred to be the 5 th one. |

| | | | |
|---|---|---|---|
| Suissa (P) | Post Office-Suissa, Police Station-Bagmundi, Panchayet-Bagmundi | The village is archaeologically a significant one, with several relics and idols, possible of Jain origin, preserved under a recent construction by the State Archaeology Department. Mostly these deities are all worshipped as local gods. There are two important Manasa *mandirs.* | The locals are aware about the temple being of historical importance. No other local lore available. |
| Harup (P) | Post Office-Suissa, Police Station-Bagmundi, Panchayet-Bagmundi | Harup *mela* on *Jaisthya Sankranti.* † concerning the Pansi Mura Hatiya Sini of this small village. | The village did not yield any significant lore associated with festivals rites and rituals or about the past history of the village. |
| Charida (P) | Post Office-Suissa, Police Station-Bagmundi, Panchayet-Bagmundi | This is referred to as the artisans village- of the *chhou* mask makers. The main residents of the village include- Kalindi *para-* at the entrance, which has Dom and Namahsudra. Others are Sutradhar, Roy, Brahmans, Gorai, Murai (on north and south) and there are scattered *adivasis,* who are available as landed labourers. The village has the festive season to be an important period of financial activities with sales going up and performances being staged during various *pujas.* This period starts with the Viswakarma | There are several lore associated with the beginning and the end of the working season of the artisans. |
| | | *puja*, followed by Manasa, Ganesh and Durga, Laxmi for Kojagori, Jagatdhatri, Kartik. Important in the village is also the Manasa *pujas-* which is there in almost every house and *puja* takes place on Bhadra (4th) or on *Sravan Sankranti.* The village also has Harinaam Sankirtan, Durga *puja.* All of these are managed by *Gram Sholoanna Committee.* No Gajan takes place and people attend the Gajan of Lohariya Siva. | |

| | | | |
|---|---|---|---|
| Kalimati (P) | Post Office- , Police Station- Bagmundi, Panchayet- Bagmundi | Important is the *Chabbisprahar Harinaam Sankirtan* as well as Durga *puja* within the Majhi *para*. In the Śiva *mandir*, no Gajan takes place. There is also the important *puja* of Duarbasini (within the 15$^{th}$ of the month of *Asad*). The officiating priest is one Manki. In front of the Sini goddess is the Jetha Mura on its right side. All people attend the Chhou of Suissa. There is also Manasa *puja* in almost every house- starting from *Sravan Sankranti* and continues till the entire month of *Bhadra*. | The Sini goddess is forbidden to be visited by women. Thus, the researcher was also not allowed to visit the site. |
| Anai &Jambad (P) | Post Office-, Police Station- Kenda, Block- Purulia 1 (they lie within 1½ km of distance within each other) | Important population of both villages include- Mahato, Brahman, Santal, Dom, Hari and others. The village of Anai is at present famous for Paresnath Mahadev Bera Ananda Asram, which is located on the southern side of the village. This asram has several *pujas*, including, Kali *puja*, Surya *puja*, special *puja* on 23$^{rd}$ *Bhadra*, *Paus Sankranti* and also on *Paus Krisnapaksha ekadasi*. Within the asram complex, several ancient Jain Tirthankara idols could be seen, where they are worshipped even in present times. Of the six Jain images, two were seen to be worshipped as Paresnath, two as Adinath and two as Chandraprabhu The village has Durga *puja* and a *mela* on *Paus Sankranti*. The asram could also be seen to have several possible herostones. Jambad is smaller in size as compared to Anai has Durga & Kali *puja* as well as Bhadu and Tusu *puja and bratas*. (A detailed report on these finds is given in Appendix-4) | The village did not yield any significant lore associated with festivals rites and rituals or about the past history of the village. |

| Ralibera (P) | Post Office- Ralibera Madhyapara, Police Station- Kenda, Block- Purulia 1B | The village is important for Śiva temple, next to primary school. On the left wall, next to the pedestal- 30 ft away (1'20" L x 1' W x 8" H). There are three Jain idols next to Śiva linga. (A detailed report on these finds is given in Appendix-4) | The village did not yield any significant lore associated with festivals rites and rituals or about the past history of the village. |
|---|---|---|---|
| Palma (P) | Post Office- Puncha , Police Station- Puncha, Block- Puncha | The village is noted for several historical assemblages, dating to Late Historical period. Several of these are also remains of possible Jain idols. Some of these are worshipped in present times as local village deities, especially fertility gods and goddesses. Several other suggested herostones were also seen within the village, which are also often the places of present worship of Ind/Indra *puja*. These herostones are also often referred | The village did not yield any significant lore associated with festivals rites and rituals or about the past history of the village. |
| | | to be grave-markers of the Bhumij community of the village, who are believed to have buried their ancestors in the past (though now, no such activity takes place). Several of the idols are also seen to be taken in within personal properties of various people of the village. (A detailed report on these finds is given in Appendix-4) | |
| Puncha (P) | 239.3'N/8639'E Post Office- Puncha , Police Station- Puncha, Block- Puncha | The village has Kaivartya- as one of the most oldest inhabitants of the village. The area is famous for the findings of Jain relics/idols, which are worshipped as local/village deities. This is across the Kangsabati river. On the western side of the village, within the Tamboli *para* is a Manasa temple.(A detailed report on these finds is given in Appendix-4). The village also has Tusu *mela*. | The village did not yield any significant lore associated with festivals rites and rituals or about the past history of the village. |

| Pakbira (P) | Post Office- Puncha , Police Station- Puncha, Block- Puncha | The village is archaeologically important with various stray occurances of *kalas*, idols and parts of broken images possibly of Jain origin- seen accumulated within an enclosure that also comprises of 3 temples of laterite stone, which also has idols within, but without *nitya puja*. Only an idol of Jain Tirthankara, locally referred to as Bhairabnath Śiva is worshipped daily and also on Mondays. The officiating priest resides in the Ray *Para* of the village. (A detailed report on these finds is given in Appendix-4) | The village did not yield any significant lore associated with festivals rites and rituals or about the past history of the village. |
|---|---|---|---|
| Budhpur (P) | Post Office- Puncha , Police Station- Puncha, Block- Puncha | The region is famous for the various finds associated with a broken Śiva temple. Many of the associated relics are referred to as herostones. Gajan takes place annually, as well as *nitya puja*. (A detailed report on these finds is given in Appendix-4) | The village did not yield any significant lore associated with festivals rites and rituals or about the past history of the village. |
| Hura (P) | 2317.9′N/8639.8′E Post Office- Puncha , Police Station- Puncha, Block- Puncha | The region did not yield any significant historical information. The regular *pujas* are- Durga, Laxmi, Siva Gajan and some Manasa temples has special *puja* every *Sravan Sankranti* | The village did not yield any significant lore associated with festivals rites and rituals or about the past history of the village. |

# Appendix 5

Location, measurements and brief information about various herostones and other related historical artifacts seen during the course of fieldwork. (The majority of the artifacts of idols and images which are worshipped as various folk gods and goddesses are mentioned in Appendix-3. The list below, includes mainly those artifacts which are referred to as herostones in the present region of study).

**Chhatna, Bankura**

Post Office- Chhatna

A visibly sculpted and heavily eroded herostone of a female warrior, worshipped as Sasti, is seen facing east, towards the Basali Temple. (5′ L x 1′22″ B x 7″ W). The image (2′10″ L) is in a running position with the left foot bent and the right foot bent and raised from the ground This sculpture stands on the banks of a local pond and under a banyan tree. Local lore has that three similar structures have gone under the mud of the banks.

**Dhumkoro, Bankura**

Location- Distance from Bankura town is 20 kms. The village lies on the left hand side of the NH 60 from Bankura Town. Thana and Block- Gangajalghati. Post office-Amarkanan.

Cluster of six herostones were seen near the *bandh*, which is located on the eastern outskirt of the village of Dhumkoro. At the time of fieldwork according to local information, three other similar structures have got submerged underground due to construction activity at the *bandh*. Much part of the six remaining herostones were seen damaged by erosion and water and construction activities, however, the images of sitting lion can be seen visible on top of three of the six herostones, measuring to about 2′ L x 1½′ B x 8″ W. One of the herostone is cylindrical in nature (2½′ L x 1½ diameter) One of the herostones displays part of an image of a warrior, facing the east, holding a bow in left hand (5′ L x 6½″ B). No arrow is visible in the image. The gender of the figure is not prominent due to heavy erosion, but the headgear and hair arrangement suggests a possible female warrior.

A Bhairab *sthan* is also located on the left of *bandh*. No regular *puja* takes place here but is visited occasionally by people for fulfillment of wish. A broken structure, possibly the broken part of an image is seen lying at the Bhairab *sthan* (1½ ′ L x 6″ W).

A herostone (5′ L x 8″ B) is seen displaced at a distance of about 20 ft from the Bhairab *sthan*, lying face-upright on the shallow water of the *bandh*. This makes measurement tabulation difficult. Sculpted on top, can be clearly seen the images of two elephants. Very close to this herostone, at about a distance of 7 ft on its right is another herostone, cylindrical in shape (6½ diameter x 5′ L) is seen standing in an upright condition. The base of this herostone too stands submerged in the shallow water of the *bandh*.

**Open field near Charra, Purulia**

Location- Amidst a field which is 8 kms from Purulia Town. The area lies on the right hand side of the Barakar Road from Purulia town. Mauja- Chharra.

11 herostones found lying in an area of diameter of 14½′ W x 16 ½′, embedded in mud in the field. Two of the herostones displayed sculpted & heavily eroded images of

a sitting and meditating male figure, facing the east and towards the north respectively. The majority part of these images lie buried underground. With its proximity to Chharra, the place looks like an extension of the ruins of the temple structures found at Chharra, possibly Jain in origin.

**Chharra, Purulia**

Location- 10 kms from Purulia Town. The village lies on the left hand side of the Barakar Road from Purulia town.

**Mauja- Chharra**

Assorted number of antiquities, found embedded in concrete and mud in front of the Dharmaraj mandir, located in the Dom para of the village in the north-western part of the village of Chharra, including an amalaka and a kalasa, possibly of Jain origin. The other images of the temple of Dharmaraj, found near the entrance and also inside, displays images possibly of Jain origin.

A herostone is seen being used at present as part of an entrance door of a village house, near the entrance of the village (6′ L x 1′ W). The structure has an eroded image of a sitting lion at the top.

***Para,* Purulia**

Location- 20 kms from Purulia Town. The village lies on the eastern bank of Harai River. Block- Panchakot.

A sculpted structure (possibly Jain in origin), seen at the rear end of the village, referred to as the Yamraj *sthan*. This place is visited by people returning from the cremation grounds outside the village after performing the last rites. The structure is approximately 5′ L and 8″ W with a sculpted, standing male figure, facing the village at present.

### Harup, Purulia

Location- 50 kms (approx) from Purulia Town. Approximately 7 kms from the juncture where the main Bagmundi road from Purulia bifurcates between Kalimati and Suissa. Post office- Suissa. Thana and Panchayat- Bagmundi.

Referred to as Hatiya Sini, an image of an ornamented male warrior is seen lying under a tree at the outskirts of the village, near Harup *bandh*. The figure has four hands and is astride an elephant. It is holding a raised sword in the right hand and an ornamented stick on the left, the end part of which looks like an axe. The area has an annual *mela* referred to as Harup *mela*. With a meager population of 45 people in the village, the *mela* is attended by people from adjoining villages of Deuli and Suissa as well.

### Suissa, Purulia

Location- 50 kms (approx) from Purulia Town. 5 kms (approx) from the juncture where the main Bagmundi Road from Purulia bifurcates between Kalimati and Suissa. Post office- Suissa. Thana and Panchayat- Bagmundi.

An assorted number of 11 images are seen kept inside an enclosure, which at present acts as a temple. There is no regular officiating priest, but *puja* is offered by locals at will and mainly for wish fulfillment. These images are preserved in the enclosure through the works of West Bengal State Archaeology Department. The sculpted images in the antiquities reveal possible Jain standing, sitting and meditating images of Tirthankaras.

### Anai, Purulia

Location- 20 kms (approx) from Purulia Town. The village is located on the Anaijambad Road that comes out of the western side of Purulia Town. This road comes under

Pradhan Mantri Sarak Yojna and has been metalled in 2007. Block- Purulia 1. Thana- Kenda.

Pareshnath Mahadev Bera Ananda Asram has the herostones. This Asram is located on the southern side of Anai village. One herostone is located on the backside of the present structure that is referred to as Shibananada Giri Maharaj's Samadhi *sthan* (4′ L x 10″ W & B). Another herostone is seen lying next to the left wall of this Samadhi *sthan* structure (visible length of the structure is 3′ x 6″ W & B). A third part of a herostone is seen jutting out from the backside of the same Samadhi *sthan* structure (visible size of the structure is 10″ L x 10″ B x 8″ W).

Open field on left bank of Kangsabati, 2 kms from Ralibera, Purulia.

Location- On left bank of Kangsabati- 50 mts from the main river bed, and moving ahead from the village of Ralibera. The area comes under village- Phatadiri. Thana-Kenda. Post Office- Ralibera.

Within an area of 50 ft (approx) in diameter stray structures can be seen with heavy marks of erosion on its body making the distinction of any visible structure difficult. In total 9 sculpted herostones and remains of old structures could be seen. There is only one ornate structure seen on leftmost part (3′ L x 1′ B x 9″ W). The one next to this (3′ 9″ L x 1½′ W) has no visible marks of sculpture or inscription on it. 5 of the structures, located approximately in the middle of the diameter area are visible 1 ft above ground. At the farthest end of the diameter area, away from river Kangsabati, are seen two more structures, one of which is ornate with a heavily eroded carved figure visible on its body (7″ L x 8″ B x 7″ W). The other one is seen devoid of any sculpture (3′ 9″ Lx 9″ B x 1′ W). This area is completely submerged under water during rainy season, this is the reason, along with heavy wind, the structures are exposed to heavy erosion at all times of the year. The area also suggests a good prospect of being part of structures underground and is a good prospective site for excavation.

**Palma, Purulia**

Location- Ralibera main road connects to Daradi More (crossroads) at a distance of about 4 kms. From this crossroad, the village of Palma is further 4 kms towards Shitalpur and Puncha. The village has Kalyaneswari River, located 1½ kms (approx) on its eastern side.

Several herostones are seen at the end of the village, displaced over an area of 200mts, at the outskirts of the village at the western end. The one farthest from the village has two vertical herostones, out of which one is carved (5′4″ Lx11″ Bx7″ W) and the one next to is devoid of any sculpting (6′4″ Lx11″ B x 9″ W).

Displaced about 100 ft on its left are 3 herostones out of which one is lying horizontal on the ground (2′4″ L x 10″ B x 9″ W). The one next to it, standing erect has a highly eroded sculpture (2′3″ L x 9″ B x 10″ W). Another herostone is seen facing the village and is partly broken on the side (6′3″ L x 11″ B x 3″ W), worshipped as Indra/Ind for blessings for rain. The *puja* is officiated by a Brahman priest, carrying a surname of Chatterjee who is from the Sadar *Para,* also known as Brahman *para* of the village. At the time of the *puja,* the horizontal herostone is used as a base to erect an umbrella over the top of the vertical one. The *puja* also has a goat sacrifice during Ind *puja.* This *puja* comes under *Gram Sholoana Commiittee.* Local lore has it that these were erected by the people from Bhumij caste who stays closest to these clusters of stones and at the rear end of the village, as memorials for grave of their deceased ancestors.

Another 80 mts from these 3 herostones is another cluster of 6 herostones. From the right, the first one measures 4′8″ Lx10′ B & W. The one next is sculpted, yet due to heavy erosion the figure is very indistinct. The side of the figure faces the village. (3′7″ L x 7″ B x 1′3″W). The third (4′8″ L x 9″ B & W) and fourth (3′7″ L x 8″ B x 7″ W) are unsculpted. The fifth one again has a sculpted and heavily eroded male figure facing the village (2′2″ L x 1′2″ B x 6″ W). The last one is again unsculpted (3′7″ L x 8″ B x 7″ B).

**Pakbira, Purulia**

Location- About 48 kms from Purulia Town and 3 kms from Puncha towards east on the Puncha Main Road. Post Office, Block, Thana, Panchayat- Puncha.

Stray examples of images, *kalas* and parts of broken images possibly of Jain origin are seen accumulated within an enclosure that also comprises of 3 temples of laterite stone. The temples also consist of images, possibly of Jain origin. No *puja* takes place at the temples, excepting at the image of Jain Tirthankara, locally referred to as Bhairabnath and thus, the image receive *puja* regularly on Mondays. Special *puja* by devotees are also performed on any other day. The officiating priest resides in the Ray *Para* of the village. Most of the structures, as mentioned in the J.D. Beglar report (A tour through the Bengal Provinces, Volume 8, pp- 193-195) could not be noticed at present, however, the extensive architectural details suggest the existence of a possible large and elaborate temple complex.

2 ½ kms from Puncha, towards Budhpur, near a field on the Manbazaar main road, Purulia Location- Post Office, Block, Thana, Panchayat Puncha.

A stray sculpted herostone is seen with a male figure, facing east, towards Puncha and is holding a shield on its left hand and a sword on its right. The feet are seen in a running position with the left foot bent and placed on the ground and the right is bent and raised. This stone is placed at the base of a Banyan tree and occasionally worshipped as Sivasthan.

**Budhpur, Purulia**

Location- 6 kms from Puncha on the South-west, going through Manbazar Main Road.

Four sculpted herostones in front of a Siva temple- the one farthest away from the temple is 4′ L x 1½′ B x 5″ W. Of the two facing each other, the one on the left of the entrance of the temple has a prominent and sculpted, though eroded, head of a sitting lion (4′ L x 1½ B x 8′ W), and the one on the right and facing the previous herostone has a completely eroded head (3′4″ L x 2′10′ B x 5″ W). The one farthest from the temple and placed on the right hand of the entrance of the temple (4′3″ L x 1′10″ B x 6″ W), has the *yupa kastha* in front for goat sacrifice during the regular *puja* on Mondays and also during the time of *Gajan*. All the herostones have images of a warrior with a raised sword on right hand and a shield on left and facing away from the temple, towards the east. The *puja* at the temple is managed at present by the *Gram Sholoanna Commiitee.*

**Deulghata, Purulia**

Location- in Arsa, 25 kms from Purulia Town (approx). This place is centrally visited by all villagers from surrounding region.

Two Siva temples of terracotta are seen. Both are heavily eroded and receive *puja* regularly on Mondays. The temple region has regular *Gajan* festival and a *mela*, attended by people from surrounding villages. The first temple on the right has an unsculpted herostone (4½′ L x 8″ B & W). Within an area of over 600 ft, surrounding these two temples, several relics, including base of pedestals, broken pieces of *amalaka* (each measuring between 1½′ to 2½′ diameter), stone bricks and broken pieces of the base of images in meditating and sitting position are seen, possibly of Jain origin. This site also contains newly constructed temples, facing the Siva temples- from right- Bhairabi, Singhi, Jagattaraini and Ranachandi. Another frequently visited Siva temple also adorns the site, where marriages take place, apart from *Gajan* festivals regularly. This is a recent construction. A Ganesha and a Kali temple, along with a temple devoted to one Suniti Pathak, who is ascribed to have erected the modern temples at the site also is found at the site. However, the images within these temples are not recent ones as is reflected through the sculptural details.

**Talajudi, Purulia**

Location- 30 km from Purulia on Kasipur-Bankura Road. Thana- Kasipur. Panchayat- Barandi.

Five herostones outside Baruneswar Siva Mandir and one inside the temple premises. Three of the herostones are sculpted with standing, eroded images, possibly of Jain Tirthankaras, with each measuring to a height of 4′ L & 7″ W. The sculpted herostone (being a worshipping image, this deity was not allowed to be touched for measurement, so the approximate measurement is 5′ L x 1½ B x 7″ W) inside the temple is worshipped as Shiva, especially on Mondays and also during *Gajan* on the 27, 28 and 29$^{th}$ of *Caitra* every year. This place also receives regular goat sacrifice.

**North Bandwan**

Location- P.O.- North Bandwan. The site is a flat area under a tree and next to the main road.

According to the local people, the idol has been lying under the tree eversince they moved into the village. They worship the image on 12th day of Magh as Kal Bhairab. The site has a total of three images- all of possible Jain origin. One of the idols stand under a peepul tree, in North Bandwan, (1 km south of Banjore )- next to the main road that connects to Banjore. The area is close to the house of one Dibakar Mahato. Possibly an idol of Adinath (90 cms L x 40 cms B x 15 cms W and 12 cms peg and 35 cms (approx pedestal). The second idol- possible of Parsvanath (75 cms L x 40 cms B x 12 cms W, 10 cms pedestal), was seen about half a kilometer from the first image and next to a pond and outside a Siva Temple and close to the main road towards Banjore- referred to as sivasthan and has four days of Gajan in Phalgun as well as 5th day of Baisakh every year. The village also had a single herostone (2m, 15 cms L x 35 cms B x 15 cms W [approx]), lying close from the main road that connects to Banjore next to a cowshed. The locals refer this to stand erect and vertical in an area about six ft away, but due to the construction of the main road, connecting to Banjore, it was removed and kept horizontally near the cow shed. The stone was removed last Kartik from its former position.

**Ranipukur**

Location- P.O.- North Bandwan.

A total of eight artifacts were seen. This had a single antiquity, resembling a *kalas* (50 cms L x 22 cms B x 22 cms W) is worshipped as Khelaicandi, with a special *puja* every 5$^{th}$ *Phalgun*, with a *mela*. Officiating priest is one Laya. *Puja* entails regular fowl and pigeon sacrifices. And mostly attended by married women for blessings for a child. A possible herostone (1m 20 cms L x 25 cms B x 15 cms W [approx]) is also seen outside a Siva temple- referred to as Siva *sthan*. Another possible herostone [1m, 75 cms L x (Upper carving)= 70 cms L x (Upper carving)= 30 cms B x

(Upper carving)= 25 cms W x (Lower carving)= 1 mts L x (Lower carving)= 28 cms B x (Lower carving)= 28 cms W] stands vertical inside the siva temple, near the Banjore road. The village also yielded a broken idol of Surya [lower part= 67 cms L x 90 cms B x Pedestal (which has the 7 horses being driven by Arun)= 35 cms]- next to a mustard field and close to a pond- named- Ranipukur, after which is the name of the village. There is Brahma and Maheswar on either sides of the image. There is also a miniature depiction of Ketu on the right side and Rahu on the left side of the deity. The lower part of idol had waist up [83 cms L x 90 cms B x 10 cms W]. The material is chloride stone, with high relief in form. The image has Gandharva, Kirti Mukha and Nabagraha around it. It has also seated images of other Nabagrahas. Another possible herostone [1m,12 cms L x 45 cms B x 25 cms W] of chloride stone was also seen amidst a tomato field. No *puja* takes place. The backside of sculpture is undressed and front covered with high relief. The top of the stone is crowned. There is a depiction of lion and also a sword. Type is also rare in Bengal and has association with Utkal. The village also had several historical antiquities, like the oval *amalaka*. Amalaka (1m, 15 cms L x 65 cms B and 23 cms W) Information regarding the site from the memory of the local people. The material is chloride stone.[65 cms L x 32 cms B x 25 cms H).

**Kurmasor**

Location- P.O.- Kuda, the area has Sindhri Barabazar in South and Rajnoagarh on North. Taking a left turn from Taldih More (close to Bandwan) near Mahara High School and go straight to Kurmasor.

Possible Jain deities (sitting under a *kalpataru* and the upper part has Dhyani Tirthankara and Vasuki) within a temple at the entrance of the village, whom the local worship as Hara-Parvati. Important *puja* on Gajan and *mela* on 1st, 2nd and 3rd of *Baisakh*, accompanied by Chchou dance of Purulia.

**Mahara**

Location- P.O.- Mahara. On Manbazar-Purulia Road and 18 kms from Manbazar.

The region yielded six artifacts. One of them, being an entire and unbroken piece of *amalaka* (located at the doorstep of a Deuli at the very entrance, close to the centre of the village). Another *amalaka* in broken fragments was seen with the housing complex (of one Neelkamal Mahato, at the entrance of village), which the villagers refer as *purono pathar* (old stone) and worship as siva. One of the artifacts is also a Jain Image (possibly Parsvanath, 85 cms Lx 50 cms B x 10 cms W), plastered against the rear wall of a Deuli, and referred to as the god in the Deuli. A herostone (1m L x 25 cms B x 10 cms W) was observed at the centre of the village and near a Deuli, which the locals sometimes use to tie cows. Another herostone (75 cms L x 22 cms B x 12 cms W) was observed close to the main road of the village. A herostone comples was seen in the *upar para* area of the village.

**Purru**

Location- P.O.- Daka Kendo. From Akhra at the entrance of the village main road connecting Sindhri to Banjore and travelling 2 kms towards Sindhri.

The region yielded one herostone (90 cms L x 22 cms B x 10 cms W), close to the main road of the village at Akhra (at the very entrance of the village main road connecting Sindhri to Banjore). The local people are aware about the stone being a *purono pathar* or old stone.

# Bibliography

## Anthropology and Archaeology


Archer, W.G. 1974. *The Hill of Flutes: Life, Love and Poetry in Tribal India- A Portrait of the Suntals*. London: George Allen and Unwon Ltd.

Allchin, B. 1994. *Living Traditions*. UK:Oxbow Books Limited.

Ball, V. 1867. On the Jungle Products Used as Articles of Food by the Inhabitants of the Districts of Manbhoom and Hazaribagh. In *Journal of the Asiatic Society of Bengal*, ed.

The Natural History Secretary. 1868. Vol XXXVI, Part II, Nos. I, II, II: 73-81. Kolkata: Baptist Mission Press.

Bandopadhyay, Amiya Kumar, ed. 1968. *West Bengal District Gazetteers- Bankura 1968*. Kolkata: Narendra Nath Sen, state editor, West Bengal District Gazetteers.

Banerjee, Amalendu 1997. *Rock Shelters of Patina (A Critical Study of the Shelters of Patina)*. Monogram, Calcutta: Processica.

Baske, Dhierndranath 1987. *Paschim Banger Adibasi Samaj (vol. 1)* [Bengali]. Kolkata: Kole Concern.

Bhattacharya, Birendra Kumar, Bimal Ranjan Chakraborti, Narendra Nath Sen, Sankarananda Mukherji, Pranabranjan Ray, Satyaranjan Sengupta, Kiran Sanker.

Sengupta, Nirendra Nath Sen, Tarapada Maity. 1985. *West Bengal District Gazetteers:Puruliya*. Kolkata:West Bengal District Gazetters.

Bhattacharya, D.K. 1993. Is Prehistory Dead in India. In *Journal of the Asiatic Society*, 35 (3): 52-73.

Bhattacharya, D.K., R.K. Chattopadhyay 1997. History in Folk Culture. In Trends in Social Science Research, Vol. 4, No. 1, June- Special Issue- Culture Studies- Selected Papers from the 6th National Academy of Psychology (NAOP), India.

Bhattacharya, R.K. 1991. *Moslems of Rural Bengal*. Kolkata: Subarnarekha.

Bhowmick, P.K. 1994. *Primitive Tribal Groups in Eastern India- Welfare and Evaluation*. New Delhi: Gyan Publishing House.

——.1980. *Some Aspects of Indian Anthropology*. Kolkata: Subarnarekha.

——.2003. *Loksamaj O Sanskriti* [Bengali]. Kolkata: *Loksanskriti O Adivasi Sanskriti Kendra. Tathya O Sanskriti Bibhag. Paschim Banga Sarkar*.

Bhattacharya, T.1963. *The Lodhas of West Bengal: A Socio-economic Study*. Kolkata: Punthi Pustak.

Bodding, Rev. P.O. 1927. *Santal Medicine*. Asiatic Society of Bengal Vol. X, No. 2. Kolkata: Asiatic Society of Bengal.

——. Skrefsrud, L.O., Sten Konow 1942. *Traditions and Institutions of the Santals: Ho koren.*

*Mare Hap amko Reak' Katha* [The Story of Our Ancestors]. New Delhi: Bahumukhi.

Chakraborty, Dilip K. 1993. *Archaeology of Eastern India- Chhotanagpur Plateau and West Bengal*. New Delhi: Munshiram Manoharlal Publishers Pvt. Ltd.

——.2006. *The Oxford Companion to Indian Archaeology- The Archaeological Foundations of Ancient India*. New Delhi: Oxford University Press.

——.2001. Archaeological Geography of the Ganga Plain:- The Lower and the Middle Ganga. Delhi: Permanent Black.

Chari, R.B., ed. 1971. *Census of India 1971- India*. Series 1. Paper 1 of 1975. Scheduled Castes and Scheduled Tribes. New Delhi: Government of India Publications.

Chattopadhyay, R.K. 1980 (March). Bankurar Pragitihasik Pratnabastur Sandhan [Bengali]. In *Puratattwik* [Bangiya Puratattwa Parishader Mukhapatra], Year 1, Issue 1, March 1980. Kolkata: Bangiya Puratattwa Parishad.

——.1989. *Early History and Culture of Bankura- An Archaelogical Study*. (Unpublished work) Thesis submitted to the University of Burdwan for the degree of Doctor of Philosophy (Arts) in History. 1989. Burdwan: University of Burdwan.

——.Rajat Sanyal and Kumkum Bandopadhyay 2007. Early Village Farming Settlements in Eastern India: a New Appraisal.

Pp 68-93. In Dikshit, K.N.ed, *Purattatva.* Number 37, 2006-2007. Bulletin of the Indian Archaeological Society. New Delhi:Indian Archaeological Society.

——.Paromita Bose and Dipshikha Acharya 2009. Archaeological Sequence of a Region:Bishnupur/Vishnupur Sub-division, District Bankura, West Bengal. pp 80-95. In Dikshit, K.N. ed, *Purattatva.* Number 39, 2009, November. Bulletin of the Indian Archaeological Society. New Delhi:Indian Archaeological Society.

Coupland, H., ed. 1911. *Bengal District Gazetteers- Manbhum* 1911. Kolkata: Bengal Secretariat Book Depot.

Dalton, E.T. 1960. *Descriptive Ethnology of Bengal.* Kolkata: Firma K.L.M.- a verbatim reproduction of the original publication of 1872.Kolkata:Indian Studies Past and Present.

Dandekar, Deepra 2000-2001. Folk Turned Sanskritic: Manasha. Pune: Dissertation for Certificate Course in Women's Studies, University of Pune (Unpublished).

Das, Amal Kumar 1964. *Koras and Some Little Known Communities of West Bengal.* Kolkata:Tribal Welfare Department, Government of West Bengal.

——.Bidyut Kumar Roy Chowdhury and Manis Kumar Raha 1966. Handbook on Scheduled Castes and Scheduled Tribes of West Bengal- Special Series No.-8. *Bulletin Of the Cultural Research Institute, West Bengal.* Kolkata: Tribal Welfare Department.

Dasgupta, P.C. 1975. The Archaeological Treasures of Tamralipta. Tamluk,Mednipur: Tamralipta Museum and Research Centre.

Ghosh, Binoy 1976. *Pashchimbanger Sanskriti* (Bengali). Bankura: West Bengal.

Ghosh, Pratapchandra. 1870, September 7. Vastu Yaga. In *Journal of the Asiatic Society of Bengal*, ed. The Honorary Secretaries.1870. Vol XXXIX, Part I, Nos. I-IV: 199-232. Kolkata: Baptist Mission Press.

Ghosh, S.N., ed. 1981. *Census of India 1981- West Bengal,* Series 23, Part IX (iv):Special Tables for Scheduled Tribes- tables 4 to 7. Kolkata: Government of West Bengal.

——.1981. *Census of India 1981 West Bengal,* Series 23, Part IX (iii):Special Tables for Scheduled Tribes- tables 1 to 3. Kolkata: Government of West Bengal.

Gupta, J. Datta, ed. 1961. *Census of India 1961-West Bengal and Sikkim.* Vol XVI, part II, Social and Cultural Tables. Kolkata: Government of West Bengal Publications.

Hunter W.W.1973. *A Statistical Account of Bengal,* vol III, Districts of Midnapur and Hugli (including Howrah). New Delhi: D.K. Publishing House.- a verbatim reproduction of the original publication of 1876. London: Turner and Company.

Latham, R.G. 1985. *Ethnology of India.* New Delhi: Abhinav Pubications. Chapter IX: 188-192. - a verbatim reproduction of the original publication of 1859. New Delhi: Manas Publications.

Maitra, Lopamudra. 2008. Change and Continuity as Means to Perpetuate Cultural Anxieties:- A brief Study of Tusu Brata Rites and the Worship of Goddess Manasa in Specific Districts of Lateritic West Bengal (India). In Mohanty, Panchanan, Ramesh C. Malik and Eswarappa Kasi, ed. 2008. *Ethnographic Discourse of the Other: Conceptual and Methodological Issues.* UK:Cambridge Scholars Publishing.

Marriot, Mckim ed. 1955. *Village India.* Chicago:U.S.A. Memoir

——.1955. *Little Communities in an Indigenous Civilisation in Village India.* Chicago:U.S.A.

Mitra, A.K. 1953. The Tribes and Castes of West Bengal, *Census of India, 1951.* Alipore Kolkata: Superintendent, Government Printing, Bengal Government Press.

——.1961. *Paschim Banger Puja Parbon O Mela- 24 Parganas and Midnapur Districts* vol III. In *Census of India- Census Report.* New Delhi: Government of India Publications.

Maini, Darshan Singh. 2000. *Cultural Anthropology- Encyclopaedia of Anthropology-3.* New Delhi: Mittal Publications. Pp. 179-203. [Chapter-8, Structural description of Subanun "Religious Behaviour" (of mountainous interior of Zamboanga Peninsula on the island of Mindanao in the Philippines).

Murty, M.L.K. 1994. Forest Peoples and Historical Traditions in the Eastern Ghats, South India. In Allchin, Bridget ed. 1994. *Living Traditions- Studies in the Ethnoarchaeology of South Asia.* New Delhi: Oxford and IBH Publishing Co. Pvt. Ltd.

O'Malley, L.S.S., ed. 1910. *Bengal District Gazetteers- Midnapore* 1910. Kolkata: West Bengal District Gazetteers, Higher Education Department, Government of West Bengal-a verbatim reproduction of the original publication of 1911. Calcutta: Bengal Secretariat Book Depot.

Pal, Anil Chandra 1992. Dihar: A Chalcolithic Site. In *Pratna Samiksha* Vol 1, 1992. Directorate of Archaeology, Government of West Bengal. Kolkata: Department of Information and Cultural Affairs, Government of West Bengal.

Peterson, J.C.K, H. Coupland, ed. 1910. *Bengal District Gazetteers-Burdwan* 1910. Kolkata: Bengal Secretariat Book Depot.

Porter, A.E. 1932. *Census of India 1931, Bengal and Sikkim,* Vol. 5, Part I. Kolkata: Publication Branch.

——.1933. *Census of India 1931, Bengal and Sikkim,* Vol. 5, Part I, Appendix I, The Depress Classes, 494-513. Kolkata: Central Publication Branch.Redfield, Robert 1941. *The Folk Culture of Yucatan*. Chicago:University of Chicago Press.

——.1960. *Peasant Society and Culture.* Chicago:University of Chicago Press Risley, H. 1915. *People of India.* Delhi: Munshiram Manoharlal.

——.1981. *The Tribes and Castes of Bengal.* Vols. I and II. Kolkata: Firma Mukhopaddhyay.- a verbatim reproduction of the original publication of 1891. Kolkata: Bengal Secretariat.

Russel, R.V. and Hiralal 1973. *A Statistical Account of Bengal.* Vol III, Districts of Midnapur and Hugli (including Howrah). New Delhi: D.K. Publishing House.- a verbatim reproduction of the original publication of 1876. London: Turner and Company.

——.1993. *The Tribes and Castes of the Central Provinces.* Vol I, II, III and IV. New Delhi: Asian Educational.

Sen, Narendra Nath, ed. 1985. *West Bengal District Gazetteers-Puruliya 1985.* Kolkata: West Bengal District Gazetteers.

Singh, K.S. 1992. *People of India:-An Introduction-National Series, Vol-1.* Kolkata: Anthropological Survey of India, Seagull Books. Pp.1-16.

——. 1994. *The Scheduled Tribes.* People of India, National Series Volume III. New Delhi: Oxford University Press.

——.2008. Shekhar Bandopadhyay, Tilak Bagchi and R.K. Bhattacharya, ed. *People of India:-West Bengal,* vol. XXXXIII, part-I and part II. Kolkata: Anthropological Survey of India, Seagull Books.

## Atlas, Dictionary and Encyclopaedia

Banthia, Jayant Kumar, general direction, Dr. R.P. Singh, technical director, Deputy Registrar General (Map). 2004. *Language Atlas of India 1991.* Government of India: 2001 Census of India, Jayant Kumar Banthia of the Indian Administrative Service Registrar General and Census Commissioner, India. pp. 16-17, 28-29.

Pearsall, Judy. 1998. *The New Oxford Dictionary of English.* New Delhi: Oxford University Press.

Maini, Darshan Singh. 2000. *Encyclopaedia of Anthropology-3-Cultural Anthropology.* New Delhi:Mittal Publications. pp. 31-45.

Mandal, Hrishikesh, Archana Datta, Pradyot Kr. Guha, Sumit Mukherjee, Sanchita Ghatak. 2005. *India- An Illustrated Atlas of Scheduled Castes.* Kolkata: Anthropological Survey of India, Ministry of Culture, Government of India.

Sumit Mukherjee, Archana Datta. 2002. *India- An Illustrated Atlas of Tribal World.* Kolkata: Anthropological Survey of India, Ministry of Culture, Government of India.

Samsad, Sahitya. 2000. *Samsad-Bengali-English Dictionary* [Revised and Enlarged Third Edition]. Kolkata:Shishu Sahitya Samsad Pvt. Ltd.

Williams, Monier. 1982. *A Dictionary English and Sanskrit.* New Delhi: Motilal Banarasidas.- a verbatim reproduction of the original publication of 1851. London.

## Culture studies, folk studies and other social sciences

Apte, Mahadev. L. 1978. *Mass Culture, Language and Arts in India* [Papers Presented at a Symposium at Duke University, Durham, North Carolina]. Mumbai:Popular Prakashan.

Bankura 2002 April. *Jela Loksamskriti Porichoy Grantha- Loksamskriti O Adibasi Sanskriti Kendra* [Bengali] Kolkata: *Tathya O Samskriti Bibhag. Pashchim Banga Sarkar.*

Bhattacharya, Ashutosh 1927. *Banglar Samskriti* [Bengali]. New Delhi: National Book Trust.

Bhattacharya, T. 1986. *Paschimbanga Darshan, Purulia.* [Bengali]. Kolkata: Firma K.L.M. Pvt. Ltd.

——.1979. *Paschimbanga Darshan, Medinipur.* [Bengali]. Kolkata: Firma K.L.M. Pvt. Ltd.

Blackburn, Stuart H., A.K. Ramanujan ed. 1986. Another Harmony:- New Essays on the Folklore of India. New Delhi: Oxford University Press.

Carey, James. W. 1989. *Communication as Culture- Essays on Media and Society.* Boston:Unwin Hyman.

Chanda, Shubhendu. 2003. *The Border Society- A Study of Network and Linkage [West Bengal and Odisha].* Kolkata: Anthropological Survey of India, Ministry of Tourism and Culture, Department of Culture.

Chakrabarti, S.B. 1986. *Around the Plough:- Socio-cultural Context of Agricultural Farming in an Indian Village.* Kolkata: Anthropological Survey of India. Ministry of Human Resource Development, Department of Culture, Government of India.

Chakraborty, Dr. Timirbaran. 1994, 21 February. *Bangla Loksamskriti Charchar Adi Yuga* [Bengali] Kolkata:Pustak Bipani.

Chakraborty, Kalyanbrata. 2007. *Emergence of Hinduism and Human Face of God.* Kolkata:Firma KLM Pvt. Ltd.

Chattopadhyay, Annapurna.2002. *The People and Culture of Bengal- A Study in Origins.* Vol I, part I. Kolkata:Firma KLM Pvt. Ltd.

——.2002. *The People and Culture of Bengal- A Study in Origins.* Vol I, part II. Kolkata:Firma KLM Pvt. Ltd.

——.2006. *The People and Culture of Bengal- A Study in Origins.* Vol II, part I. Kolkata:Firma KLM Pvt. Ltd.

——.2006. *The People and Culture of Bengal- A Study in Origins.* Vol II, part II. Kolkata:Firma KLM Pvt. Ltd.

Chattopadhyay, Debiprasad 2005. *Lokayat Darsan* [Bengali]. Kolkata:New Age Publishers Pvt. Ltd.

Crooke, W. 1994. *An Introduction to the Popular Religion and Folklore of Northern India.* New Delhi: Asian Educational Services.- a verbatim reproduction of the original Publication of 1894. Allahabad: Government Press, North-Western Provinces and Oudh.

Davidson, Kay Linda and David M. Gitlitz.2002. *Pilgrimage- From the Ganges to Graceland- An Encyclopaedia*. California, Santa Barbara: ABC Clio.Pp.145

Finnegan, Ruth. 1988. *Literacy and Orality- Studies in the Technology of Communication*. UK:Basil Blackwell.

Goswami, Prabhat. 2007. *Barnamay Bankurar Pathe Prantarey*. [Bengali] Kolkata:Shishu Sahitya Samsad.

Kaushal, Molly. 2001. Introduction. In *Op. cit.*, ed. *Chanted Narratives- The Living 'Katha Vachana' Tradition*. New Delhi: Indira Gandhi National Centre for the Arts.

Kisku, Upen, editorial head. 1998. *Loksruti* [Bengali]. Kolkata: *Loksamskriti O Adivasi Samskriti Kendra*. West Bengal Government.

Mahajan, Kamlesh.1977. *Communication and Society- The Emerging Human Concerns*. New Delhi:Classical Publishing Company

Maiti, Bankimchandra. 1990. *Dakshin-Paschim Simanta Banglar Lokayata Sanskriti*. [Bengali]. Narayangarh, Mednipur: Bidisha Prakashani.

Mitra, Sanatkumar. 2008. *Lok Sanskriti Gabeshona- Patachitrakala: Pater gan: Gurusaday Bishesh Sankhya*. Kolkata: Loksanskriti Gabeshona Parishad.

Mukherjee, Dr. Soma 2003. *Folk Deities and Matrika Cult of South West Bengal*. Kolkata: R.N. Bhattacharya.

Mukhopadhyay, Bhaskar. 2008. Dream Kitsch-Folk Art, Indigenous Media and G9/11-The Work of Pat in the Era of Electronic Transmission. In Pinney, Christopher and Graeme Were, ed. March 2008. *Journal of Material Culture*. Vol 13 (1). London: Sage.

Roberge, Gaston. 1977. *Mass Communication and Man*. Allahabad:Allahabad Saint Paul Society.

Rothenbuhler, Eric W. and Coman Mihai, ed. 2005. *Media Anthropology*. California:Sage Publications.

Roy, Samaren. 1981. *The Roots of Bengali Culture*. Kolkata:Firma K.L.M.

Sanyal, H.R. 1981. *Social Mobility in Bengal*. Kolkata: Papyrus.

Sarma, Nabin Chandra. 2001. Verbal Narratives: Performance and Gender of the Padma Purana. In Kaushal, Molly, ed. *Chanted*

*Narratives- The Living 'Katha Vachana' Tradition*. New Delhi: Indira Gandhi National Centre for the Arts.

Sarkar, Kalyan Kumar. An Unnoticed Image of Sarasvati: Some Iconographic Observations. In Ray, N.R. and P.N. Chakrabarti, ed. *Studies in Cultural Development of India- Collection of Essays in Honour of Prof. Jagadish Narayan Sarkar*. Kolkata: Punthi Pustak.

Saraswati, Baidyanath. 2001. Orality and its Complexity. In Kaushal, Molly, ed. *Chanted Narratives- The Living 'Katha Vachana' Tradition*. New Delhi: Indira Gandhi National Centre for the Arts.

Sen, Dinesh Chandra. 1939. *Banglar Puronari* [Bengali]. Kolkata: National Literature Company.

Singha, Maniklal. 1977. *Paschim Radh Tatha Bankura Sanskriti* [Bengali]. Bangiya Sahitya Parishad, Bishnupur Sakha. Bishnupur: Bankura.

Singha, Maniklal. 1982. *Radher Jati O Kristi* [Bengali] Vol II. Bangiya Sahitya Parishad, Bishnupur Sakha. Bishnupur: Bankura.

Smith, Daniel H. and M. Narasimha Chary. 1991. Handbook of Hindu Gods, Goddesses and Saints. Delhi:Sundeep Prakashan.

## Geology and Geography

Singh, R.L., ed. 1971. *India- A Regional Geography*. Varanasi: National Geographical Society of India.

Temple, R.C., ed. 1993. *A Geographical Account of Countries Round The Bay of Bengal 1669- 1679* by Thomas Bowrey. New Delhi:Asian Educational Services.- a verbatim reproduction of the original publication of 1905. London:Cambridge, Printed for the Hakluyt Society MDCCCCV.

## History

Banerjea, Jitendra Nath 1985. *The Development of Hindu Iconography*. New Delhi:Munshiram Manoharlal Publishers Pvt. Ltd.

Bandopadhyay, Rakhaldas. 3rd edition. *Banglar Itihash*. Vol I. Kolkata:Gurudas Chattopadhyay and Sons.

Basu, L. 1981. *Amader Padabir Itihas* [Bengali]. Kolkata: Aananda Publishers Pvt. Ltd.

Basu, Satyendrakumar. 1952. *Hiuen Chang* [Bengali]. Kolkata:Vishwabharati Granthalaya. Pp.91-111.

Bottéro, Jean. 1992. *Mesopotamia- Writing, Reasoning and the Gods.*

Chattopadhyaya, Brajadulal 1998. *The Making of Early Medieval India*. Delhi:Oxford University Press. pp.1-37.

——.2005. *Studying Early India:- Archaeology, Texts and Historical Issues*. New Delhi:Permanent Black. pp 172-190.

Datta, Bimal Chandra.1980. *Boudhha Bharat* [Bengali]. Kolkata:Ramkrishna Vivekananda Institute of Research and Culture.pp 118-120.

Goyal, S.R. 1993. *A Religious History of Ancient India (upto c.1200 A.D.). VOL II- Sm rta, epic- Paurāṇika and Tantrika Hinduism, Christianity and Islam.* Meerut:Kusumanjali Prakashan.

Gupta, Bipinbihari. 1989. *Puraton Prosongo* [Bengali]. Kolkata:Pustak Bipani.

Hazra, R.C. 1958. The Upapurana Literature-Its extent, antiquity and origin. In *Studies in the Upapuranas, Vol I- Saura and Vaisnava Upapurāṇas. Calcutta Sanskrit College.*

*Research Series, No. II.* Kolkata: Sanskrit College, under the auspices of the Government of West Bengal.

Hunter W.W.1965. *Annals of Rural Bengal.* Indian Studies: Past and Present. Kolkata.- a verbatim reproduction of the original publication of 1883. London.

Jash, Pranabananda. 1982. *History and Evolution of Vais avism in Eastern India*. Calcutta:Roy & Chowdhury.

Kuber, W.N. 1973. *Dr. Ambedkar- A Critical Study.* New Delhi:People's Publishing House

Macdonell A.A. 2000. *India's Past- A Survey of Her Literatures, Religions, Languages and Antiquities.* Delhi: Indian Publishers' Distributors.- a verbatim reproduction of the original publication of 1927. Oxford:United Kingdom.

Majumdar, R.C. 1971. *History of Bengal* vol.1- *Hindu period.* Patna: N.V. Publications.

Majumdar, R.C. 1978. *History of Modern Bengal* Part- 1. Kolkata: G. Bharadwaj and Co.

Mukhopadhyay, Bratindranath. 1995. *Itihasher Aloke Arya Samashya* (in Bengali). Kolkata:Paschim Banga Itihas Samsad.

Rhys Davids, T.W. 1911. *Buddhist India- The Story of the Nations.* Vol I. London:T. Fisher Unwin. Pp. 308-310.

Roy, Niharranjan.2003. *Bangalir Itihas: Adiparva* [Bengali]. Kolkata: Deyís Publishing.

Sallami, Abu-l-Fazl [translated into English by H. Elochmann]. 1927. *Ain-Akbar*. Kolkata: Printed for the Asiatic Society of Bengal. pp. 406-424, Note on the Battle of Takaroi or Mughulmari, in Odisha [The Grandees of the Empire- with bibliographical notices by the translator].

Sastri, Hirananda 1925. The Origin and Cult of Tara. In *Memoirs of the Archaeological Survey of India*. Vol. No. 20. Kolkata: Central Publication Branch, Government of India.

Sen, Dr. Amulyachandra. 1953. *Asoklipi* [Bengali]. Kolkata:Mahabodhi Book Agency.

Sen, Dr. B. C. 1942. *Some Historical Aspects of the Inscriptions of Bengal*. Kolkata:University of Calcutta.

Sen, Dinesh Chandra. 1934. *Brihat Banga- Suprachin Kal Hoite Palashir Juddha Parjanto- Vol.I* [Bengali]. Kolkata: Deyís Publishing.

Sen, S.1960. *History of Bengali Literature.* New Delhi: Sahitya Academi. 1999. *Banga Bhumika* [Bengali]. Kolkata:Paschim Banga Bangla Akademi.- a verbatim reproduction and reprint of the original publication of 1974. Kolkata.

Sengupta, Nikhileshwar. 1991. Revival of Brahmanism in Bengal Under the Aegis of Bhavadeva Bhatta. In Ray, N.R. and P.N. Chakrabarti, ed. *Studies in Cultural Development of India- Collection of Essays in Honour of Prof. Jagadish Narayan Sarkar.* Kolkata: Punthi Pustak.

Sinha, B.P. 1991. Cavalry in Ancient Indian Army 600 B.C.-300 A.D. In Ray, N.R. and P.N. Chakrabarti, ed. *Studies in Cultural Development of India- Collection of Essays in Honour of Prof. Jagadish Narayan Sarkar*. Kolkata: Punthi Pustak.

Sontheimer, Günther-Dietz. 1977. *The Joint Hindu Family: Its Evolution as a Legal Institution.* South Asian Studies No. VII. Munshiram Manoharlal Publishers Pvt. Ltd. Pp. 16-20, 214-217.

Watters, Thomas. 1961. *On Yuan Chwang's Travels In India (A.D. 629-645).* New Delhi: Munshiram Manoharlal.- a verbatim reproduction of the original publication of 1904. Vol I and II. London: Royal Asiatic Society.

# Index

Fig. 1 : Herostone- Chhatna, Bankura

Fig. 2 : Herostones- Charra, Purulia

Fig. 3 : Herostones- Open field, 2kms from Ralibera, Purulia

Fig. 4 : Herostone- Open field, 2 ½ kms from Puncha, Purulia

Fig. 5 : Chowdhury of Balsi (Bankura), displaying documents

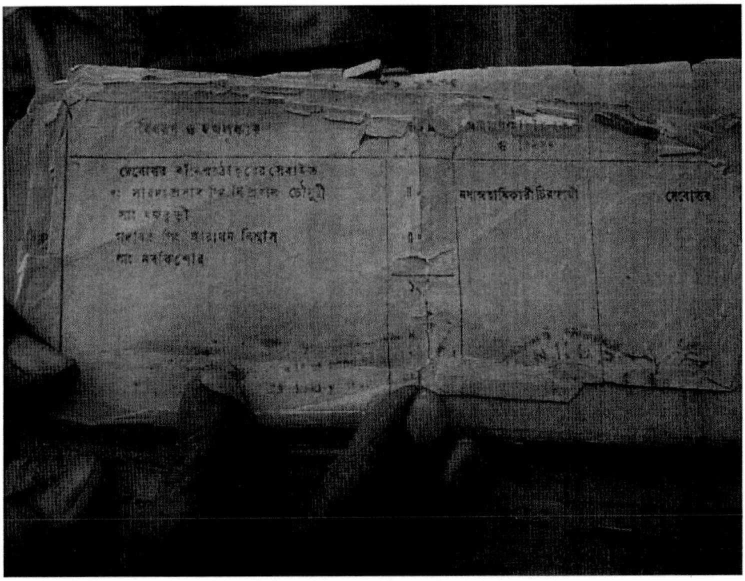

Fig. 6 : Close-up of the same documents, Balsi, Bankura

Fig. 7 : Same documents, Balsi, Bankura

Fig. 8 : Lakkhinarayan Jiu, Balsi, Bankura

Fig. 9 : Inscription at the entrance of the temple of Radhakanta Jiu at Muninagar, Bankura, displaying royal patronage under the name of Bir Singha of Malla royalty.

Fig. 10 : Terracotta at the entrance of the Radhadamodar Jiu temple, Khirpai, West Mednipur

Fig. 11 : Temple of Narayana, Hadalnarayanpur, Bankura

Fig. 12 : Temple of Lakkhinarayan Jiu, Metla, Bankura

Fig. 13 : Parbatinath temple, Khirpai, West Mednipur

Fig. 14 : Bhuteswara Siva, Tiliboni/Basantapur, Bankura

Fig. 15 : Temple of Saileswara, Dihar, Bankura

Fig. 16 : Temple of Sareswara, Dihar, Bankura

Fig. 17 : In front of the twin temples of Dihar, Bankura

Fig. 18 : Temple of Deuleswara, Kusadwip, Bankura

Fig. 19 : Temple of Buddeswara Siva, Budhpur, Purulia

Fig. 20 : Temple of Deulghata, Purulia

Fig. 21 : Dugdheswara Siva, Gamidhya, Bankura

Fig. 22 : Temple of Baruneswara, Telajuri, Purulia

Fig. 23 : Radharajrani, Jamkuri, Bankura

Fig. 24 : Raj Rajeswari, Kasipur, Purulia

Fig. 25 : Ma Brahmani, Hadalnarayanpur, Bankura

Fig. 26 : Yamaraj, Para, Purulia

Fig. 27 : Entrance of Dharmaraj temple, Chharra, Purulia

Fig. 28 : inside Dharmaraj temple, Chharra

Fig. 29 : Idol of Jain Tirthankara on the outside wall of Dharmaraj temple, Chharra, Purulia

Fig. 30 : Various idols of possible Jain origin within the temple of Dharmaraj, Chharra

Fig. 31 : Idols of possible Jain origin within an enclosure in Suissa, Purulia

Fig. 32 : Idols of possible Jain origin, Suissa, Purulia

Fig. 33 : Temple at Pakbira, Purulia

Fig. 34 : Jain idol, Pakbira, Purulia

Fig. 35 : Idols of Jain Tirthankaras housed within Paresnath Mahadev Bera Ananda Asram, Anai, Purulia

Fig. 36 : Jain idol/Nangta Syamchand Thakur Dharapat, Bankura

Fig. 37 : Parsvanath/Manasa, Dharapat

Fig. 38 : Jain idol/Khhandarani, Bheduasole, Bankura

Fig. 39 : Chhinamasta/Basulimata, Muninagar, Bankura

Fig. 40

Fig. 41

Fig. 42

Fig. 43

Figs. 40-43 : Jain idols/ village deities, Palma, Purulia

Fig. 44 : Pashan Kali, Dwarika, Bankura

Fig. 45 : Buddhadev, Radhamohanpur, Bankura

Fig. 46 : Temple of Buddhadev, Radhamohanpur

Fig. 47 : Bisahari, Bisra, Bankura

Fig. 48 : Kaliburi, Gamidhya, Bankura

Fig. 49 : Temple of Jagatgouri, Rautkhanda, Bankura

Fig. 50 : (from left)- Bipadtarini, Singhabashini Durga, Sankattarini, Penara, Bankura

Fig. 51 : Kekai Candi, Chhilimpur, Bankura

Fig. 52 : Manasa temple, after renovation/samskar, Hadalnarayanpur, Bankura

Fig. 53 : Manasa temple, Dhumkoro, Bankura

Fig. 54 : Manasa, Kapistha, Bankura

Fig. 56 : Manasa idol within temple, Palpal, Purulia

Fig. 57 : Within Manasa temple, Dhibor para, Gangajalghati, Bankura

Fig. 58 : Hatiya Sini, Harup, Purulia

Fig. 59 : Chukai Sini, Indpur, Bankura

Fig. 60 : Baner bandh Sini, next to Baner bandh (Indpur Police Station),

Fig. 61 : Bhairab sthan, Koro, Bankura

Fig. 62 : Bhairab sthan, Pataspur, Bankura

Fig. 63 : Bhairab sthan, Dhumkoro, Bankura

Fig. 64 : Bhairab sthan, Tiliboni/Basantapur, Bankura

Fig. 65 : Dharmaraj temple, Chharra, Purulia

Fig. 66 : Dharmaraj temple, Kapistha, Bankura

Fig. 67 : Dharmaraj, Kapistha

Fig. 68 : Basuli temple, Advaicandi, Bankura

Fig. 69 : Basuli, Advaicandi

Fig. 70 : Dasohara, Ayodhya, Bankura

Fig. 71 : Sarbamangala, Naricha, Bankura

Fig. 72 : Kalanjay, Patrasayer, Bankura

Fig. 73 : Rani Sati temple, Balarampur, Purulia

Fig. 74 : Nakti Durga sthan, Burda, Purulia

Fig. 75 : Nakti Durga, Burda

Fig. 76 : Terracotta figurine (broken) from recent Dihar excavation, 2008-09 Picture courtesy- Dept. of Archaeology, University of Calcutta, Kolkata

Fig. 77 : Terracotta figurine (broken) from recent Dihar excavation, 2008-09 Picture courtesy- Dept. of Archaeology, University of Calcutta, Kolkata

Fig. 78 : Terracotta figurine (broken) from recent Dihar excavation, 2008-09 Picture courtesy- Dept. of Archaeology, University of Calcutta, Kolkata

Fig. 79 : Terracotta figurine (broken) from recent Dihar excavation, 2008-09 Picture courtesy- Dept. of Archaeology, University of Calcutta, Kolkata